D1630039

·er

Tablighi Jamaat and the Quest for the London Mega Mosque

THE MODERN MUSLIM WORLD

Series Editor: Dietrich Jung of the Center for Contemporary Middle East Studies, University of Southern Denmark

The modern Muslim world is an integral part of global society. In transcending the confines of area studies, this series encompasses scholarly work on political, economic, and cultural issues in modern Muslim history, taking a global perspective. Focusing on the period from the early nineteenth century to the present, it combines studies of Muslim majority regions, such as the Middle East and parts of Africa and Asia, with the analysis of Muslim minority communities in Europe and the Americas. Emphasizing the global connectedness of Muslims, the series seeks to promote and encourage the understanding of contemporary Muslim life in a comparative perspective and as an inseparable part of modern globality.

Migration, Security, and Citizenship in the Middle East: New Perspectives
Edited by Peter Seeberg and Zaid Eyadat

Politics of Modern Muslim Subjectivities: Islam, Youth, and Social Activism in the Middle East
Dietrich Jung, Marie Juul Petersen and Sara Cathrine Lei Sparre

Transnational Islam in Interwar Europe: Muslim Activists and Thinkers
Edited by Götz Nordbruch and Umar Ryad

The International Politics of the Arab Spring: Popular Unrest and Foreign Policy
Edited by Robert Mason

Regional Powers in the Middle East: New Constellations after the Arab Revolts
Edited by Henner Fürtig

Tablighi Jamaat and the Quest for the London Mega Mosque: Continuity and Change
Zacharias P. Pieri

Tablighi Jamaat and the Quest for the London Mega Mosque

Continuity and Change

Zacharias P. Pieri

TABLIGHI JAMAAT AND THE QUEST FOR THE LONDON MEGA MOSQUE
Copyright © Zacharias P. Pieri, 2015.

First published in 2015 by
PALGRAVE MACMILLAN®
in the United States—a division of St. Martin's Press LLC,
175 Fifth Avenue, New York, NY 10010.

Where this book is distributed in the UK, Europe and the rest of the world,
this is by Palgrave Macmillan, a division of Macmillan Publishers Limited,
registered in England, company number 785998, of Houndmills,
Basingstoke, Hampshire RG21 6XS.

Palgrave Macmillan is the global academic imprint of the above companies
and has companies and representatives throughout the world.

Palgrave® and Macmillan® are registered trademarks in the United States,
the United Kingdom, Europe and other countries.

ISBN: 978–1–137–46438–5

Library of Congress Cataloging-in-Publication Data

Pieri, Zacharias, author.
    Tablighi Jamaat and the quest for the London mega mosque :
continuity and change / Zacharias P. Pieri.
        pages cm.—(The modern Muslim world)
    Includes bibliographical references.
    ISBN 978–1–137–46438–5—
    ISBN 1–137–46438–0
        1. Tablighi Jama'at—History. 2. Islam—Missions—England—London.
    3. Islam—Missions—Great Britain. 4. Muslims—England—London.
    5. Mosques—England—London. I. Title.

BP10.T323P54 2015
297.6'50941—dc23   2014036647

A catalogue record of the book is available from the British Library.

Design by Newgen Knowledge Works (P) Ltd., Chennai, India.

First edition: March 2015

10 9 8 7 6 5 4 3 2 1

To my parents, Peter and Katerina

CONTENTS

Acknowledgments

This book presents five years of ethnographic field research on Tablighi Jamaat in London and builds upon my doctoral thesis, which was completed in the summer of 2012 at the University of Exeter, United Kingdom. I am indebted to the supervision afforded by Prof. Jonathan Githens-Mazer. From our first meeting, Jonathan encouraged me in my research, critiqued my ideas, provided me with new opportunities and avenues to succeed, and nourished my academic development. Our meetings were innovative and discussion was stimulating. I am grateful to comments received from Prof. David Jacobson on the theoretical elements of the book, and for the time he allowed me to work on the manuscript during my time as a Postdoctoral Research Fellow with the Global Initiative on Civil Society and Conflict at the University of South Florida, Tampa. The publication of this book owes much to the support, encouragement, and feedback of Prof. Dietrich Jung, Series Editor of *The Modern Muslim World* at Palgrave. To that end, I am also very appreciative of the comments from the anonymous reviewers, and to Farideh Koohi-Kamali and Sara Doskow at Palgrave Macmillan in New York. Their support has been integral to the book's publication. In addition, I am personally indebted to Heather Fortson who donated a considerable amount of time and energy in the reading, proofing, and copy-editing of the manuscript.

Tablighi Jamaat has not always been open to social science research, and as such I am exceptionally obliged to those Tablighis who agreed to facilitate and take part in this study. This book would not have been possible without their time, trust, and frankness. Additionally I am thankful to Alan Craig who gave generous amount of time to questions and interviews and for sharing his experiences of leading opposition to TJ's mosque. I am appreciative of the time given by Peter Minoletti, and Sunil Sahadevan and others at Newham Council and the London Thames Gateway Development Corporation. Moreover, I thankful to Jenny Taylor of Lapido Media who shared her experiences of Tablighi Jamaat in Nizamuddin and who has been supportive of my research on Tablighi Jamaat in Britain.

ABBREVIATIONS

BNP	British National Party
CPA	Christian Peoples Alliance
CPO	Compulsory Purchase Order
DCLG	Department for Communities and Local Government
GLA	Greater London Authority
LDA	London Development Authority
LTGDC	London Thames Gateway Development Corporation
MCB	Muslim Council of Britain
MP	Member of Parliament
MPACUK	Muslim Public Affairs Committee United Kingdom
NC	Newham Concern
ODA	Olympics Development Authority
ONS	Office for National Statistics
PM	Prime Minister
TJ	Tablighi Jamaat

CHAPTER 1

Introduction

On July 6, 2005, Great Britain won the bid to host the 2012 Olympic Games. Crowds thronged the streets of London waving flags, with official parties held in East London's Stratford and centrally in Trafalgar Square. The mood in the capital was one of jubilation and triumph. The very next day, on the morning of July 7, four bombs were detonated on London's public transport system. The bombings injured several hundred people and killed 52. The celebrations were cut short; the context in Britain transformed overnight. Islamic extremists were tied to the bombings, and the religion of the bombers, Islam, was securitized. Muslim communities were viewed with suspicion. For some, this was indication that Britain's favored policy of multiculturalism failed, and that in its place the emphasis should be on community cohesion. This new context would have particular ramifications for Tablighi Jamaat (TJ)—a nonengaging, Islamic, theocratic, and missionary movement wanting to build Britain's largest mosque in the East end of London, and only a short distance from the then planned Olympics Stadium.

TJ has a long history in Britain as being one of the first Islamic organizations to be established there after World War II, although it tends to function among Muslim communities and, where possible, avoids interaction with a wider society. For a long time, TJ has wanted to construct a flagship mosque in London that would function both as a place of prayer and as a processing and dispatch center for its missionary activities. TJ acquired their 18-acre plot in West Ham in 1996 and intended to use it as a Muslim foundation, incorporating a mosque, an Islamic boarding school, and accommodation to house traveling missionary groups.

TJ erected a temporary mosque on the land consisting of interconnected portacabins and a car park. The mosque functions all days in a week and can accommodate up to 3,000 male worshipers.

After London won the bid to host the Olympic Games in 2012, TJ wanted to develop an iconic mosque dedicated to the movement's purposes and to act as a Muslim hub for the Games. Original plans for the new mosque called for a building accommodating up to 70,000 worshippers, a proposal that sparked mass controversy and earned it the epithet of "Mega Mosque." TJ leaders were forced to reconsider and downsize their aspirations. Plans were further thwarted when TJ's site gained strategic importance to Newham Council for the delivery of new housing and economic development. TJ was told that any redevelopment of the site would have to be of mixed use and of value to the wider community. TJ has been staunch in wanting the site to feature a large mosque and amenities important to the functioning of TJ.

The focus of this book is on TJ and its struggle in post-7/7 context to build a large mosque in London. The term "struggle" is used consciously, for the post-7/7 period has been characterized by the securitization of Islam and scrutiny over ambitious projects—at times with good cause—involving Islamic organizations. The book concentrates on how TJ navigates the British context to gain permission to construct the proposed mosque. It is a study of how elites shape and direct a movement in goal attainment and how movements such as TJ learn to adapt to local contexts (even if in a strategic way) as a means of ensuring the survival and growth of the organization. The politics of mosque construction become important, as do questions over citizenship, identity, and integration of minorities. Of prime importance is the question of what happens to theocratic and traditionally disengaged groups such as TJ that seek to advance major projects when government policy promotes active and engaged citizenship and uses this as the standard by which to judge groups and their proposed projects.

The securitization of Islam across liberal democracies has meant that Islamic organizations wishing to make claims on public space can no longer do so from a position of isolationism. They are expected to demonstrate that they are open, tolerant, and engaged with wider communities. This impacted the way TJ operates in Britain. Securitization is defined as

> the process of turning a community or issue from a political matter to a threat. It is something deemed to be so concerning that it bypasses normal political debate and becomes an emergency—for example imposing a control order on an individual just in case they do something wrong. (Jenkins 2011)

This book recognizes and challenges the overwhelming tendency to homogenize Muslims in Britain and Europe. There is no single Muslim community in Britain or Europe but rather multiple Muslim communities and individuals within those communities differ as much as individuals from other communities. As Lewis (2007) writes:

> Not only is Islam used to eclipse other identities, ethnic class or professional, many of which Muslims share with their fellow citizens, but Islam is in danger of being essentialized—reduced to some unchanging essence and pathologized. All too often, journalistic and political commentary on Islam supposes that actual ethnic particularities are subordinate to the aspirational rhetoric of belonging to one, undivided, worldwide community—the *ummah*. The reality is quite different.

In recent years, a number of texts emerged that further challenge the idea of a uniform Muslim community in Britain and started to impact policy toward Muslim communities (Abbas 2005b; Modood 2007; Ansari 2009; ChangeInstitute 2010; Esposito 2010). In the changing context, there has been growing demand that Muslims conform to a notion of Britishness—a concept that is still ill-defined, but which British Prime Minister David Cameron (2014) tried to better articulate. Stuart Croft argues that Britishness does not currently include people with a Muslim identity: "the rigid construction of Britishness not only excludes British Muslims but also securitizes them by viewing them as a suspect community" (Croft in Jenkins 2011).

In 1926, Maulana Mohammad Ilyas established TJ as a movement in India. It now has a presence in over 165 countries, and an estimated 80 million Muslims worldwide take part in its activities (Mohammed 2011: 2). Often described as a movement founded by Muslims and for Muslims—a revivalist organization seeking to reignite the spirit of Islam among the grassroots of Muslim communities across the globe—TJ has largely remained apart from the "mainstream" of Western societies to which it expanded (Metcalf 2004). It is a theocratic movement—"one in which persons endeavour to live according to the dictates of a religious conception of the good that is strict and comprehensive in its range of teachings" (Swaine 2006: 72). TJ fixates on working at reviving Islamic codes of conduct, including dress code, ways of eating and sleeping, manners as dictated by the *Shari'a*, nonengagement with non-Muslims, and abstinence from political activities. It is the practice of nonengagement that is viewed as problematic in community cohesion–driven contexts of the post-9/11 and post-7/7 periods and is an impediment to the prospects of TJ in Britain.

TJ is not a monolithic organization. Its modes of operation can vary depending on the context it finds itself in—sometimes varying within a country as much as between countries. TJ narratives often speak of a unified movement: unity in methods and ideology. This, however, is not always the case. TJ is able to adapt methods and reinterpret ideology in the light of local contexts. This book recognizes TJ's existence in a number of different forms. This includes TJ as a global movement based in and led from Nizamuddin, TJ in the national context (Britain, Australia, Pakistan, etc.), TJ in the local context (London, Sydney, Karachi, etc.), and, of course, TJ as lived and experienced by individuals. Distinguishing between the different forms of the movement will help to dispel any illusions about its uniformity and allow for exploration of how TJ works and adapts at local levels, as well as the extent of coordination and direction from the established hierarchy.

TJ has tried to avoid any interaction with non-Muslims for the majority of its history. To gain permission to construct a new mosque in London, TJ leaders—since 2006—tentatively embarked on a process of sociopolitical engagement. Their aim was to convince government officials and planning regulators of its openness, tolerance, and willingness to work with local government and the wider community. This has been a difficult process for TJ and has been manifested as a strategic repositioning of discourse to achieve TJ goals. Initially, the process of engagement in Western countries has been viewed by TJ as a means to an end—an instrumental strategy to allow their projects to progress, TJ leaders in London may not have anticipated the impact of sustained interaction with the "other." The argument is that through the process of engagement, TJ leaders in London began to be socialized into the expectations of liberal democracies.

In London, TJ's methods have been reexamined and reframed. It is a step too far to say that ideology changed or developed in a substantial manner. TJ leaders publicly asserted that through engagement with non-Muslims opportunities would also emerge for proselytization and a furtherance of the movement's work. At the same time, interaction with local government and planning officials allowed for the "other" to critique and challenge TJ's positions, leading the movement to reformulate messaging to resonate with wider societal norms.

A key concept reflected upon through much of the book is that of engagement. Engagement in the context of the post-9/11 and post-7/7 milieus has come to dominate the agenda in liberal democracies as the standard all groups in the society must strive to (Cantle 2001;

Home-Office 2005; Robinson 2005; Singh 2007; Kalra and Kapoor 2008). Engagement is seen as the basis for good citizenship. Michael Schudson argues that engaged citizens are those who "scan the environment and intervene or get active only when a threat is sensed" (1998: 310). Although this does not explain the exact instances when and where individuals or groups may become active within the sociopolitical sphere, it highlights that one need not be active all the time, but only when the need is felt.

Philip Lewis argues that Muslim communities in the West often go through different stages as part of the process of integration—with engagement having profound effects (2011). Requests for sociopolitical and cultural recognition often cause some form of conflict or contestation. This contestation should be seen as a positive sign—a sign that both sides are negotiating the acceptance of the other and, if managed properly, can result in adaptation and integration (Lewis 2011). This is not a one-way process, but one in which all sides involved have to recognize that some adjustment is necessary—even if the level of this may vary for each party and depend on its position within a given system. It is this process of adaptation that some TJ leaders in London have tried to negotiate and will be examined in this book.

For Lewis, the first stage in the adaptation process involves being caught between nostalgia and alienation. First-generation Muslims in a non-Muslim society are often marked by a separation from the "mainstream" of that society—both as a consequence of simply being new and unsure of the context, and because of misperceptions of migrants on the part of the host society (Lewis 2011). The second stage sees second-generation "migrants"—born in the "host" nation—no longer seeing themselves as migrants. They are familiar with the culture, can speak the language, and so expect to have some needs accommodated by their state.[1] This is where the process of engagement is important: second-/third-generation Muslims may ask for provisions such as *halal* meat in schools, *Shari'a*-compliant banking, and space for worship.

Empirical data gathered for this book are based on a mixed-method approach. Extensive observation research at a number of TJ-affiliated sites, interviews with TJ grassroots adherents and leaders, as well as a comprehensive reading of primary Tablighi literature were completed. Extensive notes were taken during talks given at Tablighi mosques and public engagement functions attended by TJ in London. The observation research and the interviews focused on the ways in which Tablighis negotiate the process of adaptation through strongly held religious beliefs and in contexts that do not always recognize the validity of those beliefs. An emphasis is also placed on understanding everyday routines and rituals of Tablighis. This allows for comprehending the subjective meanings members of the movement, and especially its leaders, assign to social processes, including that of moving isolationism to engagement. At the same time, conversations and interviews with senior Tablighis and grassroots members covered broad-ranging subjects from TJ history and its core ideologies, to what shape missionary tours take and how decisions are made. It is hoped that through the use of ethnographic techniques with emphasis on both TJ leaders and grassroots members of the movement, voice has been heard of people who may not have had a chance to access research settings, which will allow for an extra layer of analysis and interpretation.

Over 150 hours of observation of proceedings at the TJ's West Ham mosque in London were made, including the Thursday evening gatherings. A visit was made to TJ's Christian Street mosque in London, and two visits were made to TJ's European headquarter mosque in Dewsbury. Over 200 hours were spent on conversations with Tablighis "hanging out" at Muslim-owned cafes, stores, and bookshops. This allowed for more relaxed conversations and exchanges.[2] Semistructured interviews were held with adherents of the London movement, and this included two senior members. Interviews with senior planning officials involved in negotiating TJ's construction project allowed for an informed opinion on the movement's adaptation from governmental and professional perspectives. Further interviews were conducted with those who oppose TJ and who have sought to characterize the movement as steadfast in its isolationism and hence lacking the ability to engage or integrate.

Being a participant in "culture" is important to ethnographic work and implies immersion of one's self into the routines and everyday rhythms of the community one is observing—for example, building interactions with the people who can show and tell the researcher what is going on in a given setting, and who can help assign meaning to actions (Wax 1983). In recent sociological and ethnographic studies, this has been termed "deep hanging out" (Wogan 2004). Although the term "hanging out" can conjure images of a technique lacking in methodological rigor, it is one of the most effective ways of conducting sensitive research. "Hanging out" with the ones a researcher intends to study allows for a profound understanding of how people really function within a given context. In *Gang Leader for a Day,* Venkatesh makes the following comment—a comment that a participant made on his ethnographic methodology:

> You shouldn't go around asking them silly questions…With people like us, you should hang out, get to know what they do, how they do it. No one is going to answer questions like that. You need to understand how young people live on the streets. (2008: 21)

"Hanging out" was invaluable when examining the adaption of TJ's strategies and moves toward greater sociopolitical engagement and how the movement is organized. Tablighis were more likely to discuss such matters in more social and relaxed contexts as opposed to being asked structured questions in a formal interview process.

Elements of risk and security were important considerations of the research design and implementation. The safety of participants who (hesitatingly) took part in what can be a sensitive research area was considered. Anonymity was granted to all participants so as to "mitigate risks of harm," except in instances where their role was a matter of public record and their consent was forthcoming (Lambert 2010: 75). Research into a topical subject area such as this has implications, given the interest in such research from media and government. Efforts were made to ensure that research was carried out ethically, accurately, and honestly.

The book is organized in four parts. The first serves to provide a theoretical and conceptual understanding of the key themes and issues around TJ's mosque project. Chapter 2, which follows this introduction, identifies TJ as an illiberal, nonengaging, and theocratic movement that for wanting to gain permission to construct a large mosque is trying to adapt its strategies to resonate with the norms of liberal democracies. The chapter focuses on questions emerging at the forefront of debates across liberal democracies, including the role of Islam in the West, citizenship, national identity, and how best to integrate increasingly diverse populations into the nation state. The chapter explores what happens to illiberal and politically disengaged groups wanting to segregate themselves from what they regard as corrupt and immoral wider societies. This becomes especially important when such groups want to advance major projects in those societies and are judged by the standards set by political elites.

The second part of the book consists of two chapters outlining the historical and organizational development of TJ. The first (chapter 3) places TJ in its historical context, outlining its philosophical and ideological trajectories stemming from the sociopolitical writings of Shah Walliuallah, which stress the importance of Islamic revival as a means of moral correction, to the emergence of the Deobandi school of Islam in India. The Deobandi emphasis was on the centrality of the *Shari'a* acting as a symbolic marker of identity. If Muslims applied the *Shari'a* to their lives, dressed as Muslims, and abandoned local customary practices, a strong and separate communal identity would emerge. This would ensure that Muslims were not swallowed into the Hindu fold or corrupted by the Western influences of British colonialism. It is here that the ideas to revive a pristine form of Islam, unsullied by customary practices, as a means to reempower Islam as a force in the modern world will be discussed. Chapter 4 examines TJ as a practical organization—its leadership, hierarchies, and organizational structure. The chapter looks at those who join TJ and asks what has attracted them to the movement. It also outlines TJ's missionary activities and the central place these have in the lives of TJ activists.

These two chapters together offer the theoretical, historical, and practical knowledge necessary to understand the argumentation and crucial concepts around TJ as a modern Islamic movement. This is a movement that is becoming increasingly adept at negotiating shifting sociopolitical contexts. The chapters also provide a basis to understand how and why movements such as TJ undergo and manage any process of adaptation.

The book's third part moves from looking at TJ as a global movement to examining the case study of TJ in Britain. Chapter 5 examines the establishment of TJ in Britain, particularly the Tablighi community in London and TJ's European headquarters in Dewsbury. The chapter places this into the wider context of Muslim communities' development in Britain and uses figures from the latest UK Census (2011) to highlight the heterogeneity of Islam in Britain. The early and present goals and aspirations of TJ in Britain are examined and compared. The chapter tackles the questions of whether TJ is an isolationist movement that promotes the ghettoization of Muslims around its mosques, or whether it adapts to the shifting sociopolitical context in Britain. The chapter explores many of the historical debates surrounding TJ so that the ensuing chapters may focus on TJ's current aims and objectives in London.

Chapter 6 identifies how and why TJ began the process of engagement and adaptation. Since 2005, TJ leaders in London realized that their goal of mosque construction would need to involve engaging with Newham Council and wider communities. The chapter analyzes the ways in which TJ leaders sought to adapt to and engage with the state and other institutions—to advance their goals and objectives—and the effects engagement had on the movement. While debates examined in this book are specific to the TJ leaders in London, many of the methods and tactics are also typical of those used by other Muslim groups. One may need only to look at attempts to construct mosques in New York, Cologne, Berlin, and Paris to see the similarities. These include entering the arena of social and political engagement, and public relations, and demonstrating that Islam is not a religion of violence. The chapter further charts the opposition to its mosque proposals from both Muslim and non-Muslim groups in Britain. It becomes clear that TJ and their "Mega Mosque" went from a local issue to became a global topic, with the story reported from as far as San Francisco and Sydney.

The final chapter in the section (chapter 7) reconsiders the research questions in light of TJ's activities in Britain from 2010 to 2014. The ways in which organizations such as TJ learn to adapt to new norms and local circumstances are examined. This ability to adapt to local circumstances will be a key for its continued survival and expansion in the United Kingdom. TJ in London demonstrated its (strategic) adaptability by showing that it can understand what local authorities and planning inspectors want with regard to planning policy. On a different level, they have had to reassure supporters that they are remaining true to the fundamental tenets of their faith, an act inconsistent with the aims and objectives of the local authority and planning bodies. If a movement is able to do both of these in a meaningful way, then they are likely to succeed. TJ tried to do this during the first public inquiry they had to attend, and indeed since 2005 when the plans for the so-called "Mega Mosque" came to the public forefront. Of course, the question that is most important is whether TJ made a *genuine* attempt at adaptation or whether their actions signify a temporary strategic shift in methods.

The fourth part of the book consists of one chapter. Chapter 8 presents an in-depth analysis of what TJ is from the perspective of the movement's own followers. The chapter is set in parallel to the previous two chapters, for the events occur during the same period (2006–2014). The importance of the chapter, however, is that it provides a perspective on what was happening inside TJ at the same time that TJ leaders were making public statements about the changing nature of the movement. What is clear is that across the world, TJ presents a similar message to its members irrespective of context. Even if in practice, the way it operates in different local settings may differ. In essence, the argument is that TJ is a movement whose main concern is, and always has been, the "eternal"—that is, working toward the complete reorientation of life to the exact imitation of Prophet Mohammad and early generations of Muslims. The chapter places importance on how narratives of salvation, heaven, and hell affect the actions of TJ followers. Modern society is portrayed as immoral and sinful, with TJ activities providing a counterculture and safe haven from this. Tablighis are taught to take their attention away from consumerism and from all the things modern society presents as important for success and instead reinvest their time and funds in pursuit of the movement's goals. For TJ members, the primary goal aside from the construction of the proposed mosque is that of inviting others to Islam and convincing other Muslims to adopt Tablighi ways. The chapter outlines how TJ members draw upon traditional ideologies and concepts to govern their lives and how they negotiate living in a liberal democracy.

The book concludes through returning to a much broader overview of TJ and comments on the implications of the movement's strategies. The chapter reconsiders the role of resurgent religion in liberal democracies and the impact liberalism has on how illiberal groups practice their beliefs. As the context shifts in Britain from one of multiculturalism to social cohesion, questions arise over how illiberal and theocratic groups fit into society and how much of their requests can and should be accommodated. It is in this light that TJ's quest for their "Mega Mosque" should be viewed. TJ is a complex movement that is able to adapt the way it operates, even if it is a temporary and strategic shift to further its core aims. Drawing on and reframing its traditions to resonate with the wider community, TJ leaders in London sought to prove that they were willing and able to "play by the rules of the game" in Britain but ultimately fell short. From the perspective of TJ's leaders in London, the new mosque when built will act as a symbol of Islam and correct Islamic practice in the area. As such, the use of innovative methods was to be a means to an end and, from the perspective of some TJ leaders, a necessary evil. The process of sociopolitical engagement is contentious within the ranks of TJ in London, Britain, and even internationally. Time will tell if it has paid off.

PART I

Theoretical and Analytical Framework: Understanding the Context

CHAPTER 2

Framing the Context

The central concern of this book is to better understand Tablighi Jamaat (TJ) in Britain and its struggle to construct its new mosque—the so-called "Mega Mosque"—in the post-7/7 climate. Although mosque construction in Europe and especially Britain has become more common, the process is still controversial. What makes TJ's case interesting is that TJ is no ordinary Muslim group and its proposed mosque is no ordinary mosque. TJ is a theocratic and illiberal movement, traditionally disengaged and scornful of its surrounding secular/non-Muslim contexts. At the same time, it wants to build one of Europe's largest mosques in London. This is something that requires a high level of engagement with wider society. TJ's mosque if built will act not only as a place of prayer but also as a coordination and dispatching center for its international missionary activities. Most Muslim groups in the United Kingdom do not have the skills to deal with the lengthy planning processes involved with constructing such large mosques. In the current security-driven atmosphere, the process is even long-drawn-out. TJ faced two major public inquiries over its plans. Muslim leaders, however, have learned to navigate local contexts. Islamic movements are proving the ability to adapt—even if strategically. Context is a powerful force in shaping behavior, but the challenge for many Muslim groups, TJ included, is how to meet these challenges without compromising beliefs. As the case may be with TJ, there is sometimes too much of a gap between the demands (especially sociocultural demands) of the planning process and what a given group actually believes.

The story of TJ and its struggle to build its new mosque in London is one of learning to navigate a shifting sociopolitical context. It has been about an adaptation in strategies brought about as a matter of necessity, and as a means to gain permission to construct the mosque. Yet, no matter what the reasons behind attempted adaptation, the important point is that this acts as a foil for understanding how theocratic and illiberal movements can undergo a process of change in Western liberal democracies. This is especially so if the contextual pressures demand it and if they are sustained.

TJ's case is further important because it brings to the vanguard a number of wider issues and questions emerging at the forefront of national debates across liberal democracies. These are issues related to the role of Islam in the West, definitions of citizenship and national identity, and how best to integrate increasingly diverse populations into the nation state. The question with TJ is, what happens to illiberal and politically disengaged groups that wish to segregate themselves from what they regard as corrupt and immoral wider societies? And, when government policy seeks to define good citizens as those who are actively engaged in the sociopolitical life of the community? Further, how do such conceptions of good citizenship impact the activities and interactions of those groups that do not fit the definition in these societies? Moreover, how does such a group operate in a liberal "post-Christian" society (Williams 2014), especially when wanting to advance a major construction project that has wider sociocultural ramifications?

This chapter interacts with the above questions and outlines theoretical concepts that subsequent chapters will engage. Given that context is such a powerful shaper in the way groups operate, this chapter captures the context in which TJ operates in Britain. When it comes to the question of the rights of minority groups to pursue their own cultural and religious practices, the British context has traditionally been one of proactive multiculturalism. This is now changing. Urban riots in the north of England in 2001 and the July 2005 bombings on the London public transport system pushed government to rethink how well multiculturalism worked and how else to ensure integration of citizens. Indeed in February 2011, British Prime Minister David Cameron gave a high-profile speech at the Munich International Security Conference, where he said:

> Under the doctrine of state multiculturalism, we have encouraged different cultures to live separate lives, apart from each other and apart from the mainstream. We've failed to provide a vision of society to which they feel they want to belong. We've even tolerated these segregated communities behaving in ways that run completely counter to our values. (2011)

The concept of community cohesion emerged as central to how Britain would move forward. This policy is primarily concerned with shifting the context in Britain to one where citizens are integrated into a stronger British national identity (still poorly articulated) and where different communities engage with one another. This chapter captures how the context in Britain changed and the impact this had on Muslim communities, especially illiberal theocratic groups such as TJ.

Illiberal Theocrats

As argued above, a fundamental theme of this book is how illiberal groups function in liberal democracies and how they adapt and attempt to advance their goals. These are groups in which followers strive to live according to the strict and comprehensive dictates of a religious conception of the good. As Swaine argues, theocratic groups are not homogenous and, in modern liberal democracies, are divided into two different kinds: ambitious and retiring. Ambitious theocrats are "enthusiastic participants in public life, engaging in public discourse and political affairs with a view to supplanting liberal institutions with stricter laws and regulations drawn from their religious conceptions of the good" (Swaine 2006: 9). In other words, these groups engage with the wider society as a means to alter the way that society functions and to ultimately change the system so that it becomes one based on the values and principles of the theocratic group. There are many examples of such groups, including elements of the Religious Right in America, the Muslim Brotherhood in Egypt (at least until recently), and the Nation of Islam in the United States. Such theocrats are politically ambitious and have no qualms in actively promoting their doctrines. As Swaine puts it, in many cases ambitious theocrats use "a variety of means to try to topple the liberal establishment and the debased values that they believe its institutions enshrine" (2006: 9).

Retiring theocrats alternatively withdraw from everyday affairs. They are reluctant to partake in political or other civic matters, working instead to live in small communities where they may practice their religion in seclusion (Swaine 2006: 9). TJ is one such movement, traditionally operating exclusively within Muslim communities. These groups "denounce the concrete compromises elaborated informally by individual Muslims dealing with an alien environment. They shame Muslims who compromise with the dominant culture" (Roy 2002: 124). Left to their own devices, such groups would be content to operate in segregated areas and under different sociolegal frameworks (as defined by their religious conception of the good) than the wider society. Other retiring theocrats include Old Order Amish settlements in the United States, as well as polygamous Mormon communities.

Swaine argues that theocratic communities are generally nonliberal—not to mean that they reject all liberal values, but rather that they seek to preserve the sense of their religious communities by discouraging or banning outright liberal values and practices. Religious doctrines of theocratic communities are widely or fully comprehensive in the sense that they extend to cover:

> All recognized values and virtues within one rather precisely articulated scheme of thought. Theocratic conceptions of the good do not apply merely to some areas of members' lives; rather, those conceptions range across nearly all life practices, covering personal associations, familial structures, institutional arrangements, practices of ritual and worship, ideals of character, and so on. (Swaine 2006: 73)

Governments in liberal democracies often fail to understand this. The question that remains is one of how a liberal democracy may deal— in a just and fair way—with those who do not identify with liberal democracy, or whose religious beliefs do not allow them to integrate into the wider society.

David Cameron indicated that there may be little option for those who do not wish to integrate into wider British society. In his 2011 speech at the International Security Conference in Munich, he stressed the importance of promoting a more active and "muscular liberalism" (Cameron 2011). He added that it was no longer enough for a society to "say to its citizens, as long as you obey the law we will just leave you alone" or for the state to "stand neutral between different values" (Cameron 2011). The passive tolerance of multiculturalism was seen as problematic. Instead, Cameron defines a "genuinely liberal country" as one that does much more. This includes "making sure that immigrants speak the language of their new home and ensuring that people are educated in the elements of a common culture and curriculum" (Cameron 2011). In 2014, after news alleging infiltration of Islamic extremists into some British schools (Gilligan 2014; Mackie 2014), Cameron went even further. His message was simple:

> In recent years we have been in danger of sending out a worrying message: that if you don't want to believe in democracy, that's fine; that if equality isn't your bag, don't worry about it; that if you're completely intolerant of others, we will still tolerate you. As I've said before, this

has not just led to division, it has also allowed extremism—of both the violent and non-violent kind—to flourish. (2014)

For Swaine, as well as many others in liberal democracies, the type of discourse presented by Cameron is problematic, especially in liberal states where there has been a traditional emphasis on freedom of religion and conscience. As Swaine puts it, theocrats' moral right to religious free exercise "is a right largely to be left unmolested in daily life" (2006: 109). He argues that working to integrate theocratic communities in to a larger political entity "would come at the cost of the reasonable ability of theocrats to pursue their very conceptions of the good, whether the integration were forced, legislated or merely encouraged by government" (2006: 109).

Integration can, of course, take many forms. Those versions aiming to bring theocratic communities into a larger political unity, such as Britain's policy of community cohesion or France's policy of *laïcité*, would "alter the pursuits and practices of religious communities and risk homogenizing people's conceptions of the good" (Swaine 2006: 109). In the post-9/11 period, liberal states have been more willing to promote cohesive communities, as well as to better ensure national security. In this sense, problems are posed to liberal states not only by theocrats who wish to purse policies of integration but also by those citizens who opt to live in gated communities and are unwilling to engage with wider society. In reality, however, much of the policy focus has been on Muslim communities who are often seen as posing an existential threat to the way of life in a liberal society.

The Impact of Shifting Contexts

Multiculturalism has long been seen as a defining characteristic of the British context and symbolizes the celebration of cultural diversity. In simplest terms, it is the promotion of the coexistence of diverse cultures. In reality, there is no one agreed-upon definition of the concept and, indeed, governments across different countries have interpreted it in different ways. Multiculturalism is a form of integration, "not a flattening process of uniformity, but cultural diversity coupled with equal opportunity in an atmosphere of mutual tolerance" (Rex 1979: 32). So, what does a multicultural society look like? Bhikhu Parekh says that a multicultural society is one which "includes several distinct cultural, ethnic and religious communities, and needs to find ways of reconciling two equally legitimate and sometimes conflicting demands" (1998: 1). More generally, however, multiculturalism, at least in Britain, came to mean the "political accommodation of non-white, mainly post-immigration minorities" (Modood 2007: 15).

Aspects of multiculturalism have been used by local authorities in Britain since the 1970s, especially in regions with a high level of migration. It was not until 1997 and the election of Tony Blair's Labour government that the multiculturalist approach was fully promoted by government. This allowed for improved opportunities for ethnic minorities in Britain and for an increase in the provision of services and institutions to those communities. It also created resentment from some white British people. Following large-scale riots in the north of England in the summer of 2001, and closely followed by terrorist attacks in the United States, the government started to reconsider the success of multiculturalism. In particular, more than any other group, Muslims were branded as fanatics (Wheatcroft 2006).

While multicultural policies may have aided a Muslim community in construction of a landmark project in the past, the new context created an atmosphere in which such schemes were viewed with suspicion. Significantly the then Commissioner for Racial Equality, Trevor Philips, argued, "Multiculturalism has helped to segregate communities more effectively than racism" (Malik 2001). This sparked major debate over the role of multiculturalism, as well as the need for clarification on how minorities in Britain should be treated. This had profound consequences on TJ's project, which became associated with the promotion of segregation and division. By 2004 it was common to read or hear that British values were being challenged by cultural separatism and self-imposed segregation of Muslim migrants and that a "politically correct multiculturalism had fostered fragmentation rather than integration" (Modood 2007: 63; see also West 2005). This discourse against multiculturalism reached a new peak with the Islamist bombings of London's public transport system in July 2005. The perpetrators were Muslims born and raised in Britain, a country that had afforded them refuge from persecution, poverty, and freedom of worship. Many concluded that multiculturalism had failed or, worse still, was responsible for the bombings (Modood 2007: 11).

The July 2005 bombings in London were a catalyst in bringing about a profound contextual shift in Britain. The bombings had even more significant impact on TJ. The attack came only the morning after the announcement that London had won the 2012 bid to host the Olympic Games. This had cast security concerns over building TJ's proposed mosque. It would be just "a stones throw" from the Olympics Stadium (Izzard 2008). Kepel (2005) observed that the bombers were "children of Britain's own multicultural society" and that multiculturalism was the product of an implicit social consensus between Left-wing working-class movements and the public school–educated political elite. Their alliance allowed one side to monitor immigrant workers, while the other side secured votes through their religious leaders—"the July bombings have smashed this consensus to smithereens" (Kepel 2005). In other words, multiculturalism had failed to adequately accommodate Muslims into the mainstream of British society. The most damning declaration on multiculturalism came from Trevor Philips. He claimed that multiculturalism had once been useful, but is now "out of date" and makes "a fetish of difference" instead of encouraging minorities to be British (Baldwin and Rozenberg 2004).

It was not just the July 7 attacks that eroded the legitimacy of multiculturalism. Across liberal democracies, headlines appeared on an almost daily basis regarding culturally motivated attacks, many involving women or issues of sexuality and in opposition to liberal norms (Jacobson 2013: 147). Among the more prominent cases was the murder of Theo van Gogh, a Dutch filmmaker, in Amsterdam in 2004 by a Dutch Moroccan for the film he made criticizing the treatment of women in Islam (Dalrymple 2004). This was shortly followed by the controversy over Danish cartoons depicting the Prophet Mohammad in a demeaning way, which offended Muslims and caused worldwide riots and even attacks against Christians (Belien 2005). In Britain, Member of Parliament and former Secretary of State for Foreign and Commonwealth Affairs, Jack Straw, raised concerns about the increasing number of Muslim women in his constituency opting to wear the veil (Wainwright 2006). Such instances brought Muslims in the West to the forefront and provoked a context of anxiety.

TJ found itself at the centre of such controversy after a Muslim woman, Aishah Azmi, in the Yorkshire town of Dewsbury was dismissed as a primary school teacher for refusing to remove her veil in the classroom. The school claimed that the veil was obstructing the view of Azmi's facial expressions and that this was hampering classroom learning. Azmi argued that it was her personal decision to wear the veil and that she would not remove it if any male member of the staff was present—which the local authority could not agree to. It later emerged in a report by the *Sunday Times* that Azmi made her decision following a consultation with a local Islamic cleric, Mufti Yusuf Sacha, at TJ's Dewsbury mosque. The Tablighi cleric issued a fatwa stating that it was obligatory for women to wear the *niqab* in the presence of men who were not their blood relatives, including while working with children (Abdul 2006).

The much publicized efforts of Anjem Choudary, a fringe Islamist, to persuade the authorities to impose Shari'a zones in East London, and the actions of a few Muslims in the north of England to establish gay-free zones also exacerbated the situation despite Muslim community leaders condemning the actions (Pieri et al. 2013: 44–45). Most recently, an alleged campaign by Islamists to infiltrate schools in the city of Birmingham and to impart a hardline Islamic message brought the issues of citizenship, integration, and values back to the center of the debate. In one of the schools, children were taught that white women were "prostitutes" and were urged to join in anti-Christian chants (Shipman 2014). *The Times* made a reference to a report by the Education Funding Agency about the Oldknow Academy in Birmingham, stating that the primary school is "taking on the practices of an Islamic faith school and in this regard is not promoting community cohesion" (Shipman 2014). Incidents such as the ones discussed above impacted the context in liberal democracies and promoted an atmosphere of distrust toward Muslim communities. It is in this context that TJ's plans to advance the construction of their new mosque should be viewed in, and which explains why the process has been so hard.

THE CONTROVERSIAL POLITICS OF MOSQUE CONSTRUCTION

Such events served to create an image of Muslims as a set of problematic communities in Europe and resulted in a backlash against the establishment of new mosques, which began to be seen as hubs of radicalization. The building of mosques in Europe is one arena where the presence of Islam in the public sphere is increasingly visible. There are plans to build several hundred new and often magnificent mosques throughout Europe, including in London, Cologne, and Paris. Proposals to build a mosque and Islamic cultural center two blocks away from Ground Zero in New York also sparked mass debate and controversy (Ghosh and Mich 2010; Nocera and Goldsmith 2010; Rabinowitz 2010; Schwartz 2010).

Stefano Allievi (2010: 15) describes three main types of mosques found across Europe: Muslim community centers (often in converted buildings), purpose-built mosques, and Muslim prayer rooms (a loose category and often in less noticeable storefronts or residential buildings). The construction of purpose-built mosques is much more likely to be contested than the conversion or use of a preexisting building. A further category debated in France is that of the landmark mosque, or the *mosquée cathédrale*. *Mosquées cathédrales*—the category in which TJ's proposed London mosque belongs—have a far greater role in symbolic and community representation (DeHanas and Pieri 2011: 800). Purpose-built mosques, especially *mosquées cathédrales*, are controversial in large part due to their visibility, religious symbolism, and claim to public space. Katy Gardner describes the "Islamicization" of urban spaces in Britain during the process of mosque building:

> Increasingly, specific areas of Britain were becoming viable places in which to be a Muslim. In Tower Hamlets, for example, not only is the East London mosque a striking example of Middle Eastern architecture, but with its prominent position on the Whitechapel Road, and the broadcast of its azan (call to prayer), it is a graphic claim to British space by local Muslims. (2002: 109)

Also writing about the East End and the East London Mosque, John Eade (1993) considers the creation of Islamic spaces as a process of politically articulating community. Such articulations may threaten the national and community imaginaries of other local residents and political actors. They can be perceived as alien intrusions into national, cultural, or "secular" space. The Swiss referendum of November 2009 banning the construction of minarets successfully mobilized a mass resistance to the symbolic expansion of Islamic space and passed with 57.5 percent of the vote (Schindall 2009). Another powerful example of a perceived spatial threat is the controversy over the proposed Park51 Muslim community center in New York City: "It has been branded the 'Ground Zero Mosque' by opponents, touching a nerve of the September 11 tragedy, even though the proposed building is not actually a mosque and would be located at a two-block distance from the Ground Zero site" (DeHanas and Pieri 2011: 800).

Research carried out on mosque construction in the United Kingdom prior to 2005 indicated mosque construction as somewhat unproblematic there, especially when compared to other regions of Europe. Seán McLoughlin (2005) studied the minutes of the Bradford Council planning committee from 1999 to mid-2003 and found no evidence of public mobilizations against mosque renovation or construction. It was TJ's mosque—whose proposals emerged at a time of immense contextual shifts—that became the most controversial construction project in Britain. TJ's proposed London mosque was to be the largest, accommodating 70,000 worshipers (Steyn 2005). Architecture has become the field of a fierce ideological battle about the visibility of Europe's 16 million Muslims (Knofel 2008), and this is now also the case in the United States.

Community Cohesion

As debates on the construction of mosques were making headlines across liberal democracies, governments were also discussing new policies to better integrate increasingly diverse populations. Perhaps the most important of these in the British context has been the policy of community cohesion. The concern over community cohesion in the United Kingdom emerged after the 2001 riots in the north of Britain (Burnett 2004) and intensified in the aftermath of the July 2005 attacks in London and Glasgow. Community cohesion was developed as a policy concept and enacted by successive governments as a way to establish a greater sense of citizenship through the advancement of greater knowledge, respect, and contact between people from diverse cultural backgrounds. As Maleiha Malik notes, a cohesive community "is one where there is a common vision and all communities have a sense of belonging, where diversity is appreciated and positively valued" (2005: 46). Community cohesion further refers to situations where "individuals are bound to one another by common social and cultural commitments" (Lynch 2001: 70).

In Britain, community cohesion has been closely linked to New Labour's concept of citizenship and continued by the Conservative–Liberal Democratic Coalition government. It forms part of the government's strategy toward minorities, and Muslims in particular. The policy has a number of citizenship objectives—namely that a cohesive Britain requires its citizens to share a core value base and to actively participate in the electoral process (Shukra et al. 2004). The policy aims to foster a sense of citizenship and belonging "amongst minority groups and the majority communities" (Malik 2005: 58). A cohesive community, according to Malik, is one where

(1) There is a common vision and all communities have a sense of belonging; (2) The diversity of people's different backgrounds and circumstances is appreciated and positively valued; (3) Those from different backgrounds have similar life opportunities; and (4) People from different backgrounds develop strong, positive relationships in the workplace, in schools and within neighbourhoods. (2005: 55)

This impacts illiberal and theocratic groups such as TJ that traditionally disengage from the political system. It means that such groups struggle in communicating their needs and concerns to policymakers. Yet, it also means that groups also have to adapt and start to engage with the political process.

One factor closely connected to community cohesion is reestablishing Britishness as an identity that all Britons can integrate. On the right wing of the political spectrum are, according to Modood, exclusivist, even racist notions of Britishness that claim that nonwhite people can never really be British. On the left wing of the spectrum are some who feel there is something deeply wrong about rallying around the idea of Britain. It is too racist, imperialist, militaristic, and elitist, and the goal of seeking Britishness is demeaning to new migrants (Modood 2005: 6). Yet, as Modood rightly argues, if the goal of wanting to be British is not a worthwhile goal for new migrants and their decedents, what then are they supposed to integrate into "and why bother with integration at all"? (2005: 6). If there is nothing strong, purposive, and inspiring to integrate into, why bother with integration at all? We cannot, as Modood states, ask new Britons to integrate and also exclaim that being British is a "hollowed-out and meaningless project whose time has come to an end" (2005: 7).

Indeed, David Cameron reinforced this importance of British values. He said it is the duty of a liberal state to identify its core values and to then set about promoting them as mandatory for all who choose to live there:

> I believe we need to be far more muscular in promoting British values and the institutions that uphold them. That's what a genuinely liberal country does: it believes in certain values and actively promotes them. It says to its citizens: this is what defines us as a society. What does that mean in practice? We have already taken some big steps. We are making sure new immigrants can speak English, because it will be more difficult for them to understand these values, and the history of our institutions, if they can't speak our language. We are bringing proper narrative history back to the curriculum, so our children really learn our island's story—and where our freedoms and things like our Parliament and constitutional monarchy came from. We are changing our approach further in schools. We are saying it isn't enough simply to respect these values in schools—we're saying that teachers should actively promote them. They're not optional; they're the core of what it is to live in Britain. (Cameron 2014)

Muslims in Britain, however, already identify as British even if elements of the British population do not view them as such. As DeHanas argues, "survey after survey has shown the very opposite—minorities within British society are the highest identifiers as British" (Hailes 2014). Governments in liberal societies would do well to remember the increasing level of Islamophobia faced by Muslims and the impact this has upon communities and ultimately how Muslim communities interact with government policy.

Research by the Change Institute highlighted that many of their Muslim interviewees expressed concern at the level of Islamophobia in the media; one interviewee commented, "the British media makes it sound as if the whole Muslim community is rife with extremism—this is so far from the truth" (Change Institute 2009b: 53). Islamic movements face difficulty engaging with the British press if the starting point for relations between the press and the Muslim groups is already one of such imbalance. This will be a significant point when considering and analyzing strategies adopted by TJ in London since 2006.

ENGAGEMENT

One of the primary ways in which illiberal and theocratic groups start to adapt to liberal democracies is through the process of engagement, in particular civic engagement. Engagement under the community cohesion–driven context in Britain is seen as the basis of good citizenship and a standard to which each individual must be held. It is further especially important for TJ's case, as their opponents have branded them as disengaged and actively in pursuit of segregation from the wider societies. TJ leaders deny this and claim that they are deeply concerned for the wider community and are active across communities in a number of ways.

The concept of engagement has at times been seen as a catchall phrase—something difficult to define. This book builds on Adler and Goggin's works and sees this as a process involving citizens participating in "the life of a community in order to improve conditions for others or to help shape the community's future" (2005: 241). The understanding is that to be engaged is only to participate in a community and with a view to "shape" that community's future. This is a version of engagement that chimes with TJ. As will be seen, TJ is active across Muslim communities, working to reorient Muslims to a Tablighi understanding of Islam. At the same time, the movement seeks to combat drug and alcohol addiction among young Muslims and to give a purpose to those young peoples' lives. For TJ, this is active participation in the community and also a way that shapes and improves the future of that community. The majority of TJ's dealings, however, stem from a position of wanting to introduce a Tablighi version of Islam. As such, engagement (at least with non-Tablighi communities) is viewed more as a means than as a process that is beneficial in and of itself.

For some, political participation forms another important part of what constitutes engaged citizens. Brady notes that political participation is an "action by ordinary citizens dedicated toward influencing some political outcomes" (1999: 737). He emphasizes that we should think about political participation, first, as marked and discernable actions that people voluntarily take part. Second, "people" means ordinary citizens, not political elites or civil servants. Third, the concept refers to deliberate attempts to influence the people in power to make a difference. To be interested in politics and societal issues is not enough. It is an attempt to influence others—any powerful actors, groups, or business enterprises in society—and their decisions that concern societal issues (Ekman and Amna 2012: 286). This has been somewhat problematic for TJ, although the group vows that it is completely apolitical. In order to gain permission to construct the proposed mosque, the London branch of the movement attuned to be political.

For TJ, being engaged politically could give rise to a fear of confrontation or of heated discussions, which may take time and focus away from their more important missionary work. The movement also understands that Islamic groups that take a political stance are also more likely to draw attention from the government and ultimately face restrictions. In the case of TJ, a distinction needs to be drawn between a movement that engages in a political process out of necessity and a movement engaging in wider political debates (such as the global situation of Muslims). For TJ, their entrance on to the political stage in Britian has been out of necessity—that is the desire to construct their new mosque. The movement still disavows all other forms of political engagement, and even engagement over mosque construction has for the most part been limited to Tablighi leaders and elites. While TJ leaders in London have negotiated a process of engagement with political elites and institutions, their followers are told that politics is a dirty business.

Even so, one cannot deny that TJ has what Gaborieau terms a "vision of the political future of the Muslim community" (2006: 62). Political engagement in order to further one's objectives is not necessarily a bad thing; it has to be achieved in the correct manner. This view of political engagement is particularly clear in the work of Mohammad Zakariyya (1898–1982), TJ's chief ideologue. He argues that to those whom "Allah has granted bravery and courage, and who are able and capable, having the necessary time, should definitely spend it in religious as well as political affairs for the general welfare of the Muslims" (Kandhlawi 2001: 36). The point here is that political engagement may be an option to those few people who have the abilities and strength to engage with the profane, but only in so far as that engagement furthers the cause of Islam. In this sense, political engagement may even be viewed as a form of *jihad*. As later chapters will argue, TJ leasers in London came to view their engagement strategy as a necessary evil—necessary because without it negotiations over mosque construction cannot progress, and evil because sociopolitical engagement has the power to corrupt an individual and take time away from the work of spreading the faith.

ADAPTATION

Engagement is important because it has the capacity to induce adaptation. Adaptation is a process of change made by a given population in interaction with its environment that enhances its survival and continuation. This is particularly clear in the example of TJ in London. With becoming socialized into the expectations of the planning system though a process of engagement, TJ has attempted—at least through discourse—to say that they have changed their ways. The claim is that they recognize their violation of planning regulations in the past and are now committed to abiding by the rules. At the same time, they admit that there is no place for social isolationism in Britain and, as such, are working on becoming more inclusive.

Yet, as Barger and Reza argue, change in and of itself is not adaptation. The "ultimate measure of the adaptive success of change is how much it contributes to the survival and continuation of a group. A change is most adaptive when it maximizes the group's continuation as a distinct unit" (Barger and Reza 1994: 11). This point is key. Groups such as TJ do not change for the sake of change, but rather embark on a process of adaptation, even if strategic, as a means of ensuring the group's survival in as distinct a form as possible. For TJ, the process of adaptation is a means to an end. TJ elites sanctioned the use of innovative methods to gain permission for constructing the proposed new mosque. But once built, the mosque will act as a beacon of correct Islamic practice and missionary activity for the region.

TJ is not the only theocratic or illiberal movement to have undergone a process of adaptation. In fact, there is a set pattern that many such movements have followed. Literature from the sociology of religion outlines this process. A given movement will face a period of intense problematization or opposition. The movement will become an object of popular scorn, taking the form of angry mobs, a hostile press, the emergence of counter groups, etc. In order to survive, the movement "learns" to be more adept at defusing, deflecting, and shielding itself from hostile social reaction. It is during this period that it becomes proactive in shaping a more benign public definition of itself (Harper and Le Beau 1993: 175). This is the same process to face TJ in London. After announcing plans for building a mosque initially set to be larger than St. Paul's Cathedral, TJ came under intense scrutiny and pressure. Moral entrepreneurs emerged to mobilize popular opposition, define TJ as threatening, and articulate grievances against it. This led to a large-scale public petition against the mosque and a series of hostile articles in the press. To protect the image of the movement, and to deflect accusations, TJ leaders hired public relations consultants, identified areas of public concern, and sought to address them. They changed their public discourse to reflect the changing context of Britain. They reiterated that they were open, tolerant, and willing to engage with wider communities in developing a mosque site that would benefit all.

A key point is that adaptation does not necessarily mean a change of doctrine or ideology. Illiberal or theocratic movements are more likely to modify the implications of belief for social practice and social relations than the beliefs themselves. For Harper and Le Beau, doctrine has the capacity to remain constant and "does not change much as [movements] move from high problematization to accommodation (though its mode of public presentation does). It is possible to maintain both unorthodox beliefs and high social accommodation" (1993: 178). TJ has not managed this to date, but there are examples of movements that have made the shift. Perhaps the best example is the Church of Jesus Christ of Latter Day Saints (the Mormons) in the United States. Mormon religious beliefs do not fall into the mainstream of American society. Yet their social adaptation allowed for a committed Mormon (Mitt Romney) to be nominated as the Republican Party's presidential nominee. Herein lies an important message to illiberal and theocratic movements. Sustained engagement over a period of time combined with elements of contextual adaptation can yield results without necessarily compromising doctrine.

What is important to remember is that the problematization of a movement is more likely if it is associated with practices or arrangements that are nonconventional. For example, if a movement appears to be deviant in the context in which it operates, it is far more likely to face opposition. Nonconventional attributes can take the form of people's appearances (fully veiled Muslim women; Muslim men with long beards and South Asian attire; or the shaved heads, orange robes, and chanting of the Hare Krishnas in the streets). Structural nonconventional arrangements can also be problematic (as in the case of polygamous communities, or where the spiritual and political authority of a group rests on one person who in turn defines what actions members may be allowed to enact). In varying degrees, these social and structural attributes have the potential to call into question the legitimacy of established values, about individualism, secularism, democracy, materialism, and in some cases national security. Mormons have been successful in the United States because their story is quintessentially American. "It has all the features we associate with being American: patriotism, country, entrepreneurship and capitalism all bound together" (Roof in Fitzgerald 2014).

As Gordon Melton puts it, "religions have to adapt if they're going to survive" (Melton in Fitzgerald 2014). Religions do not, of course, have literal DNA, but they can parallel how species mutate (Fitzgerald 2014). Theocratic movements must have certain key properties of successful genetic mutations if they are to succeed. The properties are inheritance, variation, and selection. It is a trademark of religions to claim not to have changed significantly in their core beliefs. Yet the ability to change without followers feeling like they have changed is a formidable adaptive tool (Fitzgerald 2014). Religions emphasize continuity to avoid appearing effervescent and to maintain their relation to the sacred and to those things that made them important in the first place. Religious movements want to stay connected to the sacred, to those aspects that sparked their founding and development. Rituals tend to endure, while behaviors adapt to social norms.

Commenting on the adaptive process, David Snow noted that movements can cultivate a style of "accommodative flexibility," not only by abandoning those attributes that make it socially problematic (such as dress),but also by endeavoring to "finess" its structural liabilities through deliberately contrived "public relations" (Snow 1979). To do this, "movements seek to build alliances with powerful established groups and agencies and to receive endorsements from notables, thereby gaining protection and some measure of social legitimacy" (Harper and Le Beau 1993: 183). It is about the process of becoming integrated into a nation's citizenship and gradually becoming accepted as part of the fabric of that society. This is something TJ leaders in London are working to achieve.

PART II

Conceptualizing Tablighi Jamaat

CHAPTER 3

Conceiving Tablighi Jamaat

INTRODUCTION

Tablighi Jamaat (TJ) is one of the world's largest religious movements. From its humble origins in "small town" colonial India, it grew to have a presence on every continent, and in almost every country in the world. Although its members are from diverse backgrounds, all share one key common interest—the propagation of Islam for the salvation of souls. To understand TJ's development and success as a movement, a closer look at its history is necessary. A number of studies provide detailed historical overviews of the movement (Haq 1972; Metcalf 1982; Sikand 2001; Nadwi 2002; Ali 2012), and this chapter focuses on the key factors that shaped the movement to what it is today.

Movements such as TJ are best understood through comprehending both the context from which they emerged as well as the context in which they are currently found. The sociopolitical and cultural milieu at the time of its formation explains how it emerged as well as why it takes on certain forms. Understanding contexts as well as contextual changes can explain why movements adapt over time and how the adaptive process is undertaken and managed.

TJ as an Islamic revivalist movement was born of efforts to rectify the ways in which Muslims practised Islam, as well as to increase the number of Muslim subjects in colonial India. This was part of a wider movement to increase the share of political power for Muslims in India under new openings for political participation being enacted toward the end of British rule. The aim was to increase Islam's significance, and this continues to be one of TJ's goals to this day. It is this historical examination of the movement—the factors that led to its inception, the ways the early movement shaped, and the ways these early influences characterize TJ's modes of operation today (in its transnational contexts)—this chapter aims to do.

The chapter argues that early strategies and recruitment methods as devised by Mohammad Ilyas (1885–1944), TJ's founder, as well as some of the difficulties encountered therein, are central to understanding how TJ formed and expanded in new contexts. When looking at how TJ forms in areas outside of its traditional South Asian base, the original establishment of the movement becomes important, as the new branches were to mirror the original. The movement Ilays founded in rural India provided the blueprint, inspiration, and structure to launch the movement elsewhere.

TJ's core philosophies and objectives—what have since become its myths, memories, and symbols—are outlined in this chapter. It is through invoking and embodying these that members of TJ today feel themselves "part of a dense network of Muslims, both dead and alive, and cherish a commitment to relive the Prophet's own time when he was part of a faithful few among a population sunken in ignorance" (Metcalf 1982: xv).

HISTORICAL CONTEXT: FROM WALLIULAH TO MOHAMMAD ILYAS

Mohammad Ilyas Kandhalawi founded TJ in circa 1926 in the Mewat province of India (southwest of Delhi) in response to the increasingly depraved state of Islam in the region. Since then, the movement has grown to a transnational organization. Its annual gatherings in Pakistan and Bangladesh are attended at times by more Muslims than *Hajj* would attract (LapidoMedia 2010). While this book is interested in the ways TJ adapts to new contexts, it is first important to understand the history of the movement. Tablighis themselves ascribe much importance to their history and to the revivalist strand of Islamic sociopolitical thought prevalent on the Indian subcontinent at the movement's foundation. To appreciate this context, attention must be turned to the demise of the Mughal Empire, the ascendancy of "British India," and the evolution of Deobandi Islam.

The Mughal Empire ruled over vast tracts of the Indian subcontinent in the early 1500s, extending from Bengal in the east to Balochistan in the west, Kashmir in the north to the Kaveri basin in the south. Its establishment heralded the consolidation of Islam in the region (Richards 1995: 163). The political suzerainty of the Mughals over the region continued to be exercised, at least in theory, until the mid-nineteenth century. In reality, however, the power of the Mughals began to fade with the death of Emperor Aurangzeb in 1707, formally coming to an end after the failed Mutiny of 1857 and deposition of the last reigning emperor by the British (Sikand 2002; Dalrymple 2008). For Muslims in India, the collapse of the Mughal Empire carried with it connotations of the waning of Islam. Hinduism, long present in the region, was in ascendance, not to mention the emerging influences of Christianity and later secularism. It was this threat, perceived or real, to the Islamic way of life—the shifting of the balance of power—that inspired Islamic reformists in the region and the founding of movements for the reinvigoration of the faith.

Crucial to the intellectual formation of these revivalist movements—TJ was one of them—was Shah Waliullah[1] (d.1762). Waliullah grew up watching the crumbling of the Mughal system. He was an Islamic scholar, reformer, and protagonist who attempted to reassess Islamic theology in light of changes taking place at the time. He believed that it was the moral collapse of society—a deviation from the path of Islam—and the decaying of the social order that caused the decline of the Mughal Empire (Upadhyay 2003; Al-Ghazali 2004). Waliullah bemoaned the urgent need for moral regeneration and a return to the ways of Mohammad and his companions—the *Sahaba* (Haq 1972: 67; Jones 1989: 51).[2] TJ leaders would later view this as essential in their mission—to reorient Muslims back to what they regarded as a correct practice of Islam. Waliullah was a key protagonist in instigating the spiritual revival of Muslims, spreading the message of Islamic spiritualism to the Indian masses and emphasizing the propagation of Islam to his students (Mortimer 1988: 67–9).

Waliullah supported the well-established tradition of Sufism in South Asia and promoted a pathway to God through devotion and transformation of the heart. While this devotional aspect of Sufism was important to him, he condemned what he believed to be external influences and innovations in Sufi practices such as worshiping at graves. He advocated the idea of a pure Islam devoid of what he saw as innovative practices. He believed Muslims should assert an independent identity free from the influence of Hindu polytheism (Mortimer 1988: 67–69; Jones 1989: 51). It is to this more orthodox interpretation of Sufi Islam that TJ was to situate.

By the middle of the nineteenth century, the Mughal Empire was nearing its collapse. Waliullah had watched with trepidation. British Imperial rule was firmly established and Mughal Emperors reduced to a position of compliance. In the same way Waliullah wanted to revive the temporal and spiritual power of Islam in the wake of the decline of Mughal power during his own time, so too did the founders of Darul Uloom at Deoband in the wake of the 1857 Indian

Mutiny.[3] The aftermath of the Mutiny was severe: the British evacuated the whole population of Delhi, exiled the Mughal king to Burma, and occupied the mosques of the city (Metcalf 1982: 84). The Muslims of Delhi were disproportionately blamed for their part in the Mutiny, "for the British believed that Muslims had fought from political grievances, Hindus from economic; and the former motive was understood to be more invidious and more dangerous" (Metcalf 1982: 85). It was due to the decline of the predominance of Islam and a breakdown of the social order following the Mutiny that many Muslims turned to a purer interpretation of Islam for patterns of action in their lives.

The founders of the school at Deoband looked toward the creation of a post-Mutiny community of Muslims, both observant of detailed religious laws and committed to a spiritual life of renewal and reinvigoration in the path of Islam (Reetz 2006: 84). The Deobandi emphasis was on the centrality of the *Shari'a* acting as a symbolic marker of identity, uniting Muslims and at the same time clearly distinguishing Muslims from their Hindu neighbors (Sikand 2007: 132). If Muslims applied the *Shari'a* to their lives, dressing as Muslims and abandoning local customary practices, a strong and separate communal identity would emerge. This would ensure Muslims were not swallowed into the Hindu fold or corrupted by the Western influences of British colonialism.

For Metcalf, the Deobandis' uniqueness lay in the extent to which they insisted on a responsible, reformist interpretation of Islam on the part of their followers. It was not enough for a follower of a Deobandi *shaykh* to turn to him, as one might to a Sufi *pir*, for intersession, but was expected to abandon suspect customs, to fulfil religious obligations, and to be responsible for their own actions (Metcalf 1982: 140; Jones 1989: 60). Deobandis were concerned that through their standard of correct belief and practice, they would be defined as a group not only separate from but also morally superior to the British (Metcalf 1982: 153).

It was from this tradition that TJ emerged in the 1920s, stressing and intensifying many of the concepts around individual renewal and moral purity. The mindset of the time, where great import was placed on cultivating a strong Islamic identity in the face of a wider hostile culture, has remained strong among members of TJ to this day. Per later chapters, many Tablighis view the contexts in post-9/11 liberal democracies as similar to those present in the Mutiny's aftermath and, thus, demanding a similar response. That is, to retreat to an observant community of Muslims who focus on living their lives according to a prophetic model and abstaining in as far as possible from wider, non-Islamic societal activities.

TJ was not alone in stemming from Deobandi Islam. The Taliban in Afghanistan and the Jamaat Ulema-e-Islam in Pakistan share the same ideological origins. While all three may share the same fundamental core—the establishment of communities based on the *Shari'a* and a lifestyle based on the prophetic model—the different sociopolitical contexts in which these movements were founded led to each taking a different approach in the way they operate. This highlights the diversity and adaptability of Deobandi-inspired movements. Commenting on this adaptability, Metcalf notes that "none of the Deobandi movements has a theoretical stance in relation to political life"; each adapted its strategy according to local contexts (1982: xxi). This becomes important when explaining why TJ branches can differ in operation depending on the contexts in which they function.

The Barelwis also emerged from the revivalist strand of Islam present on the subcontinent at the time. Founded by Ahmed Reza Khan (1856–1921) in the North Indian town of Barielly, the movement was in direct opposition to TJ and the Deobandi-inspired movements. What made them distinct was that "they used their position and their legal scholarship to justify the mediational, custom-laden Islam, closely tied to the intersession of the *pirs* of the shrines, that was characteristic of that area" (Metcalf 1982: 296). The Barelwis guarded traditions such as "reading the *Fatihah*, observing the Prophet's birthday and calling on saints for help" (Metcalf 1982: 296). As with other *ulama* of the time, they cherished religion as an ever more important part of their identities, but in a period that was seen as threatening that identity, "they blamed not only the colonial ruler—but perhaps even more—the reformist Muslims" such as the Deobandis and Tablighis (Metcalf 1982: 296). The Barelwis wanted to "preserve Islam unchanged: not Islam as it was idealized in texts or the historical past, but Islam as it had developed to the present" (Metcalf 1982: 296).

Both the Barelwi and Deobandi movements aimed to preserve Islam as a complete way of living. Their methods were different and they often condemned each other's interpretations of the faith. The historical differences between the Barelwis and the Deobandis (both originating in close proximity in India) become important in Western contexts, as the rivalries have often been maintained, reproduced, and intensified. This has had an effect on Muslim community politics, especially in Britain, which has large South Asian Muslim communities. It sometimes serves to split those communities. A prime example of this is the Barelwi opposition to TJ's London mosque proposals.

There are a number of specific events that were catalysts to the formation of TJ. Some are distinct from those of other Deobandi-inspired groups. As a rule, movements are formed through the identification of grievances in a society coupled with the desire to change these. For TJ, these grievance factors can be traced to Muslim–Hindu interreligious tension and strife of the 1920s that climaxed in Hindu conversions of Muslims (Reetz 2006: 85; Hardy 1972). While Islam had no known missionary movements for most of its existence, the need was felt following the impact of Christian and reformist Hindu missionary activities in India toward the end of the nineteenth century. Muslims feared numbers would decrease as a result of reconversion of Muslims who had once been Hindus (Reetz 2006: 75).[4] The *Arya Samaj*[5] and *Shuddhi*,[6] in particular, developed a concept of reconversion of former Hindus.[7] In practice it was mainly directed at Muslims in general and could be interpreted as an attempt to discard the influence of non-Hindu civilization on Indian history (Reetz 2006: 148).[8]

TJ was one of several Islamic movements established in this context, all focusing on the reconversion of Muslims swallowed up into the Hindu multitude.[9] That Muslim and Hindu groups were locked in competition with each other shows the extent to which concern over individuals' religious beliefs had come to dominate the scene. This is reflected in Mohammad Ilyas' words:

> My friends! There is still time to make an effort. Shortly there will be two great forces against Din [religion]. One is *Shidhi* [a Hindu political movement], which will propagate *kufr* [apostasy] among the ignorant and general masses. The other danger is atheism. This is coming with the rise of western governments and politicians. These two deviants will rise like a wave, whatever you want to do, do it before this happens. (Maulana Ilyas as cited in Lambat 1998: 8)

For revivalist movements such as TJ, cleansing popular Islam of Hindu traces and bringing it to greater conformity with scriptural Islam became key. The adoption of external markers of identity and community boundaries that marked Muslims as distinct was seen as vital. This reaffirmed them in the faith and made them resistant to conversions.[10] This has remained vital to TJ's work to this day. Yet, in order to understand the so-called race for numbers spurred on by revivalist Hindu and Muslim groups, we must also consider the actions of the third major actor on the Indian scene at the time, the British.

It was a British decree that called for a decennial census (1871). Communities would be delineated on the basis of religion, and power allocated on a proportional basis to each religious community (Hardy 1972; Jones 1989: 184). The granting of separate electorates linked religion, the census reports, political power, and political patronage (Jones 1989: 184; 1981: 78). In effect, colonial policy had the impact of politicizing religious communities in India.

Due to the often fluid boundaries over religious practices among certain communities, those who followed a mixture of Hindu and Muslim traditions were, in 1871, forced to identify themselves as either exclusively "Muslim" or "Hindu." These terms were defined according to a reified understanding of religion (Oberoi 1994: 17). What really invested these categories with importance for both Muslims and Hindus was that, by 1910, British policy had shifted to granting greater participation to Indian elites in government services based on numerical strength of each community (Sikand 2002: 25). In short, the greater the number of a religious community, the greater its share of power in governance. This not only awakened the political appetite for each of the different communities but also led to movements for reinvigoration of faith.

TJ and other revivalist groups were born of an effort to increase the number of co-religionists in a struggle to increase power share in a community. It is this political importance attached to religion that gave rise to revivalist movements on the subcontinent, and now seen as a concern in the context of liberal democracies. For example, TJ faced accusations that their efforts to increase its members were linked to a political vision, whereby the movement would eventually be in a position to wield political power (Alexiev 2005; Gaborieau 1999). It is worth noting, however, that proselytizing movements do not solely act from a desire to increase their adherents for power purposes, but because they are convinced they have the answers to the ills of the world, and in many cases the only path to salvation. While TJ is only one of several movements established in this context, it is one of the few to have achieved transnational status and support throughout the world today.

GENESIS OF THE TJ

Much of the early history of TJ is connected and intertwined with the biography of its founder, Mohammad Ilyas. Although there are a number of biographies and texts outlining the early years of the movement, these sources are somewhat hagiographical and may not accurately capture the movement's genesis. What we know is that Ilyas was born in 1885 in a pious family with an established scholarly tradition routed in the Sufi practices. After completing his basic studies, Ilays continued his education at Deoband under the tutelage of Muhammad ul-Hassan Deobandi and Ashraf Ali Thanwi. Ilyas' time at Deoband cannot be underestimated for it played a "significant role in shaping Ilays' intellect and theology" (Ali 2012).

The Deobanis were well-versed in Islam's scriptures—the Qur'an and the Hadith. They used the power of knowledge to condemn the syncretic practices, celebrations and rituals, saint worship, and traditions of the Shi'a as inauthentic Islamic practices. Ilyas was an integral part of this intellectual phenomenon and later in his life annexed knowledge with practice to launch what became the TJ of spiritual renewal (Ali 2012). In 1918, Ilyas was appointed to the position of imam of the Nizamuddin mosque, the mosque that was later to become TJ's primary world center and global headquarters. Ilyas initially believed that with the establishment of Islamic schools young Muslims could be educated in Islam. He soon became aware, however, in "the slow spread of the fundamental principles of Islam in Mewat and the presence of syncretic elements in Meo living. Ilyas embarked on the quest for a better way of reforming the Meos who had abandoned basic Islamic principles" (Ali 2012).

In April 1926, Ilyas, while on *Hajj*, felt he had been divinely ordered to undertake a lifetime's work of preaching (Haq 1972: 91). Ilyas felt that the Prophet Mohammad instructed him to found his movement and to return to India with the task of preaching the masses. Tablighi sources state that while spending time at the Prophet's Mosque in Medina, "Ilyas saw Mohammad in a dream, who addressed him saying, 'Oh Ilyas! Go back to India where God shall take work from you'" (Sikand 2010b). Tablighi narratives focus on divine inspiration—a foundation myth claiming direct instruction from God.

Such auspicious beginnings are not unique to TJ and are recurring events in Islam's history. Scholars who came to Mecca from outside Arabia and who for some time lived there "often returned home to inaugurate a radical reform movement" (Schimmel 1991: 166). Having experienced a "pure" Islam unsullied by the influences of Western powers or the complexities of heterogeneous societies inspired scholars to share their experiences of "higher Islam with their coreligionists who, as it seemed, were deeply entangled in sinful syncretistic, nay outright pagan practices and belief" (Schimmel 1991: 167).[11] On return from *Hajj*, Ilyas began to see that Muslims in India were devoid of religious fervor and not eager to seek knowledge of the faith.

The early workings of the movement were in the Mewat region of India. Mewat provides a noteworthy example of shifting sociopolitical contexts in which TJ was able to establish strong roots in a local environment. To some extent, this environment of shifting sociopolitical contexts has a number of parallels with modern liberal democracies, with objectives established in Mewat still resonant for TJ in cities such as London, Sydney, and Toronto. Ilyas regarded Mewat as "backward," where the inhabitants, although nominally Muslim, had lost touch with what it was to be true Muslims. In other words, they were in a state of *jahilliyah*—that is the state of ignorance prevalent before the revelation of Islam (Nadwi 2002: 29–59). Mayaram comments that the Meos—those who live in Mewat—professed a "happy combination of Hinduism and Islam" (1997: 43); Ibbetson comments that "they worship countless gods and symbols"; Shams comments that "their Islam did not go beyond male circumcision and burial of the dead" (1983: 187); and Singh notes that they lay "between religions" (2004). Major Powlett, a member of the British armed forces operating in the area in the early 1900s, best represents the situation with this extract, recorded by W. Crooke:

> The Meos are now all Musalmans in name; but their village deities are the same as those of the Hindus, they keep several Hindu festivals...They often keep Brahmin priests to write the note fixing the date of marriage. They call themselves by Hindu names...As regards their own religion the Meos are very ignorant. Few know the *Kalima* and fewer still the regular prayers, the seasons of which they entirely neglect. (1906: 489–90)

In this sense, the Meos were the very people that revivalist movements targeted since they had hybrid identities. To both Hindus and Muslims they were "fair game." To Hindus, Moes appeared to follow Hindu customs, and Muslims wanted to ensure that Moes dropped remnants of Hindu culture and embraced Islam in its totality. The bringing back to Islam of lapsed Muslims is a clear objective of TJ. It is one that resonates today in liberal democracies. In most secular societies, many Muslims (in TJ's view) have deviated from the straight path of Islam. They are Muslim in name but secular in custom. In fact, so important is this analogy to TJ that some Tablighis stress that many Muslims in the West today have deviated more toward secular society that they have become modern-day Meos.

Missionary movements other than TJ had targeted Meos in the past, with Ilyas drawing his inspiration in developing a comprehensive program for Mewat from his teacher Maulana Ashraf Ali Thanawi. Thanawi, a leading Deobandi scholar in India at the time, prepared a program of *dawah* and *tabligh* focused at instructing the *ulama*. The Tablighi objectives of Ilyas, however, differed in two respects. First, Ilyas dismissed the perception that *tabligh* is solely a function of the *ulama* and educated Muslims. Second, he stressed the importance of the physical movement in small groups—or *jamaats*—to propagate the word of Allah (Masud 2000b: lvi).

The Meos had worried Ilyas and other Muslim reformists for some time. Ilyas felt the preliminary *dawah* work he carried out in the area was not enough as it left the bulk of the people untouched. The only way to reform the Meos was to spread "true" religious knowledge among them and to inculcate in them an awareness of *Shari'a* (Haq 1972: 107). This, Ilyas felt, could partly be achieved through the construction of schools and mosques.[12] The construction of places of worship and education as a means of spreading the knowledge of the *Shari'a* emerged as a key Tablighi objective in Mewat—and one that TJ has followed the world over. In 1934, Ilyas called for a meeting to promote his vision for the region. He brought together notables in the area, including landlords and village elders. The vision remains at the heart of TJ activities and one that aims to foster better Muslims. At his 1934 meeting, Ilyas presented a program of objectives and actions, which included the following points (Masud 2000a: 10–11):

1. Correct memorization of the formulae of the faith
2. Regularity in the performance of prayers
3. Education and promotion of knowledge
4. Formal appearance in accordance with Islam
5. Adherence to Islamic customs and elimination of idolatrous practices
6. Purdah (veiling) for women
7. Abiding by the Islamic faith and rejection of other religions
8. Necessity of the participation of responsible persons of the community in all meetings
9. Efforts for the propagation of religion
10. Protecting each other's honor

Ilyas demanded of the Meos (and this was directed at the men) the following:

1. Every week they should preach in their own locality about the basic principles of religion; forming a regular group under a leader and adopting the proper method, they should tour their neighborhood.
2. For 3 days every month they should go to nearby villages within a distance of a few miles to preach and hold meetings to persuade the local people to undertake similar tours.
3. For at least 4 months (3 *chillah*[13]) they should leave their homes and go to centers of religious studies.[14]

(Haq 1972: 116)

This has become the main method in which TJ operates. Small groups of Muslim men leave their locales to preach the correct version of Islam to other Muslims and encourage them to do likewise. Because of the work in Mewat and a growing popularity of Ilyas as a holy man, the movement expanded rapidly, and many followers started to give in time for missionary activity. By the time of Ilyas' death in 1944, his movement expanded across the subcontinent. Tablighis stress that the movement remains true to Ilyas' teachings and methods established for the Mewat region—that it is this same model that Tablighi groups follow whether in Lahore or London, Calcutta or Cape Town.

WHAT IS IN A NAME?

It is worth noting here that TJ is not what Ilyas had called the movement at its inception, nor in his view did it adequately represent the movement. For Ilyas there could be no new *jamaat* because Mohammad had established the first and only legitimate *jamaat*— that is the community of Muslims, the *ummah*. Why then has the movement come to be known as such?

The word *tabligh* derives from the Arabic root *b-l-gh*, meaning "to reach one's destination, to arrive, to achieve one's objective, to come to hear and to come of age" (Masud 2000b: xx). Further meanings derived from the Arabic root connote thus: "the transmission, conveyance or delivery of information" (Wehr 1960: 74). *Tabligh* has come to have the stronger meaning of "propagation" or "proselytization" (Nadwi 2002: 43), and the word *Jamaat* simply means "party" or "organized collectivity." The term *Tablighi Jamaat* may be translated as "propagation party" or "preaching party" (Sikand 2002: 8). The underlying meaning of *tabligh* in the current context is "calling others toward one's religion" (Masud 2000b: xxi).[15] This meaning of *tabligh* can be attributed partly to the developments spurred on by colonialism in the twentieth century, especially within the context of Hindu and Christian missionary activities.

The reason that Ilyas did not name his movement "Tablighi Jamaat" is that his aim was not to proselytize non-Muslims, but to work among Muslims, or rather "so-called" Muslims, to bring them back into the fold of Islam. It would be incorrect to say that one can proselytize fellow Muslims, although it is possible to strive to reinvigorate the faith of Muslims who may have lapsed. This desire to only work among Muslims was relaxed by TJ's second *amir*, who allowed for the propagation of the message to anyone (Gaborieau 2000: 125). Therefore, TJ has been referred to by a number of different names by its followers and commentators. At times TJ has been called *Din Da'wat* (call to religious renewal), and Ilyas called it *Tahrik-i-Iman* or Faith Movement (Haq 1972). This stressed the more complex character of the organization, which included more than a crude assertion of proselytization. The movement in France calls itself "foi et pratique," again distancing itself from just mere proselytization and highlighting the importance of the practise of the correct version of the faith (Kepel 2000).

When Ilyas was asked to suggest a name for the movement, he reportedly said that he was not founding a *jamaat*. The *jamaat* of the Muslims had already been formed—"it has for its constitution the *Qur'an*, the mosque is the place of its activities, its centres are Mecca and Medina and in its program are Hajj, Ramadan and prayers" (Haq 1972: 45). Ilyas did not want to be seen as establishing a rival *jamaat* to the one already established by Mohammad. The name *Tablighi Jamaat* was perhaps first used by Nadwi, Ilyas' close friend and biographer in the 1940s, and has become the standard name for the group (Nadwi 2002). Most scholars, analysts, and many of the members of TJ acknowledge the "label" and, as such, is the one used for the purposes of this study.

IDEOLOGY AND OBJECTIVES

It was under Ilyas' tutelage of the movement that its core ideologies and objectives were formed, and many remain resonant to this day. TJ grew out of the Deobandi strand of Islam, and its activists stressed then as they do now features central to Deobandi Islam. These include traditional Islamic practices linked to worship, dress, and behavior as a path to personal improvement and regeneration, and to distinguish from non-Muslims (Friedman 2005: 3). At its heart, however, TJ is based on a six-point program devised by Ilays. For Tablighis, the implementation of this program is the best way to achieve an Islamic existence and ultimate salvation. The six points incumbent upon the members of TJ are (Ilyas 1967; Elahi 1992, 2007):

1. Recitation of the *Kalimah* (Article of Faith)
2. *Salat* (ordained prayers)
3. Knowledge (of the principles of Islam) and remembrance (of God)
4. Respect for Muslims
5. Sincerity of intention
6. Donation of and good use of spare time in the path of God

Elahi, a Tablighi ideologue, states that the significance of the six-point program is that it aims at the revitilization of faith, as well as reforming the whole character of the individual (Elahi 1992: 11–12). The six points for Tablighis reflect the entirety of Islam, providing a complete system and structure for living in the world. Tablighis believe and make it an objective to ensure every Muslim is able to make a correct declaration of the faith, know how to perform ritual prayers correctly and with regularity, and inculcate a habit of remembering God through repetition of his name until it is internalized. Objectives also include ensuring respect for other Muslims as all Muslims are united as Allah's illuminated community in the form of an indivisible *ummah*—behaving honestly and with integrity in all actions and, importantly, spending time in passing on this message to other people (Sardar 2006). Taking a grassroots approach, every Tablighi has a responsibility to spend time in disseminating the message, and eventually every Muslim will be brought back to a TJ understanding of Islam. In the longer term, this may lead to the voluntary conversion to Islam of all peoples.

As well as the six points, central Tablighi ideologies can be found within the *Fazail-E-Amal*,[16] TJ's core text that every member is required to consult and study on a daily basis. The *Fazail-E-Amal* is a compilation of texts predominantly written or gathered by TJ's most eminent ideologue, Mohammad Zakariyya. Chapters focus on stories of the *Sahaba*, commentaries on the *Qur'an* and *Hadith*, as well as advice on moral regeneration.[17] The manual contains a chapter by Ihtishamul Kandhalawi ("Muslim Degeneration and its

Only Remedy") and Maulana Ashiq Elahi's ("Six Fundamentals"—essentially a commentary upon Ilyas' six points). In his introduction to the volume, Zakariyya explains that the book serves a number of purposes. This includes inspiring the spirit of Islam in children who listen to the stories, helping to remedy bad practices of millions of Muslims who "indulged in manifest false worship" and who live in an "ignorance of Islam," and providing concrete examples of legitimate Islamic lifestyles upon which readers may base their own life (Kandhlawi 1997a: 12, 1997b: 5–6).

The *Fazail-E-Amal*, and in fact the majority of TJ's literature, is meant to be used as a stimulus to everyday behavior and provides the pattern to orientate one's life. Using such literature to help reorient lifestyle patterns enables followers to feel "part of a dense network of Muslims, both dead and alive, and cherish a commitment to relive the Prophet's own time when he too was part of a faithful few among a population sunk in ignorance" (Metcalf 1982: xv). This serves to strengthen the imagined community of Tablighis across the world as they all share in the simultaneous striving for the reformation and reorientation of their lives to the very model of that lived by Mohammad.

Through preaching a simplified version of Islam and a return to the basics, many TJ adherents subscribe to a dichotomous view of the world. For Tablighis our time here (on earth) is a fleeting moment, with all efforts directed at attaining entry to the hereafter. At one TJ gathering in London, a Tablighi preacher made the following point:

> The real life is the life hereafter. The time in this world is just like a needle dipped into the sea, just a small drop on the tip of the needle. The whole ocean is like the hereafter. Very temporary is life. Allah wants to bestow on us the success and favor of never ending life after death. This is why Allah has made this world. The time will be when we cultivate our deeds for the hereafter. And everything is being made for *insan* [mankind] and *insan* [mankind] has been made to prepare for the life after death.

It is not the here and now but the eternal—where one is to reside forevermore after earthly life passes—that counts. Tablighis are encouraged to shun the bright lights of this world and retreat to a rhythm of working on the path of Allah. A popular saying among the TJ is, "this world and whatever is in it is cursed by Allah, with the exception of prayers, knowledge of Allah, the religious scholar and the religious student" (Elahi 1992: 13). All efforts must be directed at religious obligation. All other matters are anathema.

In a section on his commentary of the six points of Tabligh, Elahi builds on the theme of shunning the affairs of the world and building up faith:

> Though there may not be sin in many activities and hobbies, yet they are a sheer waste of time. This is the characteristic of a true believer, that he spends his time only on virtuous deeds, remembers Allah as much as possible and avoids all forbidden things (1992: 37–38).

A clearly written indication of this ideology in the literature of TJ comes in the introduction of Ilyas' *Six-Points of Tabligh*:

> We all know that this world is mortal. Everyone who is born here is destined to die one day, and everything that flourishes here is to meet its decay sooner or later. We are therefore bound to believe that this is not our permanent...abode: we can never succeed in living here forever...We are here on a journey and our original and real destination is yet to come. We are born here only to decorate our eternal home. We cannot be called wise if we prefer this mortal existence to the eternal one. It is a fact and we must bear it in mind permanently that our sole duty is to strive for the betterment of our real home. (1967: 9)

A key objective of the movement, therefore, is to encourage its followers to abstain from the trials and tribulations of this earthly world and instead focus their attention at the "betterment of their real home"—their heavenly abode. This led to a split in opinion over the implications of this on Tablighis' relations with the wider society. For Metcalf, participants in TJ make a "lifestyle choice; they have found a stance of cultural identity; they have opted for a highly disciplined life of sacrifice; they have found a moral community of mutual acceptance and purpose" and, as such, must be viewed as positive (1982: xv). An alternative view is that this encourages disengagement from wider society, leading to a distinct separation of Tablighis from other communities. For TJ followers, the goal is to retreat from an increasingly fast-paced world, which they view as immoral and damned. This refuge-like role of the movement partly explains its success, as well as why it is struggling with new policies in liberal democracies geared at integration and cohesion.

Whether on a proselytizing tour or as part of everyday life, Tablighis are encouraged to follow a rigid set of regulations to moderate their behavior for correct emulation of the pious ancestors. These rules include the following and can be found in much of

TJ's literature (Miah 2001: 69–74; Ilyas 1967: 47–50; Kandhlawi 2007b):

- Dust your bed three times before you go to sleep.
- When sleeping, lie down on your right side, put your right hand under your right cheek and recite "Oh Allah in your name I live and die."
- Eat always with your right hand.
- Always eat from the corner of the dish.
- Always use a tablecloth.
- Do not put your hands in the middle of the dish, for it is in the middle where the divine blessing descends.
- Lick up the fingers if they bear some of the food.
- Always drink water while sitting; use the right hand and take three pauses in drinking.

Tablighis strive to emulate the ideals or spirit of what the Prophet Mohammad and his companions said and did to the very letter. Even though it is difficult to ascertain what the Prophet Mohammad did at that level of detail, this is not an issue for TJ members. What matters is that this system of behavior is tied to a system of points and rewards. One Tablighi told me that depending on which action one follows, one is rewarded a certain amount of points. If one cleans their plate and licks their fingers, they are awarded "x" number of points. If they sleep on their right side and dust their bed, they receive a different number of points. At the end of a Muslim's life, "Allah will tally up the points and decide on who can enter the hereafter."[18] In this way, emulating the pious ancestors is not just a way of life while on earth, but also a way to ensure entry to heaven.

Because TJ strives to emulate early Islamic patterns of living, it has at times been characterized as a movement that follows a "salafist" ideology, bracketed into the same category with movements such as Al Qaeda or the Wahhabis. Salafis strive to emulate the lives and actions of Mohammad and "the first three generations of Islam referred to as the pious forefathers as much as possible in all areas of life" (Meijer 2009b: xiv). For Reetz (2003), the entire way of life the Tablighis follow is "structured by their desire to relive the early Islamic community" and, in this sense, TJ is salafi. Despite this similarity of wishing to emulate the first generations of Muslims, something that most Islamist groups follow, one should be careful of drawing too strong a parallel between Salafis proper and TJ who stem from the Deobandi strand of Islam. As Reetz (1999) notes, the main difference between the two is that the Salafis rejected Sufism outright, and TJ remains firmly within the tradition of Waliullah and, for the most part, retain significant elements of *Sufi* practices. Salafis usually reject the "blind following" of the four canonical law schools supporting individual interpretation of the *Qur'an* and *hadith*, albeit along strict lines (Meijer 2009a: 4). Alternatively, TJ and the Deobandis are very much grounded in the canonical law schools, especially the Hanafi.

The ultimate objective of TJ, according to a number of commentators, is similar to that of Abul Ala Mauwdudi (d. 1979) *Jamaat-i-Islami*—that is, to establish an Islamic world order focusing on the centrality of the *Shari'a* (Gaborieau 1999; Alexiev 2005; Sikand 2006; Horstmann 2007). Indeed, in 1939, Mawdudi (who has influenced Islamists from Sayyid Qutb to Ayatollah Ruhollah Khomeini) visited Ilyas in Mewat to observe the work of TJ. He wrote of the TJ as a "major milestone in the onward march of Islamic revival" (Sikand 2002: 96). Ilyas reciprocated by declaring that Mawdudi was involved in the real work of Islam, adding that his own endeavors were merely laying the foundations (Nadwi 2002: 135). Although TJ might have ambitions of seeing the establishment of *Shari'a*-based governance, the claim is different to that made by TJ leaders in Western liberal democracies. Instead, they declared such objectives as completely apolitical (Mohammed 2011).

It is difficult, however, to ignore the political context from which TJ emerged. There were the demands of the Muslim League calling for a separate Muslim state in Pakistan, while many of the *ulama*, especially those from a Deobandi tradition, were arguing in favor of a united India, which in due course could be Islamized (Ahmed 1991: 168; Pearson 2008). For TJ, the establishment of an Islamic world order is a long-term objective. Movement leaders argue that the goal of an Islamic state cannot be achieved through political means. For Ilyas, Muslims must first reorient their lives toward Allah and prove to him they are capable of the task to be bestowed upon them. Allah decides when that time should be. In this sense, then, TJ follows a quietist version of political Islam. They leave the hard politics to God and instead focus on Islamizing the society at the grassroots level.

CHAPTER 4

Tablighi Jamaat: Organization, Structure, and Methods

The ways in which theocratic movements are structured, how movement elites function within a given context, and a movement's abilities to adapt to and shape its environments are very important. This is even more so the case in an era where globalization, new technologies, and a greater push for transparency have merged to transform contexts in Western liberal societies and which give nonengaging theocratic movements a deep sense of unease. In later chapters, the book focuses on how Tablighi Jamaat (TJ) elites have navigated the changing sociopolitical context of Britain as a means to construct their proposed new mosque. This has entailed TJ leaders to switch from a stance of social disengagement to claiming that they are an open and tolerant movement, and in tune with the values of a modern, liberal, and Western state.

Before examining how and why TJ elites in London decided to embark on a process of adaptation, it is first important to understand how the wider movement is structured. The chapter presents an organizational map of TJ. It identifies the different levels and hierarchies within the movement, describes their functions, and how they relate to one another. Important is the relationship between TJ's international headquarters in Nizamuddin, India, and other branches or "franchises" of the movement. The chapter asks how decisions within the movement are made and how TJ operates in its methods across a number of different contexts. The chapter further considers the type of people who are drawn to the movement and sets the stage for better understanding how and why TJ leaders in London have been able to act in the way they are.

TJ is a highly complex, structured, and hierarchical movement. It has an established and close-knit (often blood-related) leadership, as well as a large and committed grassroots following with different tiers of membership. TJ is also a fluid movement. Any Sunni Muslim may join TJ activities for a given period of time without having to be a committed Tablighi. They may leave the organization at the time of their liking. Indeed as Sardar notes, many South Asian Muslims living in the West have at one point or another found themselves dipping into TJ activities—some stay on to become committed activists; many do not (2004: 15). Officially, TJ does not keep records on who its members are, and given the fluid nature of the moment at its lower echelons, it is difficult to estimate its membership levels. Difficult though this is, a senior Tablighi in London placed the size of the movement at 80 million followers worldwide.

The organization and structure of TJ may be analyzed at both permanent and temporary levels. The permanent include the official leadership and hierarchies, as well as the level of prominence ascribed to each of the Tablighi-affiliated mosques and centers. The temporary levels include the composition of individual *jamaats* that are sent out on missionary tours. The two are closely related. The ways in which the permanent structures are organized directly influence the structure of the individual *jammats*, even if that structure only lasts for as long as each *jamaat* is out in the field. Each individual *jammat* is named as such, so as to "signify that it is a micro-representation of the movement as a whole" (Masud 2000a: 29).

Despite attempts to understand how TJ is organized, there is still confusion surrounding the power dynamics and structure of the movement. This is further complicated by the international nature of the movement leading to complex systems of communication between the international headquarters, regional headquarters, and local mosques. This becomes especially important when trying to understand why TJ leaders in London veered so far from traditional Tablighi methods in the pursuit of their proposed mosque, as well as when investigating claims that TJ's international advisory council opposed such a big mosque in London. Gaborieau comments that TJ has from the very beginning remained "centralized and the leadership jealously kept by the lineage of the founder" (1999: 21). Gaborieau quotes sociologist Felice Dasetto, who describes TJ as "a total institution" comparing it to a sect, citing evidence that "none of those having reached the inner core have ever spoken" of the workings of the movement (1999: 21).

LEADERSHIP

TJ's leadership started with Mohammad Ilyas (1885–1944). He grew the movement from its humble origins to having an established presence in India and the subcontinent for Islamic renewal by the time of his death in 1944. As with many large movements in which a few select families are invested in leadership positions, the process of succession after Ilyas' tenure became ever more complicated with fewer sources shedding light on the internal process of progression. On his deathbed, Ilyas called upon three of his most trusted colleagues and asked them to consider his successor from a list of six people[1] (Masud 2000a: 12–13). After discussion with senior members,[2] two names were returned to Ilyas: Mohammad Yusuf (his son) and Hafiz Muqbal Hasan (a close relative). Ilyas decided on Mohammad Yusuf to take the movement's leadership. Being his own son, the wider population would favor him more (Masud 2000a: 13).

It was under Mohammad Yusuf (1917–1965) and his successors that the movement expanded from its South Asian base and transformed into the transnational organization it is today. Tablighis tell of the immense spirituality and closeness to God of Mohammad Yusuf. It is claimed that he learned to recite the entire Qur'an at the age of ten and was involved in the work of TJ from an early age under his father's supervision. While Ilyas centered his activities in Mewat and expanded to other areas of India, it was Yusuf's belief that TJ's message and methods had to be expanded outside the continent, as well as that Arabs should be at the forefront of Tablighi work. He pushed for spread of the movement to Arabia. Yusuf identified Islam's holy cities of Mecca and Medina as the ripest areas for expanding the movement as Muslim pilgrims from throughout the world visit them. Sending *jamaats* to these cities, pilgrims were taught the message and methods of TJ. Leaving the holy cities and returning to their own countries, they could establish their own branches of the movement.

Mohammad Yusuf's death was sudden and not anticipated by TJ leadership. Mohammad Zakariyya (1898–1982), TJ's chief ideologue, took the initiative to decide on a successor. Zakariyya was Ilyas' paternal first cousin and also married Ilyas' daughter. His one daughter married Yusuf while another daughter married Inaam ul-Hasan (Gaborieau 2006: 57). Zakariyya proposed his son-in-law Inaam ul-Hasan as successor to Yususf. He was claimed to be Yusuf's closest companion and the architect behind the internationalization of the movement (Masud 2000a: 18). As such, in 1965, the leadership of TJ passed to Inaam ul-Hasan (1918–1995), a nephew of Ilyas and one of the candidates proposed for the position by Ilyas before his death (Gaborieau 2006: 57).

Inaam ul-Hasan was educated by Ilyas and later by Zakariyya. He was deeply ingrained in Tablighi thought and methods from an early age. Having been nominated as one of Ilyas' successors by Ilyas himself, and for being one of Yusuf's closest companions, he was a popular choice as TJ's new leader. It was under his supervision of over 30 years that the movement fully grew to what it is today. Following his death in 1995, TJ leaders decided that due to the movement's mass expansion, a different type of leadership structure was necessary. TJ elders concluded that a small council should be elected to oversee the movement.

The initial members of this council were Izhar ul-Hasan (a close family member), Zubayr ul-Hasan (son of Inaam ul-Hasan), and Saad ul-Hasan (son of Mohammad Yusuf) (Masud 2000a: 19). Since Izhar ul-Hasan's death in 1996, the governing executive council was made up of Zubayr and Saad (Arshad 2007).[3] In the strictest sense, the final decision-making powers in the movement fell to these two men. TJ leaders demand the loyalty and support of all those beneath them. Although TJ leaders wield large amounts of decision-making power as on the direction and broader vision for the movement, the day-to-day running of TJ falls to a much wider consultative process, where senior members of the movement from across the globe can add input.

In 2014, there was yet another change in TJ's leadership with the passing away of Zubayr ul-Hasan. Zubayr was seen as the senior leader in the movement and teacher of the current leader Maulana Saad. In line with retaining blood relations among the senior TJ leadership, Zubayr married Tahira Khatoon in 1969, daughter of Ilyas. Three sons and three daughters survive him. TJ's world advisory council is now headed by the remaining Maulana Saad and includes input from Maulana Izhar from India, Maulana Zainul Abdeen and Haji Abdul Wahab from Pakistan, as well as members from Bangladesh (Asim 2014).

Mayaram argues that the process of succession has not been fluid. Some in TJ allege that after Yusuf's death, his brother, Hazrat Kandhalawi, started to "dominate the decision making structure at Nizamuddin," with even the official *amir* having to consult him before decisions were made (Mayaram 1997: 224). It was from this split that the trend toward a dual hereditary leadership emerged (Mayaram 1997: 224). Adding to this, Reetz commented that even before Maulana Zubayr's death, Maulana Saad moved to the center of the movement and was seen as the "spiritual and symbolic head" attracting immense popularity on an international level (2004: 302, 2008: 109).

HIERARCHICAL STRUCTURES

TJ has a larger consultative (*shura*) council operating from the *Markaz* at Nizamuddin. This council comprises 15 members and consists of TJ's most senior elders. The council meets daily in private and also holds an open meeting on Thursday, the day of their local *ijtima* (Reetz 2004: 302). Not all members of the council have to attend every meeting. A rotational system of sharing responsibilities guarantees that any decisions pertaining to incoming or outgoing preaching groups "are not left undecided" (Reetz 2004: 302). Tablighi participants also commented that while the council is largely comprised of elders from India, it takes inputs from other senior Tablighis from across the globe. For example, TJ's leader in Pakistan, Haji Abdul Wahhab, was noted for being prominent within decision-making structures of the movement.

Directly beneath TJ's world advisory council based at Nizamuddin, each country where TJ operates has its own national council that, in consultation with Nizamuddin, makes decisions on TJ operations within that region. For example, TJ's national center in Britain is in Dewsbury, a town in North England. This is also home to the TJ's European headquarters. In some larger countries—India, for example—the movement has councils at the level of each of the federal states. Business and decisions made at these councils are passed up to the national and, at times, the international councils for final approval. Penderson adds that regional meetings are held in different countries every 3 months. At least one leading member from each country should attend the region council, and a grand council is held in India every 5 years where representatives from around the world are instructed in best practices (Penderson 1999: 140). International objectives of the movement are set at these "grand council" events.

Below the national level, TJ has councils at what are known as key city/district zones. The Tablighi centers in these zones are under the oversight of the national center, which in turn is accountable to Nizamuddin. Some centers have more autonomy than others. It is not clear what makes some centers more important than others, although membership levels, geographical location, and proximity to political influence are likely to be key. One center that has displayed a high level of autonomy is TJ's West Ham site in London. TJ leaders here have veered away from how TJ acts in other parts of Britian, adopting a public relations–driven image, claiming to be open, tolerant, socially inclusive, and engaged. This is part of a profound desire to gain permission to build their proposed mosque.

In an interview, one British Tablighi explained that for logistical purposes a country is divided into a number of zones. A Tablighi center (*markaz*) in the zone oversees the work carried out there and coordinates with other zones in terms of where preaching groups will be sent. As one participant told me, coordination across all the different levels is particularly important because the movement does not wish to send out multiple *jamaats* to the same area:

> That would be a bit like the Jehovah's Witnesses knocking on your door one morning, and then half an hour later a different group of Jehovahs knocks, and then an hour later yet another, and you just get really angry and tell them never to come again. It's like with our work, we don't want to pester people and anger them. It's important to be organized and professional and that is why information about *jamaats* is shared across the different levels.

In Britain, for example, TJ has eight regional *markaz* that oversee the work of the movement and serve as central hubs for smaller TJ-affiliated mosques in the zone. At each *markaz*, there is a *shura* council that meets on a daily basis to tend to smaller and administrative matters and holds council on more prominent matters during TJ's *ijtima* in that zone. It is at such meetings that TJ leaders in London make strategized plans for the construction of their proposed new mosque and then seek permission from Dewsbury and ultimately Nizamuddin. There have been claims that a new and iconic TJ mosque in London could take precedence over Dewsbury. This is unlikely to be the case. Dewsbury, and especially Savile Town where TJ's European headquarters is based, is a Tablighi enclave, and given long-established TJ roots there, it will remain as TJ's key British location. A new center in London, however, will act as the movement's major dispatch headquarters for sending out missionary tours. This is because of the relative ease for Tablighis in other parts of Britain to get to London and also because of London's excellent transportation links to Europe and rest of the world.

It is understood that members to these councils are often appointed from councils at more senior levels, with positions kept by the incumbent until death. Further to TJ zonal centers, each TJ-affiliated mosque (which is always under the oversight of one of the regional centers) has its own council to take care of the running of the mosque and to assist with visiting and outgoing preaching groups.

At the bottom of the movement's power structure comes the individual Tablighi preaching groups—the *jamaats*. These are temporary structures established for the period of a given tour (3 days, 40 days, etc.). They are composed of no more than 15 members. One of the members is elected to serve in the capacity of a leader or *amir* for the duration. Even though these *jamaats* are at the bottom of TJ's hierarchy, they carry out the central task of the movement—to preach the message of Tablighi to fellow Muslims and to bring them back to a correct understanding and practice of Islam.

While TJ elites take decisions as a means of navigating local contexts, these *jamaats* are tasked with preaching TJ's message. That is the same message the first *jamaats* preached in Mewat under the guidance of Mohammad Ilyas. The *jamaats* are not concerned about multiculturalism, social or community cohesion, or the government policy of the day. Their job is to preach a return to a correct version of Islam as understood by TJ, and they believe this is the only path to salvation. Further, it is only through active and sustained participation in these *jamaats* that members rise through the ranks of the movement.

Each individual *jammat* reflects and mirrors the structure of the main TJ organization. Ilyas made it clear in his six points that each individual *jamaat* is to work under the instruction of an *amir* selected by the group for the duration of the tour (Ilyas 1967: 51). Ilyas stipulated that an *amir* has the overall responsibility and oversight of the mission. This "helps maintain the discipline and smooth running of the system" (Ilyas 1967: 51). It is expected that all members of a *jamaat* obey the *amir* and carry out his instructions willingly while on tour. The *amir* on his part is to consult with colleagues on all matters before making a decision, and further, it is his responsibility to ensure the cohesion and success of the mission (Ilyas 1967: 51; Miah 2001: 66). The *jammats* are also requested to choose from among themselves a speaker and a guide, with the latter having knowledge of the area being targeted.

As the structures of *jammats* reflect the structure of TJ as an organization, they also differ. The organizational structure of the individual *jammats* is more egalitarian than the movement as a whole. Theoretically any male Muslim can take part in a preaching tour, and anyone from among the group has the chance of being elected as *amir* by his peers for the duration of the tour. In theory, while on tour, the *amir* must consult with every member in the group before making a decision. This is not the case with TJ's overall leadership, which has remained in the hands of the Kandhalawi family, and which sometimes follows a closed or secret agenda, "which is deliberately kept away from the public eye" (Reetz 2004: 301). This is further expressed in the sentiments of Mohammad Yusuf, TJ's second leader, who claimed that at the higher echelons of the organization "majority opinion is not our basis of decision and it is not necessary to ask everyone's opinion on every issue" (Hasani 1982: 777).

Even though Mohammad Yusuf claimed that TJ is not a traditional organization in the sense that it does not have offices, registers, or funds, TJ's activities are coordinated through specific centers called *markaz*. In the Tablighi system of mosque organization, there exists two types—the *markaz* (center) and the *masjid* (mosque). The *markaz* is a center that oversees other mosques. The *markaz* carries out all the functions of a *masjid* but has further responsibilities in organizing and dispatching missionary tours. The most important of these *markaz* is the one at Nizamuddin.

So important is the *Markaz* at Nizamuddin that it has been metaphorically described as "the heart circulating blood through the body" of TJ (Mayaram 1997: 228). It is the center of the Tablighi universe, a place where people are trained for missionary work, where worldwide tours are organized, and where communication and dissemination of information for Tablighis all over the world takes place (Khan 1986: 34). It is also where the *amirs* and councils of the movement reside. Apart from the *Markaz* at Nizamuddin, two other geographical areas of importance identified as such from the early days of the movement are Mecca and London.

According to Gaborieau, the first priority after India was to have a center in the holy places of Islam in order to promote the movement throughout the Muslim world and target those on the annual Hajj pilgrimage. The second priority was to establish a center in London that could be used as a bridgehead to promote the movement throughout Europe and the West (Gaborieau 2000: 131). TJ leaders in London are currently working to achieve this. Although London is no longer the center of a world empire, it still holds a position of prominence for TJ. There is a large and active Tablighi population in Britain; they have strong links with Tablighi communities in India, Pakistan, and Bangladesh, and London is well situated for easy access to global places.

Further, there have been suggestions that the real power of the movement shifted from the *Markaz* at Nizamuddin to the *Markaz* at Raiwind, Pakistan. The elderly Mohammad Abdul Wahhab (b. 1923) is *amir* of the regional *markaz* and is one among the few surviving people who personally knew Ilyas (Khattak 2009;

Gaborieau 2000: 130). Wahhab gave up his job and donated his time exclusively to working for TJ in Pakistan. The *markaz* at Raiwind is also said to be more politically oriented than the one at Nizamuddin. It often attracts senior politicians and dignitaries to its gatherings. It should be remembered that it is the context in Pakistan that has allowed the *markaz* in Rawind to be more politically influential, just as the context in London has demanded of TJ leaders to act in more engaged way. The *markaz* near Dhaka in Bangladesh is also noted as a center whose progress should be watched, as the annual gatherings there attract vast numbers of pilgrims (Gaborieau 2000: 130; Lapido Media 2010). Tablighi interviewees denied Raiwind's elevation over Nizamuddin, commenting that Nizamuddin always has been and will be the most important Tablighi center. Reetz was told by a senior Tablighi that the extension of ablution facilities at Raiwind had to be sanctioned by Nizamuddin. Hence Nizamuddin acts as a regional and even global point of reference and authority (Reetz 2008: 111).

Even though information regarding the structure of the movement may be difficult to come by in literature, it is a question that can be explored through interview and conversation. One adherent explained how the system for appointing leaders within the movement works: "the international council based in Nizamuddin selects the leaders of the different countries, the country leaders then pick the local leaders and each preaching *jamaat* is free to choose its own leader." When asked if there was consultation between the international and national branches before selecting the leaders, the respondent was not sure. He mentioned that TJ usually employed a method of consultation before making major decisions.

PARTICIPANTS IN TJ

TJ claims that up to 80 million Muslims across the globe are engaged in its activities. Given the vast numbers involved in TJ, as well as the huge geographical reach of the movement, it is difficult to stereotype individuals who join. Its members are men and women, rich and poor, varying ethnicities, and people of all ages. It may be possible to more accurately describe the composition of TJ members at national and regional levels, and this is done for TJ in Britain in a later chapter. From conversations with Tablighis, it is clear that the largest contingent within the movement is South Asian Muslim men. It is from this group that the majority of the influential positions in the movement are recruited. It is men from South Asian families in the diaspora who are most active in TJ in a number of its Western contexts. In Britain, and in other areas such as Africa and Southeast Asia, the movement has also been successful in recruiting from the indigenous populace. In Mali, for example, TJ was specifically successful with a branch of the Ifoghas clan. An entire branch of that clan joined the movement (Pieri 2014: 96).

As mentioned earlier, TJ at its lower echelons is a fluid movement with many Muslims joining its activities for a brief period without necessarily becoming full-fledged members. A distinction must, therefore, be drawn between those who attend TJ's meetings and those who are committed and become active members for a sustained period of time. On a superficial level, committed Tablighis are often easy to spot—the men grow beards to a fistful in length, have their trousers stopping at the ankle, and wear leather socks, all in imitation of Prophet Mohammad. The committed followers also abide by stringent rules affecting all of their behaviors, for example, only entering a toilet with the left foot and exiting it with the right. At a more practical level, committed members are initiated as such due to the level of service they have given to the movement.

At its most basic form, each TJ member must commit at least 3 days per month in service of the movement. For a *jamaat*, these 3 days are for venturing to a local area to convince Muslims to start attending TJ meetings. Many Muslims at one point or another in their lives join one of these *jamaats*. Committed members, however, are expected to do so at least once a month. At the next level of membership are Tablighis who, in addition to the monthly *jamaat* tours, spend a consecutive period of 40 days per year in the work of the movement. This involves the individual joining a *jamaat* being sent to a destination in another region of their country or to another country. Again, the purpose is to preach TJ's message and methods as the path to salvation. An even higher level exists whereby members are expected to devote one third of each year to the movement. This service is known as a grand *chillah*—that is 4 months of engaging in the missionary work and almost exclusively in a different country than the individual's own. Those who accomplish this are given the title "purani sathi" or, as Reetz terms it, the "old comrades" (2008: 114).

A number of Tablighis commented that completion of the grand *chillah* is a necessary precondition of attaining any position of authority or seniority within the movement. As well as this, many Tablighis aim to complete the grand *chillah*—not because of the possible positions of seniority that it may bring but more so due to belief that it is the best way of dispelling the devil from their lives and bettering their chance of salvation. In addition to spending 4 months in missionary work, individuals are encouraged to live frugally and turn their complete attention to the sacred, the abandonment of consumerism, and the salvation of their souls. On completing the grand *chillah*, members are rewarded at special gatherings where they could meet national and international leaders and receive more input on the direction of the movement's activities.

TJ has also been fortunate in its recruitment campaigns due to the publicity it received from a number of prominent Muslim celebrities who joined the movement. A number of British Tablighis interviewed were pleased to inform that many members of Pakistan's cricket team are active members of TJ, including Mohammad Yusuf, a convert to Islam who was one of the few Christians to ever play for Pakistan's national team. It was after attending TJ sermons that he became a Muslim and a Tablighi. Given the importance of cricket as a sport in Pakistan, this new recruit served to raise the profile of the movement. Another interviewee mentioned that Pakistani singer and fashion designer Junaid Jamshed was an active member of the movement. TJ also had a large level of support from prominent politicians and military personnel in Pakistan and Bangladesh, as well as from India's Muslim populations.

TJ's Methods

Since the inception of the movement, TJ leaders claimed not to be introducing new or innovative methods, but were reviving the methods of *tabligh* as practiced by the *sahaba* in the early periods of Islam.[4] Each Tablighi mosque or center sends out *jamaats* of several men each week on *dawah* missions—these form the nucleus of Tablighi activity at the base level. Going out on *jamaat* is the process whereby individuals voluntarily donate their time in traveling to places and proselytizing other Muslims. This "effort," according to Tablighi literature, is the same work that the Prophet Mohammad himself was engaged in. For example, Elias comments that the Prophet and one of his companions left Mecca and traveled "60 kilometers...on foot to invite the people to Islam" (2004: 7). Mohammad met the chiefs of the people and presented to them his case, staying among them for 10 days (Elias 2004: 7). Elias extrapolates that it was prophetic method for groups to go out on foot, meet with leaders, put their case for Islam to them, and spend a set number of days preaching Islam among the population.

For Elias, the structure of TJ was derived from this method, as Mohammad himself had been an *amir* and spokesperson and consulted with his companions (2004: 8–12). In the words of Mohammad Ilyas,

> The main object of our *jamaat* is to teach the Muslims the original and genuine religion taught by the Holy Prophet. This is our real object; as far as our Tabligh and tours, this is a preliminary means to carry out our mission; the instruction of *kalimah* [articles of the faith], *Tayyibah* [purity] and *Namaz* [prayer] is the alphabet of our course. (1967: 62)

In fact, the objective of preaching tours is twofold. The participants should reform themselves and propagate the faith to Muslims who remained disinterested or ignorant in the ways and practices of Islam. These preaching tours became the hallmark of the movement. Today the tours traverse the globe and put the Tablighi program into practice, which they must all be familiar (Reetz 2008: 101).

TJ's methods of *dawah* differ from the Islamic norms of concentrating on preaching in mosques. The major departure point has been the emphasis on traveling to spread the message of Islam as opposed to propagation through fixed centers of Islamic education. In this sense, TJ has built upon and furthered the work of the "nineteenth century Muslim reformers such as Sayyid Ahmad, who had been stimulated to travel by example of Christian missionaries" (Mayaram 1997: 228). TJ, rather than waiting for individuals to come to the mosque to be instructed in the faith, goes out into the people and stresses participation, group work, and a focus on renewing and revitalizing the faith of current Muslims at the grassroots level.

TJ encourages its male members to go on missionary tours away from their local area.[5] This change of environment and travel out of one's place of work and residence will allow each individual Tablighi to focus on the work of *dawah*, as well as enable them to meet other Muslims and remind them of their duties as prescribed by the *Shari'a*. This process of traveling away from the familiar to the unknown is essential for the development of the individual. It is only through leaving familiar surroundings that one is able to discriminate between the "vital and trivial in one's life" (Masud 2000b: xvi) and thus make a conscious step toward hearing the call of Allah. As Ilyas commented,

> So long as we are surrounded by our domestic affairs and occupational environment we can hardly make our mind realize due importance of the hereafter…our minds remain occupied with whatever we do or come across in our daily life and seldom make time to study the life of our beloved Prophet. (1967: 37)

Masud describes this physical movement from one's current sur-roundings to others less familiar as comparable with the concept of "*hijra*," both in the sense of migration and withdrawal (2000b: xvi). The process can be regarded as not only physical travel but also a spiritual journey—of traveling within oneself. The Tablighi travels from worldly pursuits to working in the path of Allah.

Traveling away from one's locale to spread the word of God and to develop one's own sense of spirituality is also seen as important in other proselytizing movements such the Church of Jesus Christ of Latter Day Saints (Mormons). For the Mormons, the period spent on mission is an important rite of passage. It is a time when young Mormons completely dedicate themselves to preaching the gospel and often "gain a degree of status within the Mormon world that may last a life time" (Davies 2000: 175). The word "mantle" is often used to refer to a "special religious state" of missionaries. This state is a sense of being "spiritually guided or empowered by God, or able to provide words of encouragement that seem to possess a depth over and above that which a nineteen year old might expect to command" (Davies 2000: 175). This is remarkably similar to the Tablighi expe-rience of mission—a process in which Tablighi men often claim to return changed.

This notion of working in the path of Allah is best summed up by Siddiqur Miah:

> When we are on Tablighi tour our main objective is to purify our heart and to prepare ourselves for the life after death. We should therefore be more particular about our time and by avoiding all sorts of futile affairs. We should utilize every moment of this limited time to gain something good. (2001: 59)

The traveling groups usually first arrive at the mosque of the area they want to target. They cook, eat, and sleep in the mosque for the duration of their stay.[6] After prayers, the *jamaats* divide themselves into smaller teams and go into the community knocking on doors to invite people to the mosque and telling them about the work of *tabligh* and *dawah*. Some remain in the mosque to receive any peo-ple going there. Hasani quoted Maulana Yusuf as having set a tar-get at one person from each household to go out for three *chillahs* with the TJ (Hasani 1982: 772). According to Reetz, the success rate of these missions—in convincing people to attend prayer—varies from 2 to 10 percent, and some may have already been regulars at the mosque (Reetz 2004: 297, 2008: 101). Once a sufficient number have gathered at the mosque, prayers are said followed by an inspirational talk based on the principles of the six points. This is followed by further readings from the writings of Zakariyya, and finally, people are asked to volunteer for tours.[7] At the Markaz Ilyas, on an average Thursday evening, between 5 and 15 percent of those gathered will volunteer.[8]

To ensure best outcome, these travels are organized according to strict discipline and program. This includes learning sessions and the practice of the six basic tenants of *Tabligh* (Masud 2000a: 24–25). There is a set pattern for Tablighi tours that every Tablighi male is expected to abide by. As Hasani (1982: 772) has summarized, (Muslim) men should donate:

- Three days per month on a preaching tour to an area outside of their locality;
- Forty days per year (also known by the Sufi phrase *chillah*) which involves a longer period of withdrawal from one's own way of life to focus on the work of *Allah*. This could involve travel to a distant location from one's own area, and possibly even to another country;
- A once in a lifetime "grand *chilla*" which consists of three consecutive *chillahs* (equating to 120 days) usually in another country;
- Year long tour—this is for the most devoted Tablighi and usually consists of travelling by foot, from mosque to mosque in a given country to call other Muslims to the work of the Jamaat.

This structure of Tablighi tours is also well documented by other Tablighi writers (Elias 2004; Kandhlawi 2007b). Elias comments that TJ's adoption of these timeframes is well grounded in the *hadith*. With tours lasting 3 days, justification is taken from Prophet Mohammad instructing a number of his companions to go to certain tribes, present them with the case for Islam, and then stay among them to allow them time to contemplate the choices (Elias 2004: 15). Three days is not just a period of time when those being proselytized should consider their options, but also a time when those on mission should contemplate their own commitment to the faith and to the movement.[9] Mohammad himself spent 10 days in Taaif for *dawah*. The justification for 40 days is taken from the fact that Moses was instructed to spend 40 days on Mt. Sinai (Elias 2004: 17–18).

Ilyas' most extraordinary contribution was to organize *jamaats* in which disciplined members—fired with religious zeal and leading lives of piety, simplicity, and abstinence—traveled far and wide to acquire and impart Islamic knowledge, inviting "the attention of people toward Islamic practices, spreading the message of Allah" (Hasan 1997: 318). Each member of the *jamaat* is responsible for paying on their own for the tours; they are encouraged to share in the cooking, cleaning, and other menial tasks that they would usually not engage in at home (Mayaram 1997: 229). This, much like in the Mormon tradition, was to serve as a training ground for developing the character of missionaries and "seen as helping to qualify men as better husbands and fathers" (Davies 2000: 195). Ilyas' strategy was to persuade Muslims—despite how little learning they had—to go out in groups to approach even the *ulama* and to remind them to fulfill their ritual obligations (Metcalf 1982: xiii). By following correct codes of Islamic practice and rituals, they would inspire others to see the benefits of the movement, to bring people and their lives closer to the path of Allah, and to empower and provide them with the necessary knowledge of the means to salvation.

While the preaching tours of TJ have became the most common method of advancing the movement and fulfilling Ilyas' six points, in recent years the movement's congregations (or *ijtima*) symbolize another key feature and method. Congregational gatherings take place in a number of different ways and at different levels. Congregations take place on the national and international levels, and the annual TJ meetings in India, Pakistan, and Bangladesh have the largest gathering of Muslims (and sometimes exceeding the *Hajj*), with representatives coming from all over the world (Reetz 2004: 298; Perlez 2007b; Hicks 2009; LapidoMedia 2010). These international events attract not only millions of lay people but also the world's television and press and presidents and ministers. Events follow on a grander scale during Tablighi tours. People bring their own bedding, cooking utensils, and provisions. They are expected to attend talks around the six points, network and learn from each other, while renewing their commitment to further preaching tours. Even though these international "grand national" meetings attract millions of people, Reetz questions the extent to which those attending are actually committed Tablighis. Reetz notes that the closing prayers of these meetings have a special social significance in that they confer a blessing from learned and respected Tablighi elders on those attending. This attracts swarms of locals seeking blessings in a culture where this is still very much seen as sacred (Reetz 2008: 103).

On a more local level, each Tablighi *markaz* is expected to hold a weekly congregation with talks and readings based on the six points.

This is primarily aimed at the Muslims in the local area and so serves as a community orientation meeting. A further method utilized at these meetings is that regular Tablighi attendees bring food that is shared at the end of the meeting to create an atmosphere of hospitality and increase social communication and networking opportunities.

What remains, however, is that TJ, just as with the Church of Latter Day Saints, is in essence a missionary movement and, therefore, difficult to conceive of outside this ethos. Tablighis, as with many other missionaries, give themselves to living in a highly controlled fashion with a seeming total dedication to spreading the truth of their faith. Any decisions TJ leaders take in London, or indeed in any other part of the world, will be guided by the basic principle of how it could advance salvation. Government policies are made; they are subject to change and at times may demand certain groups to act or adapt in certain ways. Ultimately, however, it is a controlled and structured living (in the face of what is perceived to be a society in free fall) that contributes to TJ's growth. The movement in London (as examined in the following chapters) has to decide how to navigate between its theocratic and salvation-oriented core and government demands of liberal, open, and inclusive values.

PART III

The Quest for the London Mega Mosque

CHAPTER 5

Tablighis in Britain: Adapting to Shifting Contexts

INTRODUCTION

In his forward to Philip Lewis' *Young, British and Muslim*, Jon Snow, a veteran British broadcaster, poses the following seminal questions:

> How is our society coping with the significant influx and development of Muslim populations in the United Kingdom? In turn, and as important, how are those populations managing to survive, prosper and integrate within British society? Sadly it seems to have taken the 9/11 attacks in the United States, and the London bombings of 7 July 2005 to spark the debate. But debate there now is, at last. (Snow in Lewis 2007: ix)

Snow's questions are of paramount importance for they rearticulate the growing importance of identity, integration, and citizenship in modern liberal democracies. This chapter attempts to engage with the above questions through examining the development of Muslim communities in Britain and specifically Tablighi Jamaat (TJ) in the post-9/11 and post-7/7 contexts.

The chapter provides an historical overview of Muslim communities in Britain and draws from the 2001 and 2011 Census to outline the development of those communities. Following this, the chapter focuses on the establishment of TJ in Britain. Attention will be paid to TJ's headquarter mosque in Savile Town in Dewsbury. The chapter will explain how TJ in Britain is structured and how the movement has traditionally operated in areas where it has been relatively free to pursue its own methods. Of importance are assertions based on observations from Savile Town that TJ is isolationist in nature and disengaged from wider non-Tablighi communities. This is the very same image the movement in London is attempting to battle.

Whether TJ is able to integrate into life in a liberal democracy is critical to the success of their proposed mosque construction in London. Following an examination of TJ in Dewsbury, the final part of the chapter focuses on the development of TJ in London. The chapter provides an ethnographic mapping of TJ's current London mosque through describing where the mosque is situated, what services it offers, and the types of people that attend. The chapter further looks into the difficulties TJ have faced over their plans to convert this site into what would be Britain's largest mosque. The chapter concludes through arguing that TJ in London is becoming socialized into what is expected of them and that TJ leaders are becoming more adept at adapting their strategies to fit the local context.

MUSLIMS IN BRITAIN: AN HISTORIC OVERVIEW

Britain, due to its colonial presence on the Indian subcontinent, has long been in contact and interaction with Islam(s) and Muslim populations. These populations were for the most part in foreign lands—part of Britain's exotic, expansive, and diverse empire. H. A. Hellyer has noted that much of current scholarship has analyzed Muslims in Britain through this colonial lens and argues that Britain's interactions with Muslim communities pre-dates the colonial era. Hellyer traces the settlement of small Muslim communities in the British Isles since the seventh century. He notes that during the reign of Queen Elizabeth I, England had a more cordial relationship with the Muslim state of Morocco than with other European powers such as Spain (Hellyer 2009: 145–147). This challenges the dominant strand of history, where Britain's contact with Muslim people has been presented as somewhat alien. It serves to show that Muslims in Britain are not an entirely modern phenomenon. Due to Britain's position as a naval power with large and active ports, some Muslims, originally seafaring Yemenis, settled in the cities of Liverpool and Cardiff during the nineteenth century (Ansari 2009: 37; Hellyer 2009: 148; Saggar 2010: 34). Toward the end of World War II, Britain saw an influx of immigration, including many Muslims that would start to alter the demographics of the British population.

Muslims, since the end of World War II in 1945—as well as the crumbling of Britain's "age of empire" (Hobsbawm 2003)—formed an increasing part of the British population. They are the largest religious minority group in the United Kingdom. Following the immense devastation caused by the war, both in terms of loss of lives as well as destruction of industries and manufacturing, the British state had an economic incentive to encourage the migration of foreign workers to help reconstruct British cities and take jobs that British people did not want (Siddiqui 2001: 185). The most obvious candidates to be drafted to help in postwar reconstruction efforts were subjects of the British Empire and Commonwealth. Indeed, important to the immigration of minorities to Britain was the British Nationality Act of 1948—one of the most liberal pieces of legislation to ever pass in Britain on citizenship and immigration. The Act allowed for any one of the 800 million subjects of the British Empire to live and work in the United Kingdom without needing a visa. Any subject of the Crown in the colonies was to enjoy the same civil and legal rights as subjects of the Crown born in Britain (Fetzer and Soper 2005: 27). The irony should not be lost that these Imperial subjects were invited and encouraged to migrate to Britain and were a vital part of (re) building a postwar modern Britain.

Migration to Britain for most people, Muslims included, in the postwar period was for economic reasons (and during this period, emphasis was not on the religion of the minorities in question, but rather on ethnicity) (Rex 1979; Ansari 2009). For example, wages for laboring jobs in Britain in the early 1960s stood at over 30 times above those offered for similar jobs in Pakistan (Lewis 1994: 16). Working in Britain could be relatively lucrative. Initially it had been single Muslim men who arrived in Britain with the idea of working there and then returning home in a strong financial position. They would establish themselves in society and provide for their families. By the early 1960s, however, economic migrants to Britain from South Asia (mainly Pakistan, Bangladesh, and India) increased dramatically, with two key reasons cited. The first reason was to preempt the 1962 Commonwealth Immigrants Act. This Act was to alter the British Nationality Act of 1948 and closed the door on automatic entry into the United Kingdom of Commonwealth citizens. This was in response to a heavy influx of immigrants into Britain since 1948. This had propelled the Conservative Party, and especially the Monday Club (a group affiliated to the Conservatives but to the right of the party), to argue in favor of a system permitting only those with government-issued employment vouchers (which were limited) to settle and work in the United Kingdom. Bari notes that by the mid-1950s there was intense debate in Britain as to the impact of black immigration on housing, the welfare state, crime, and other social problems, with the 1958 riots in London's Notting Hill and in some areas of Nottingham paving the way for "the development of racialized politics in Britain" (Bari 2005:28–29). The second reason was that wives and other dependents increasingly chose to join their husbands in Britain. Linked to the Act of 1962, spouses and dependants could settle with their relatives who were already working in Britain before the new legislation introduced complications (Lewis 1994: 17). When dependents (i.e., wives and children) of Muslim men began to join them in the 1960s and 1970s, demands for Islamic institutions in Britain began to grow. This migration of women and children was part of a process that led to a more stable and permanent settlement, an indication that Britain would not be just a temporary abode but rather home for the long term. Hellyer notes that this period can be seen as the end of the "myth of return." Migrant communities, Muslims included, were on the whole here to stay (Hellyer 2009: 154). The education of Muslim children became a pressing need, as did maintaining a Muslim identity. Migrating to Britain from different parts of the Empire or Commonwealth would have entailed a dramatic cultural shock for many of the individuals, as during this time there would be little or no multicultural provisions. Mosques and other Islamic institutions had yet to be established, and *halal* meat and traditional spices used in South Asian cuisine were difficult to come by. According to Nielsen, interest in religious matters had been minimal among the male migrant workers living in boarding houses—apart from avoiding non-*halal* meat, there was little time to focus on spiritual matters (Nielsen 1987: 387). With the arrival of their dependents, this was to change.

It was in this context, among the newly arrived Muslims of the South Asian subcontinent, that TJ was able to initially disseminate its ideology and establish itself in British society. It helped to build mosques, hold meetings, and educate Muslims in the way of Islam much as they had done in Mewat (Faust 2000: 140–141). For TJ, a movement that had arisen at the height of British colonialism in India, the myths and memories of the desire to spread the faith and set themselves on a morally superior path to their colonial masters still resonated in the 1960s' British context—a period when many in society were awakening to a cultural and sexual revolution (Lent 2001: 5). The desire to provide for the needs of Muslim communities spurred a marathon of institution building. Importance was placed on establishing mosques and religious schools. In its early history, TJ in Britain was actively involved in establishing and shaping new Islamic institutions. TJ in London, in the current context of wanting to construct their new mosque, draws upon this history as an important and resonating factor. TJ saw Britain as the new Mewat, a land in which Islam had to be built. They would take the same methods used in Mewat and give importance to building mosques—to be centers of Tablighi expansion. This is a fact that should remain at the forefront of understanding why the construction of TJ's new mosque in London is so important to them.

MUSLIMS IN BRITAIN IN THE
TWENTY-FIRST CENTURY

Muslims have come to form one of the key religious communities in Britain. While the situation of many Muslims in Britain is improving, traditionally these communities have been rather disadvantaged in socioeconomic terms and tend to underperform in the education system and workforce. The Muslim Council of Britain (MCB) highlighted that many Pakistanis and Bangladeshis living in Britain (both predominantly Muslim communities) remain underprivileged. Among other issues, the MCB notes that Pakistanis and Bangladeshis are among the poorest ethnic groups in the United Kingdom, and that Pakistani and Bangladeshi men on average are likely to earn £150 less per week than white men and that over two thirds of Pakistani and Bangladeshi households are living below the line of relative poverty (MCB 2003). In a more recent study, Miqdad Asaria found after controlling for characteristics and accounting for coefficient differences, being Muslim still drastically reduces the odds of being employed in Britain. "The odds of a non-Muslim male being employed are double the odds of a Muslim male being employed while the odds of a non-Muslim women being employed are four times the odds of a Muslim women being employed" (Asaria 2006: 13). While Asaria found that there was some level of discrimination against Muslims in the workforce, the study also noted that many Muslims of working age were born outside of the United Kingdom and, as such, face language barriers that reduce their ability to find work. There are pressures on Muslim women from within Muslim communities not to enter the workforce and stay at home to raise families (Asaria 2006: 14).

The 2001 UK Census was unique in that it was the first time since 1851 that questions of religious identity were asked. The Census in 1851 was only interested in church attendance (Peach 2006: 629). In 2001 the majority of the British population still regarded themselves as Christian (71.8%). The second most definite category, at 15 percent of the population, was those who did not classify themselves as religious at all. The Census established that there were 1.6 million Muslims residing in the United Kingdom in 2001, approximately forming 3 percent of the British population. This made Islam in 2001 the second largest religion in Britain. The 2001 Census also confirmed that the majority of the UK Muslim population originate from the Indian subcontinent, "with nearly 68 per cent from Bangladeshi, Indian and Pakistani backgrounds" (Change Institute 2009a: 9).

Since the 2001 Census, there have been significant changes in the demographics of the UK population, and these are best exemplified in the Census data for 2011. As with the Census of 2001, the question on religious identity was the only voluntary question, with only 7.2 percent of the population choosing not to answer. Perhaps the most significant and commented upon statistic to emerge from the 2011 Census with regard to religious identity is that between 2001 and 2011 there has been a significant decrease in the number of British people who identify as Christian. In England and Wales, those who identified as Christian in 2001 made up 71.7 percent of the population, and in 2011, this fell to 59.3 percent (ONS 2012: 1). Another significant finding was that those who identified themselves as having no religion rose from 15 percent of the population to 20 percent in England and Wales (ONS 2012: 2). A third, much commented upon finding was that Islam saw the largest increase in adherents across all religions in Britain, with Muslims in England and Wales rising from 2.8 percent of the population to 4.8 percent. Muslims, however, are not evenly distributed across the country, but rather tend to be concentrated in particular areas (ONS 2012: 3). In over half of local authorities, the proportion of the population who self-identified as Muslim was under 1 percent, and in over three quarters of areas, it was under 6 percent (ONS 2012: 8). The areas with the highest proportion of Muslims were in the London boroughs of Tower Hamlets and Newham with 34.5 and 32 percent, respectively. Redbridge and Waltham Forest had proportions of the population higher than 20 percent (ONS 2012: 8). There were also a number of areas outside London with Muslim proportions higher than 20 percent, including Blackburn with Darwen in the northwest, Bradford in Yorkshire and the Humber, Luton in east of England, Slough in southeast, and Birmingham in the west midlands (ONS 2012: 8).

It should be noted, however, that even though the 2001 and 2011 Censuses asked questions on religious identity, these questions did not measure the depth of religiosity across the population. As such it is difficult to discern from the census data whether Muslims are more observant of their religious practices than, say, Christians or Hindus. The fourth Public Studies Institute (PSI) survey of race relations in Britain did note the centrality of religion to people's lives, concluding that religion has a more central role in the lives of Muslim citizens as opposed to any other major UK religions. The survey at the time found that "74 per cent of Muslims, 46 per cent of Sikhs, and 43 per cent of Hindus" reported religion as "very important to them compared with just 11 percent" of Church of England attendees (Modood et al. 1997: 310).

It is clear that the majority of Muslims in England are concentrated in the boroughs of London (approximately 40%), cities of the west midlands (approximately 14%), the northwest of the country (approximately 13.5%), and Yorkshire and the Humber (approximately 12.5%). The fact of the matter is that three key English cities—London, Birmingham, and Bradford—account for over half (51.7%) of the Muslim population.

The majority of Muslims residing within the United Kingdom (40%) live in England's capital and surrounding areas, Greater London. Due to the density of Muslims in London, it is important to have a more detailed understanding of the Muslim population here, not least because this is the area TJ wanted to construct their new mosque. The population of London is 8,173,941, of which 1,012,823 declared themselves as Muslim. In other words, 12.4 percent of London's population identify as adherents of Islam (Nawhami 2013). The Muslim population of London increased 67 percent from 607,083 to 1,012,823. This is a change of 405,740. This figure is high when compared to London's general population growth of 14 percent. However, when compared to the growth of Muslims in other regions of the country, it is one of the smallest increases, with other regions seeing increases of up to 111 percent (Nawhami 2013). While London may have a strong Muslim population, some boroughs have larger populations than others. As already noted from the results of the 2011 UK Census, the strongest concentrations of Muslims may be found in Tower Hamlets and Newham. There are also sizeable Muslim populations in the London boroughs of Waltham Forest, Hackney, Brent, Ealing, and Redbridge.

One indicator of the vibrancy of religious communities is that of worship provisions. In other words, what is the level of access to and the quality of that community's worship facilities? London has the best provisions in terms of mosques and Islamic institutions for its Muslim communities. The number of mosques in the United Kingdom has grown considerably in the past decade. In 1963, there were a total of 13 mosques registered in the United Kingdom, by 1975 the number rose to 99, and by 1985 there were 338. By far, the majority of mosques in Britain are Sunni-controlled and specifically in London are oriented toward the Deobandi strand of Islam, including TJ. For example, there are approximately 800 Deobandi mosques in Britain compared to 350 Barlewi mosques and roughly 60 Salafi mosques (Naqshbandi 2010).

TJ IN BRITAIN

Britain is currently one of the main foci of TJ's activities in the West, although the movement has been successful in many European countries. The desire of establishing what TJ leaders hope to be a new world center has brought the most attention to the movement in Britain and especially London. London has special significance to TJ. It was selected as part of a strategic triumvirate of regions—Delhi, Mecca, and London—from which the Tablighi version of Islam could be propagated to wider geographical reaches (Gaborieau 2000: 131). This was because of Britain's then position as the colonial power in South Asia, one of the world's super powers at the time, and a prime location for South Asian migration after the end of World War II. Some commentators have gone as far as to argue that this desire of establishing a world center in London will function as the basis for the conversion of Europe to Islam (Gaborieau 1999: 21; Alexiev 2005).

Although the Muslim population of London is far greater than that in any other city in Britain, TJ tends to be better established in the north of England, as seen in the predominance of Tablighi regional centers there. The most important of these is TJ's Markazi Masjid in Dewsbury's Savile Town. It functions as the movement's British and European headquarter mosque and also incorporates a private Islamic boarding school for boys. In fact, the midlands and north of England have particularly strong Deobandi communities, with extensive networks of mosques, schools, and seminaries. Lewis notes that the links between Deobandi mosques controlled by different regional groups are being strengthened and with particularly close ties between the Deobandi seminary at Bury (established 1975) and TJ's Dewsbury center (established 1982) (Lewis 1994: 90). The closeness of the Deobandi communities in Britain's north were reinforced by ties dating back to colonial India. Lewis reports that the principal of the Bury seminary, Yusuf Motola, was a student of Maulana Zakariyya, "one of the most influential figures in the TJ" and who made a number of visits to TJ's Dewsbury center (Lewis 1994: 91).

It was not until after the death of TJ's founder, Mohammad Ilyas, in 1944 and under the guidance of his son and successor, Muhammad Yusuf, that the movement started its operations in Britian. TJ leaders were always serious about Britain becoming a key area of its activity.

They selected London as a site of importance since the early years of TJ's inception (Gaborieau 2000:131). TJ activists were at the forefront of helping to establish mosques and other Islamic institutions in Britain, with three initial goals: "to impart knowledge of the basic rituals and beliefs of Islam to the children; to combat western and Christian cultural influences; and to instil in children a spirit of dedication of Islam, which could later be channelled for Tablighi activity" (Sikand 2002: 220).

These early goals are still at the heart of TJ's objectives and lead to allegations that they are a separatist and culturally isolationist movement. For Sikand, the Tablighi ethos "works to minimize contacts with people of other faiths, withdrawing from the wider society to protect Islam from the threat of secularism and materialism" (2002: 232). TJ in London, if they are to succeed in developing any proposed mosque, will need to demonstrate that this is not the ethos of the movement and that they are willing and able to maintain sustained interaction and engagement with wider communities.

The first large gathering or *ijtima* of TJ in Britain took place over the Christmas period toward the end of the 1950s. The gathering was a 4-day event "attended by around 100 people, and participating in it were *jamaats* from Manchester, Birmingham and Sheffield, besides activists from London itself" (Sikand 2002: 221). The aim of this gathering was to provide opportunities "for activists from across the UK to meet up and plan for the future expansion of the movement" (Sikand 2002: 221). These gatherings, as well as similar ones taking place on a regular basis, were geared toward establishing a firm Tablighi presence in Britain. A goal was to ensure the movement had a network of mosques from which it could operate and spread Tablighi tenants to all Muslims in Britain. The first leader or *amir* of the TJ in Britain, who was also at that time responsible for the TJ's activities in Europe in consultation with TJ headquarters in Nizamuddin, was a first-generation migrant named Hafiz Muhammad Ishaq Patel. Patel came to Britain as an ordinary worker. When he was on *Hajj*, he came into contact with Yusuf, then TJ's global *amir*, "who was apparently so impressed by his sincerity in the cause of Islam that he took him in front of the *ka'ba* and there offered supplications to Allah to make him the instrument of winning the whole of Britain to Islam" (Lewis 1994: 135; Sikand 2002: 225; Ansari 2009: 348).

It was Patel who established the Tablighi community in Dewsbury and eventually led the construction of the movement's European headquarter mosque and Islamic seminary there. He also encouraged regular visits from senior international Tablighi leaders such as

Maulana Zakariyya. Indeed in 1979, Zakariyya visited Dewsbury and offered "special supplications for its future success as the center of Tablighi activity in the west" (Sikand 2002: 225).

TJ IN DEWSBURY

As noted, TJ's European headquarters is at the Markazi Masjid in Savile Town in West Yorkshire's Dewsbury. Construction of the mosque began in the late 1970s with the building completed in 1982, with suspected financial support from Saudi Arabia (Langley 2006). The mosque itself is a large and imposing square building, with a wide frontage, large doors, and topped by a green dome and piercing minaret. The mosque is traditional in its architectural style and based on the plan of the great mosque at Medina in Saudi Arabia. It has a capacity for up to 4,500 men, is one of the biggest mosques in Britain, and one of the largest purpose-built mosques in Europe. The main prayer hall is composed of a large rectangular carpeted space. It is here that members of the movement meet to pray, to listen to Tablighi instruction, and where teaching circles are held.

As well as providing space where Muslims can perform their daily prayers, TJ's Dewsbury *markaz* is the center of TJ authority in the United Kingdom. As is common practice with TJ, the United Kingdom is divided into regions. Each region has its own *markaz* and regions are then grouped into smaller subregions or what TJ refers to as *halaqa*. Each *halaqa* is linked to a local *markaz*, and in turn these *markaz* are under the oversight of the headquarter *markaz* at Dewsbury. TJ currently has eight *markaz* or main organizational mosques in Britain—Dewsbury, Leicester, Birmingham, Glasgow, Blackburn Newcastle, Bristol, and West Ham in London. Dewsbury is where major decisions on the direction of the movement in Britain are made. It is also the *markaz* that communicates on a regular basis with TJ's international headquarters in Nizamuddin. The mosque hosts TJ's Thursday evening gatherings, dispatches Tablighis on propagation missions worldwide, and the attached school serves to educate and train new generations of Deobandi scholars. The mosque has faced some criticism, with allegations that its ethos is counter to the cohesion of local communities contributing to ethnic segregation (Norfolk 2006).

Visiting TJ's Dewsbury *markaz*, it is clear that it sits at the very center of the community, with the area surrounding the mosque almost entirely oriented to the mosque. To outsiders the mosque and its surrounding area are seen as imposing and separatist. Conway notes that since 1992 the area around the mosque "has seen its Indian population grow by 25 per cent, and its Pakistani population grow by 60 percent. Its 5,000 strong population is now 88 percent Asian" (2009: 16). From walking around the area it is apparent that Muslims there adhere to the strict dress and behavioral codes recommended by TJ. Women walk together in small groups and are fully veiled, men wear traditional Muslim clothing and beards, and most shops advertise produce and products in Urdu.

As a result, *Times* journalist Andrew Norfolk asserts that "it is now possible for a Muslim child to grow up [in Savile Town] in the family home, at school and in the mosque and madrassa—without coming into contact with Western lifestyles, opinions or values" (Norfolk 2006). A qualitative research report on Savile Town by CJS Planning in 2013 found that even in a time of economic recession, the outlook in Savile Town has been "positive" and that a "community spirit was evident." The report goes on to say that "in Savile Town it is evident that Islamic religious faith binds the community together and provides a very strong family cohesion" (CJS 2013: 11). The report also acknowledged that the Muslim community of Savile Town "frequently referred to self help, hard work and family strength. In contract [*sic*], the wider community did not and called for government investment to stimulate employment growth" (CJS 2013: 13). What is clear is that the Muslim community of Savile Town is strong, flourishing, and bound by strong ties to Islam and family.

Even though the Muslim community of Savile Town appears to be content in its situation, the issue arises in that it may not be meeting the government's definition for what constitutes cohesive community. Indeed the CJS report articulated:

> The overwhelming conclusion from the site visits and conducting research is one of a closed Savile Town community which is happy and tolerant within itself, but not able or wishing to interact with other diverse elements of the population. Effectively, Savile Town is not a mixed or balanced community, it is a type of monoculture within a geographic area of Dewsbury. The scale of that monoculture appears to be commensurate with the scale of the mosque. (2013: 14)

While self-containment does not create problems in Savile Town, it has served to cause community friction and resentment within the wider Dewsbury area. Some respondents found "concentrated Muslim society unpalatable" and questioned the restricted role of women in Savile Town (CJS 2013: 13). At the same time, within Savile Town itself there was fear of racism outside of Savile Town and this has caused the desire to keep the Muslim community there self-contained.

Arguments abound that mosques are instrumental in changing the demographics of the communities in which they are built, encouraging the influx of Muslims and the pouring out of other communities. Indeed the CJS report on Savile Town found that a "principle reason for residents choosing to reside in the locality" was the "important function in the daily lives of Savile Town residents...of the Markazi Masjid" (2013: 12). Other research finds that ethnic clustering is sometimes a result of structural inequalities. Indeed, one recent study found that it is difficult for South Asians to move into white neighborhoods and cited examples of people who tried to do so but, due to feelings of isolation, returned to areas with higher populations of their own ethnic backgrounds. The report argues that there is usually a feeling that "no matter how much minorities try, the majority community will never accept them—'if they don't want us why should we bother?'" (Change Institute 2009c: 48).

The school attached to TJ's mosque is one of two Deobandi seminaries in the United Kingdom. The Institute of Islamic Education provides education for boys from the age of 12 to 16 and is part of an Islamic seminary that caters for boarders and day students. The school was established in 1982 and works to provide a primarily Islamic education to "create competent native Islamic scholars endowed with knowledge and skills that enable them to cater for the changing needs of British Muslims and the wider community" (Ofsted 2011: 3). The Institute is oversubscribed each year, with admission to the school being selective, including consideration of the educational attainment of students. All students are Muslim. The day at the school is split into two halves where the morning is instruction in Islam and the afternoon is subject matter of the English National Curriculum.

The Islamic curriculum is based on the *Darse Nizaami* (Islamic curriculum). It prepares students to become scholars in Islam. Subjects include Arabic grammar, Qur'an Tafsir (interpretation of the Qur'an), Hadith literature, Fiqh (jurisprudence), Urdu grammar, Islamic history, stories of the prophets, Islamic philosophy, logic, and Qur'anic recitation in Arabic (Ofsted 2011: 4). The secular curriculum is taught in the afternoon and includes the core subjects of English, mathematics, science, and information and communication technology. Conway notes that the school does not allow students to read newspapers or watch television, nor does it take them on any organized field trips other than to go preaching (2009: 15). In the past, concerns were also noted about children not having adequate cultural development at the school and that "the school needed to develop how it made pupils aware about British public institutions" (Conway 2009: 16).

Commenting on the relationship between the Islamic and secular portions of the curriculum at the school, Philip Lewis argued that "what seems evident is that students in the morning and afternoon, live in two unrelated linguistic and cultural worlds" and that "a possible discordance between these worlds is neither acknowledged, nor addressed" (1994: 94). Although a series of reports by Her Majesty's Inspectorate of schools—Ofsted—noted a significant improvement in the quality of secular education taught at the school, concerns still remain about the way science is taught and the limited level of access students have to parents and others outside of the school when in residence:

> The curriculum for science is very knowledge-based and does not offer sufficient opportunities for investigative and practical activities. Students who spoke to the inspectors and the questionnaires they returned made frequent comments about this. Also, students, parents and carers are right to raise issues about the lack of educational visits and/or visitors. The absence of these hinders the enrichment of students' curriculum experiences. (Ofsted 2011: 4)

Unsurprisingly, Ofsted reports consistently highlight the exceptionally high-quality provision for spiritual and moral development of students at the school. It noted that there are very high expectations placed on students to behave in respectful ways and that teachers at the school are good role models. More than this, Ofsted claimed that the school succeeded in keeping young male students away from crime and other undesirable activities. This is best exemplified in what one student commented to Ofsted inspectors:

> I don't have enough words to praise my school, it kept me away from a bad environment. If I wasn't at this school I would have been a criminal and drug dealer, like my mates, but school saved me from that, I will never forget this great favour of my teachers at this school. (Ofsted 2011: 5)

Despite the school having a good record of shielding students from a life of drugs and crime, this does not mean that students are always prepared for an integrated life in modern Britain. Ofsted noted that while students have an excellent understanding of "their own Muslim culture and learn about contrasting cultures through the curriculum...there are no firsthand experiences to enable students to extend their empathy with differing cultural groups in society both at home and overseas" (2011: 6).

While it is clear that TJ made efforts to improve the way in which secular education is taught at its school, the discourse from TJ's gatherings is still one of Britain being a society fraught with moral impurities and ungodliness. It is this form of discourse that, argues Sikand, serves to promote TJ following paths of insularity, or at least feeling most comfortable in almost wholly Tablighi communities. TJ "excluded from the dominant British society in the midst of whom they live, see society as ungodly and immoral and thus respond eagerly to the calls for social separatism and insularity" (Sikand 2002: 232). Adoption of a higher moral ethical code compared to their colonial masters in India was intensified in Britain by TJ as a way to find comfort in a society generally viewed as immoral and to reinforce boundaries of purity. Having said this, contextual shifts in Britain, Europe, and the United States post-9/11 and post-7/7 put pressure on TJ to become more engaging with wider communities, and this will be instrumental to the success of any future construction project.

TJ in London

Furthering the already established research on TJ in Britain, this chapter uses account of the movement's settlement in the United Kingdom from Solad Sakandar Mohammed, a senior member of the London TJ. Mohammed notes that TJ in Britain was "founded in 1944 at 448/450 Commercial Road, Whitechapel, London" and the movement later moved to Christian Street in London's Aldgate East in 1979 "as a result of the redevelopment of our former premises by the local council" (2011: 4). Establishment of the movement in London was earlier than previously thought, but the movement will have only had a small presence at this time.

In 1996, TJ made a significant step in establishing a larger and more active presence in the city of London. After a period of seeking land for a new mosque that would serve as the movement's new home in London, TJ's trustees purchased 18 acres at Abbey Mills, in London's eastern borough of Newham for £1.6 million ($2.7 million). TJ already had a significant presence in East London at that time, including their Christian Street Markazi Mosque, and use of a myriad of Deobandi-affiliated mosques in the city. Abdul Khaliq Mian, a businessman involved in TJ, drove forward the fundraising and the purchase of the Newham site. Mian, who came to Britain from Pakistan at the age of 11, was encouraged by Muslim members of the Newham Council to invest in the property: "I was told it was a very, very strategic site and they said, 'Get a planner and the best architect you can and build the biggest mosque you can'" (Perlez 2007).

During the time TJ has been in possession of their Abbey Mills site in West Ham, they erected structures but without always obtaining planning permission. TJ further failed to submit a timely masterplan for the redevelopment of the site. Temporary planning permission for the use of the structures on TJ's site for faith-based worship ended in November 2006 (Pieri 2012: 52–53). Shortly after this, designs circulated for a mosque structure that would accommodate up to 70,000 people, earning it the epithet "Mega Mosque." In February 2010, Newham Council issued an enforcement notice requiring the cessation of faith-based use and removal of all unauthorized buildings and fixtures associated with the temporary mosque. TJ's London trustees appealed against the enforcement notice, and a Public Inquiry was held in London in February 2011 (Pieri 2012: 52–53). At this Inquiry, Planning Inspector Graham Dudley extended TJ's permission to remain on the site for a further 2 years, in which time a plan for the redevelopment of the site had to be submitted. One of the stipulations was that the plan had to be of genuine mixed use. A planning application was submitted in February 2012, but Newham Council refused this in December 2012, as the plan was for a single faith-based use of the site. The "proposed development was not in accordance with the development plan policies" (Panton 2014: 3). TJ appealed the decision, with the effect that the Secretary of State will make a decision based on the recommendations of a Public Inquiry, on the basis that the proposals give "rise to substantial regional or national controversy" (Panton 2014: 3).

The initial land purchase, despite its huge cost, was not seen as controversial at the time. The Tablighis were understood to be an apolitical movement, and the site was significantly far into East London, in the West Ham area of the London borough of Newham and out of the public eye (DeHanas and Pieri 2011: 805). Further, TJ's newly acquired site was situated on the premises of the former Abbey Mills chemical works, one of the most contaminated pieces of land in the capital, and not particularly desirable for commercial developers.

TJ set up a temporary mosque structure on their site that consisted of a series of interconnected portacabins. The temporary mosque structure has a capacity for 3,000 (male) worshippers, and this is usually reached on the weekly Thursday evening gatherings. On other days of the week, only between 75 and 100 members attend, with the exception of Friday congregation prayers where there could be up to 500. During Ramadan the numbers attending the talks are smaller, with members more committed to Tablighi teachings. The mosque attracts worshipers and adherents from all over the United Kingdom and acts as a dispatching center for missionary groups to other areas of Britain. It has an Islamic shop where those attending can purchase items such as the group's literature, recorded sermons, prayer beads, and religious garments. There is also a kitchen where food is prepared to share among worshipers after meetings. These facilities are important because it means that the mosque is more than just a place of worship, but rather a place where Tablighis and other Muslims can meet to socialize, discuss theological and community matters, and partake in a meal in like-minded company.

The Mosque is divided into three separate prayer halls, and when possible, it is encouraged that all worshipers pray at the same time in the main payer hall. The reason for three prayer halls is that they also serve as rooms where translations of the talks and sermons are relayed. In the main prayer hall, the Thursday evening speech is given in Urdu—the main language of instruction for Tablighis (Pieri 2012: 50). The same speech is then relayed in English and Arabic in the other two rooms respectively by a qualified member of the movement. Given that the talks are of central importance to the religious teachings of the movement, every effort is made for the talks to be accurately translated, although not transliterated. Moreover, certain key words (e.g., *amal, iman, haq*) are not translated but rather relayed in Arabic or Urdu due to the assumption that the majority of those present will have an understanding of the original Arabic or Urdu words.

The Thursday evening inspirational talks or *bayan* allow for visiting national and international Tablighi leaders to speak to gathered congregations about articles of the faith. These talks prove a valuable source of the movement's overarching objectives, albeit in a general manner. The talks follow a similar pattern. The speaker outlines the depravity and ills of society and builds up to the antidote. That is donation of time to go in the path of Allah. As TJ is a missionary organization, Tablighi mosques are not used just for worship, but also as a hub for spreading the Muslim faith as interpreted by the group. Tablighi mosques, including the Markaz Ilyas, accommodate jamaats where those on missions reside for the duration of that *chillah*. The mosque is used as a base for going out into the community to invite Muslims in the locality to listen to the talks. The purpose of inviting other Muslims to the mosque is to ensure that local Muslims know how to correctly perform their prayers and other Islamic duties and to convince them that they too should give time and go into the community to call other Muslims back to a truer interpretation of Islam.

As it currently stands, TJ's London *markaz* is the regional center for a large geographical area covering Greater London, the southeast of England, East Anglia, Oxfordshire, Cambridgeshire, Hertfordshire, and Bedfordshire. TJ leaders have also said that the London *markaz* has some jurisdiction over their Bristol *markaz*, whose geographical jurisdiction extends to the West Country, Plymouth, Southampton, Portsmouth, and into Wales. Smaller local mosques are under the jurisdiction of the London *markaz*, with TJ leaders saying that between the London *markaz* and the one in Bristol over 400 mosques adhere to the TJ version of Islam.[1]

The London *markaz* holds two weekly gatherings. The first is on Tuesday evening and takes the form of a consultation. At this event, TJ's London leader, Zulifqar Ali, meets with representatives from mosques under his jurisdiction. The purpose of the gatherings is to inform all mosques within their region of what needs to be done in terms of Tablighi effort. The second gathering is held on a Thursday night; it is open to all Muslims and features an inspirational talk around the six points of Tabligh. According to TJ leaders, each regional *markaz* is further responsible for holding other events geared at different sections of the Muslim population. For example, TJ in London hosts specific events geared at Muslim students, restaurant workers, business people, and activists who had dedicated their time to the activities of the movement. Such gatherings are meant to increase solidarity between different sectors of Muslim communities and TJ, as well as to elicit more missionary activity from these groups.

Many of TJ's adherents traditionally come from the lower to lower middle class and are South Asian and of older age. Ethnographic research at TJ's London *markaz* suggests that this is changing. The gatherings attract men from different ethnic backgrounds. This shows that TJ has to some extent managed to expand from its predominantly South Asian base. A study commissioned by TJ trustees via ECORYS group confirmed the same. Their survey was during a Thursday and then a Friday gathering in 2010 and included 426 responses. The results of this indicate a strong trend to a youthful population (41% in 20–29 years of age) and one that is ethnically mixed (Pakistani 35%, Bangladeshi 32%, Black African 17%, and Indian 11%) (ERCOYS 2010: 12–13).

While not taking into account even half of the users of the facility, and the probability that many more young people participated, the results are the first and only official source of the mosque attendees. Even though the results in part correlate with what has been observed, it is still important to note that the majority of adherents are older than the survey suggests, and though an increasing number of people from different ethnic backgrounds may use the facility, the majority still originate from a South Asian background. TJ is no longer the same organization that it was in the 1980s and 1990s, and at least in London, the movement has managed to attract a wider following.

The following observation remains important in exploring the extent to which TJ has undertaken a process of adaptation:

> What is particularly striking about the TJ in Britain, and in the west, is how a movement such as the TJ, known for its firm commitment to a conservative understanding of Islam, has not just managed to survive in what it sees as a hostile environment, but has actually flourished despite all odds. (Sikand 2002: 214)

The remainder of this book argues that TJ has been successful in liberal democracies, and especially in London because it not only continues to provide a safe environment for its adherents but also has been able to adapt its strategies to suit local contexts. This does not mean that ideology has changed, but rather that TJ leaders have identified the tools and tactics that are needed to advance the movement in a given context. TJ leaders through a process of engagement have started to become socialized into what is expected of them, as well as how to frame their needs in a way that resonates with policymakers and wider communities. The chapters that follow delve into different aspects of how TJ operates in Britain, and especially how it has attempted to gain permission to construct its new mosque.

CHAPTER 6

Tablighi Jamaat in Transition:
2005–2010

INTRODUCTION

Breaking from traditional methods in 2007, Tablighi Jamaat (TJ) leaders in London reconsidered the movement's previously stated apolitical nature and embarked on a process of engagement with local and national institutions, in order to achieve the goal of constructing their proposed new mosque in West Ham. This chapter charts the London TJ's attempts to adapt from a movement fixated on salvation—in essence a religious theocratic movement—to an organization attune and adept to politics of modern society. In doing this, the chapter seeks to understand the ways in which TJ is willing to undergo change to advance its objectives. This chapter demonstrates how engagement works at a practical level and emphasizes catalysts in TJ's process of adaptation.

The chapter is divided into four parts, each exploring a different aspect of London TJ's process of adaptation. The first places London TJ's attempts at constructing the new mosque in a post-7/7 context. It charts the project's recent history and shows how what could have been a mildly controversial scheme, once imbued with symbolic significance and affected by shifting local and global contexts post-9/11 and post-7/7, came to represent one of the most fiercely contested construction projects. It is precisely because of the mounting scale and increasing symbolic value of the project post-7/7, and at the time of the 2012 Olympic Games, TJ leaders in London had to reevaluate their strategy and take a more community-minded approach.

The second part examines initial attempts of TJ leaders to alter modes of operation in London to secure permission for the project. This includes why planning consultants and public relations (PR) experts were hired, establishment of a project website, a YouTube site with videos from senior Tablighis, a public consultation day held at the site of the mosque, as well as a number of public debates between TJ activists and opponents. This marks a shift from a position of isolation to one of engagement—something traditionally alien to TJ as a movement.

The third part examines opposition to TJ and their proposals and shows how the movement's objectives can be stifled by local and national campaigns. This provides opportunity to view "framing battles" between TJ and its opponents and to see how movements frame and reframe messages to ensure resonance with the widest audience. With the securitization of Islam post-9/11 and post-7/7, Islamic organizations often have a difficult time ensuring their perspective resonates with wider society. TJ has not been helped by numerous allegations that individual movement members were associated with and in some cases prosecuted for acts of terrorism. This encouraged TJ leaders in London to take a more robust approach to community engagement with a strong emphasis on countering allegations of terrorism.

The fourth and final part analyzes proposed mosque construction from the perspective of senior planning officials involved with the project. This serves to provide perspective on TJ's attempts at engagement and interaction from policy and decision makers. In other words, to question how effective TJ has been in its new strategy.

THE CASE OF THE MARKAZ ILYAS

Two events served to drastically alter the way in which TJ would have to interact in Britain and had a significant impact on discussions regarding the proposed mosque. The first was London winning the bid on July 6, 2005, to host the 2012 Olympic Games. The second came the next morning—terrorist attacks on London on July 7, 2005. Prior to the July 7 attack, TJ was a little known albeit global Islamic movement.

The fact that TJ's site for redevelopment was situated next to the land designated for use by the 2012 Olympic Games transformed the nature of the project and propelled the movement into the spotlight. What was once seen as a comparatively worthless piece of contaminated land on the edge of East London suddenly became a significant portion of land at the center of London's Olympic development proposals. The land became imbued with national and symbolic worth— this was a piece of land that potentially billions of people viewing the Games on television might see. The land and what was on it would be symbolic of twenty-first-century Britain. What would have once been a mildly controversial project suddenly became a matter of national and international importance. The still open wounds of the July 7 bombings further complicated matters. Commentators speculated over fears of terrorist activity, especially in light of the fact that the attacks on London came after announcement of London's successful bid. They linked the atrocities to fears that the attacks were a taste of what Muslim extremists would attempt during the Games (Doward 2006c; Langley et al. 2006; O'Neill and Boyes 2006).

For Muslim communities, mosques have come to symbolize the setting where Muslims can join in worship as well as an expression of their religious identities. Historically, however, Islamic structures have been isolated within "invisible" prayer rooms found in private homes or in the backrooms of Muslim businesses.[1] These "garage" mosques have not carried any public symbolic value and were for the most part hidden from wider society. The founding of mosques represents an evolution of Islam from the private to the public sphere and accords Islam symbolic significance in the architectural landscaping of towns and cities. Although this has sometimes been described as the "Islamicization" of urban spaces (Cesari 2005: 1017), on another level, mosques can be seen as a symbol of an ethnic population having settled and put roots into an area, a territorial marker that also acts as a reassurance for the community to allow its members to stay connected with their ancestral heritage (Manco and Kanmaz 2005: 1107). In the post-7/7 period, the British public has at times viewed the mosque as a conveyer belt for terrorism. Programs such as Channel 4's *Undercover Mosque* showed covert footage of extremism and intolerance from mosques across Britain and furthered this image (Dispatches 2007). Despite debates over the accuracy of the footage, the view came to be that what was going on in one mosque was likely to be occurring in all, thus lending succor to those who argued that the mosque would be a barrier to cohesion in the community. This would be another hurdle for TJ leaders to overcome.

TJ was propelled into the spotlight on publication of the design of the proposed new mosque and accompanying facilities by London-based architect Ali Mangera. The design for what was called the "London Markaz" came in 2005. This was after the July 7 bombings and after Mangera won the competition to design the new building. In light was the site's new position of prominence next to the location of the 2012 Games (Vaughan 2007). The symbolic importance of the proposed new mosque situated near the Olympics Stadium was not lost on Mangera or TJ. Mangera's vision for the development of the site centered around designs for a modern, almost futuristic, and ecofriendly mosque with a capacity for 70,000 worshipers. It would feature an Islamic garden, library, Muslim boarding school, and residential accommodations.

For Magera, it was important that the mosque not only be an iconic new structure highlighting London as a multicultural capital, but that it would also reflect something of the character of TJ. On his website, Mangera stated that the project would adopt the idea of *dawah*, or the invitation to Islam and that which is central to TJ's beliefs. Mangera hoped this would be achieved by the mosque "physically and metaphorically reaching out to provide large urban connections which invite people into the building from West Ham Station, the Greenway and beyond."[2] Foreseeing the controversial nature of proposing a building where a main objective was proselytization of people to the Tablighi version of Islam, Mangera added the caveat that for him this also meant the creation of a space where "Muslims and non-Muslims interact, debate and promote a greater understanding between ideology, faith and humanity."[3]

Many commentators questioned Magera's assertions over the interfaith aspect to the mosque, not least because TJ has traditionally shunned interfaith dialogue as a waste of time:

> [TJ] was born from Hindu-Muslim conflict and from proselytizing competition between the two communities in conflict. It cannot therefore be said that the discourse of the Tablighi Jamaat on other religious communities is irenic and only aimed at facilitating religious coexistence. This movement was born out of conflict; and the defence of the community and of its religious boundaries is central in its motivations, as it is central in the whole Deobandi tradition. (Gaborieau 2006: 61)

More than anything else, it was the size of this proposed development that caused a major public outcry. One newspaper article noted that the proposed mosque "will be the biggest house of worship in the UK: it will hold 70,000 people—only 10,000 fewer than the Olympic stadium, and 67,000 more than the largest Christian Cathedral" (Steyn 2005). Another commented on the scale of the project, saying that due to its size "you would end up having a completely Muslim community...it would create a separate district, a parallel society" (Doward 2006a). It was at this time that Newham Borough Councillor and foremost opponent of the scheme, Alan Craig, described the project as the "Mega Mosque."

As part of the ongoing debate over community cohesion, Mangera's designs sparked a national discussion as to the acceptability of such a colossal mosque in London and put a spotlight on TJ as the movement behind the mosque. The *Architects Journal* in 2007 reported that Mangera had been sacked from the "controversial" project, noting that Mangera's design had "attracted a mountain of negative press coverage," which made TJ's position untenable (Vaughan 2007). When questioned about this, the response from TJ's team was:

> Unfortunately the vision that the architect Ali Mangera was producing for the Site did not match that of the community and it was determined in May 2007 that a full architectural competition should take place to appoint an architect who could deliver in accordance with a development and design brief for the site. (Jones 2011: 25)

It was at this point that London TJ leaders considered an alternative strategy to the development of their proposed mosque. This strategy would require a clean break and an emphasis on community engagement and partnership. TJ leaders in London distanced themselves from the original proposals, commenting that the plans were Mangera's and did not reflect the movement's vision. TJ leaders further appointed Allies and Morrison as the new architects and capped the size of the mosque to a capacity of 12,000 worshipers (Jones 2011). The switch to Allies and Morrison highlights one of the ways movement leaders can attempt to overcome negative publicity, namely through positive association. Through being associated with Allies and Morrison, a British firm entrusted with national architectural projects such as the Royal Observatory at Greenwich and the Royal Festival Hall in London, TJ leaders hoped that their scheme too might be recast as a national project. This was also the idea when TJ leaders employed Malcolm Reading Consultants, a firm with royal connections and entrusted with the trusteeship of the Historic Royal Palaces—"a government appointment—including the Tower of London and Kensington Palace" (Lapido Media 2011).

The controversial and contested nature of the "Mega Mosque" project is not something that has been exclusive to TJ or to London, but rather a part of a more marked phenomenon. Among the most striking changes in urban space in the West has been the establishment of a visible and physical presence of Islam, represented through the symbol of the mosque (Eade 1996: 217). This at times caused unease and increased public debate over Islamic architecture. For Allievi the issue is not just about mosque architecture but rather "the real problem is the relationship of Europe with Islam, on the one hand and the relationship that the Muslims have with Europe and the west, on the other" (2010: 47). Cities have been key sites for the spatialization of power projects, whether political, economic, or religious (Sassen 2003). As Cesari puts it, it is the mosque that is "central to Islam's urban visibility and is the centre of Muslim communal life" (2005: 1017).

Every project that concerns the construction of a mosque demands exhaustive and time-consuming processes in which Muslim community leaders are impelled to deliberate, consult, and negotiate with local, city, and regional authorities (Cesari 2005: 1018). A failure on the behalf of the developers to engage in the correct way can often result in disastrous outcomes for the project. As has been seen in the case of the "Mega Mosque," TJ leaders' initial inexperience and inability to interact with the local authority at the level expected of them left a sour note. It is part of the construction process of mosques that Islam goes from being invisible to being unwanted (Cesari 2005: 1018). When deciding on the construction of any structures, planning authorities must take into account what effect the building will have on the local environment and the extent to which the new development will be harmonious within its environment (Dwyer 2000). After 2005, TJ leaders in London awoke to this realization. It has been their desire to make the mosque more "wanted" that has motivated their strategic adaptation.

TJ ENTERS THE TWENTY-FIRST CENTURY

Having discussed the context and early developments to TJ's proposed mosque, this section focuses on early strategies leaders used to mitigate criticisms to the project. These included hiring of project management and PR consultants, establishment of media and web resources, and efforts to engage with local and national publics, the media, and government institutions. Of course, such strategies are not unique to TJ or to Muslim groups and often used by organizations wishing to advance major construction projects in any given city. What is unique to the Tablighi case is that this is a movement that traditionally rejects any form of publicity and remains aloof from the processes of engagement. The mantra for the movement has been "concern yourselves only with the heavens above and the grave below, and never about the world in between."[4] The London TJ's adoption of new strategies in 2007 marks a turning point.

Between 2005 and 2007, TJ leaders allowed their project to be defined by its opponents. Their public silence during this period served to promote their image as an "isolated and secretive network" (DeHanas and Pieri 2011: 808). Following the large-scale negative debates in the media around the project, London TJ leaders made the unprecedented step of hiring a PR firm, Indigo Public Affairs, to advise and manage the movement's media relations. This was a bold move indeed. For TJ members, their absolute belief in Allah made them to hope that the movement does not need Western techniques and innovations or the hiring of consultants. Why then did London TJ leaders in 2007 break with the norms of the movement and hire a PR firm? In 2006, amidst the public furore around the mosque, TJ leaders sought advice from Sohail Sarbuland. This local Muslim was sympathetic to TJ, but not a member, and importantly he was director of London-based Crossier Properties Ltd, with professional knowledge of advancing property developments (Perlez 2007a).

As both a Muslim and TJ sympathizer, TJ trusted Sarbuland and allowed him to act as an intermediary between TJ and the complex world of property development and media engagement. Sarbuland pledged to financially back a part of the project and to manage the planning process through to submission of a formal planning application to Newham Council (Pieri 2012: 55). In early 2007, he was responsible for bringing in the triumvirate of Indigo Public Affairs, new architects Allies and Morrison, and property consultants GVA Grimley (Gilliat-Ray and Birt 2010: 145). This put new direction and energy into the project and spurred on a round of media and public consultation initiatives that came to define TJ during the period 2007–2009.

London TJ leaders sought out a specialized firm with wide-ranging experience and political connections that could help advance the project. Indigo Public Affairs is a London-based PR firm specializing in community consultation and political communications advice. Indigo lost no time in establishing a website for the project and aimed at providing relevant facts and up-to-date information on the progress of project to the media and public. The website[5] was further developed as part of a response to a website by TJ opposition group, Newham Concern.[6] The use of the Internet and social media as means of providing information about the movement resulted in both framing the debate around the mosque as well as reframing the image of the movement to resonate with British society.

For the najority of organizations, the establishment of a website is an ordinary part of everyday life. For TJ in London it was controversial—a move many in the wider movement saw as an unacceptable innovation, a reliance on Western methods, and allowing worldly desires to be the driving force. It was something the movement in Britain had not done before. While the website was still operational, one could access different relevant facts and figures surrounding the project and TJ.

Due to the limited information available about TJ at the time, it came as no surprise that one of the sections on the website was dedicated to providing a "brief overview" of the movement. It explained TJ as a Muslim missionary and revival movement, which has an estimated 70–80 million followers worldwide. The website clarified that TJ's goals are to "bring spiritual awareness to the world's Muslims, promote good morals, social integration and cultural exchange with other communities."[7] Having identified social integration and cultural exchange as key concerns for the government, TJ leaders were keen to tap into this and to rebrand themselves in this way. In reality, the statement had been developed by Indigo and did not resonate with messages imparted to the grassroots members. Until then, TJ leaders had stressed detachment from mainstream society.

One of the most important elements of the website was the FAQ page, which aimed to answer many of the recurring questions being asked about the project. The page was titled "some myths explored," giving the impression that much of what had been said in the press and other public arenas concerning TJ and the proposed mosque was not wholly accurate. A prime example of this was the response to the question over the size of the mosque. Figures ranged between 40,000 and 70,000 worshipers. The website addresses that these figures were "widely exaggerated" and that the mosque would only accommodate up to 12,000 worshipers.[8] It was true that the original designs for the mosque proposed a structure accommodating up to 70,000 worshipers, but TJ leaders clarified the situation. The latest designs for the proposed mosque suggest that the capacity will be 9,500 worshipers (Jacobs 2012).

The FAQ section denied that funds for the project came from the Saudi Royal family and refuted claims that TJ intended the mosque to be a part of the Olympic Games.[9] These FAQs were important because they allowed TJ leaders to interact with questions that had already been posed and allowed them to clarify the facts. It was hoped that this page would be used by journalists, politicians, and the public as a first port of call when trying to decipher who and what TJ is. It would also provide basic facts on the project for use in reporting.

This desire to reframe the movement as forward-thinking and actively engaged in bringing about integration and cohesion to the local area stems from emerging government discourse on citizenship, identity, and integration. At the same time, Alan Craig made assertions that TJ is a "separatist" and "isolationist" sect (Gilliat-Ray and Birt 2010: 146). Unlike TJ, Craig and his Newham Concern group were quick to use modern technologies to forward their arguments. Comparing the two webpages, it is apparent that Craig directly understood the importance of visual aids as a means of supporting claims-making. Newham Concern's website included pictures of Craig with people from different ethnic and religious backgrounds, and this was something lacking on TJ's website. Gilliat-Ray and Birt note that:

> In the early stages of its campaign, the TJ did not see the importance of reaching out directly to build local consensus about how much the project would be geared towards serving the whole community, relying instead on the stated outward-facing and multi-functional nature of the project to carry public opinion without providing further reassurance. (2010: 146)

Tablighi leaders in London were initially experienced neither in the planning process nor in information campaigns surrounding their project. This was to change as TJ leaders realized that a concerted effort would be needed if they were to achieve their objective.

Given the ways in which the context in Britain has changed since 2005, a passive reliance for TJ on the self-explanatory nature of the project was misguided. This changed once Indigo took the helms of PR management. In a further break with TJ traditions, Indigo helped movement leaders to establish a YouTube page where key spokesmen could engage with relevant topics in short video sound bites. The establishment of a YouTube site marks the height of efforts to develop a new strategy focused on actively engaging with ongoing discussions about the project. As with the hiring of PR consultants, this again marks a significant departure from the message presented to grassroots adherents and signals the extent to which TJ leaders were willing to make compromises on their methods.

As part of the attempt to counter the allegations of separatism and isolationism, one of TJ's YouTube videos speaks to the question of who the project will benefit. The questions are: "What is the truth? Will this just be for Tablighi Muslims?" TJ spokesman, Abdul Rashid Bhatti, responded thus:

> Absolutely unfounded! The whole thing behind Tablighi Jamaat is to welcome all schools of thought which encompass Islam, so that's

definitely not the case and on the other aspect with the non Muslims, we welcome every faith. We provide facilities for people who do not have the same mother tongue as us, to be able to participate in the lectures. They'll be given translations. So everybody is welcome, and this a bridge between all communities.[10]

By 2008, TJ's campaign to demonstrate that they were an active part of the local community was reaching its peak. TJ leaders were engaged in dialogue with the press and local authority. It shows the extent of TJ commitment to making a success of redevelopment of the site. Faisal Iqbal, another TJ spokesmen, stated that TJ was so committed to fully integrating that "we want to show that this new mosque can be just as much as part of the community as a football ground" (Izzard 2008). Another TJ spokesman said, "We're keen to keep people updated on our future plans and how we want to involve people in this exercise. We want to ensure that local people are at the heart of what we do."[11]

It was precisely this desire to put local people at "the heart of what we do" that led to the staging of a day of public consultation around the proposed plans for the new mosque on the weekend of March 15 and 16, 2008. TJ threw open the gates of the site and invited local residents to tour existing structures. There was opportunity to meet with TJ members and their consultants and to ask any questions related to development plans. As with the other more technology-based strategies, this was an attempt to engage directly with local residents and demonstrate that TJ was ticking the boxes of engagement and interaction expected by the local authority. A pamphlet (supposedly distributed to local residents) advertised the open day. Mosque spokesman, Abdul Sattar Shahid (2008), noted, "we feel it is the right time now to have a meaningful conversation with local people surrounding our site and we believe that the views of the residents of the Newham community are vitally important." Shahid continued in explaining that "this is a first step in actively engaging local residents in West Ham and the wider community in Newham" and reiterated that the project will benefit "people from all walks of life" (2008).

At the open day, TJ leaders were keen to stress the movement as a peaceful and reserved organization. Traditionally, Tablighis have been reluctant to engage the media, but given the current context, "we recognize that communication discussions using written and electronic means have become a necessary part of helping people understand our purpose and ideas" (Shahid 2008).

TJ leaders understood that success relied upon the credibility of claims-making. There has to be congruency between a movement's stated beliefs and its actions (Benford and Snow 2000: 619). Through the above comments, TJ leaders tried to preempt their opponents' assertions that what the movement now says does not correlate with how the movement behaved in the past. What TJ leaders in London tried to say is that despite valuing traditions, there is a willingness to adapt to and accommodate local contexts. This goes as far as directly engaging with the media, which was initially "banned by our founder" (Shahid 2008). The argument is that TJ be not judged by past actions but rather by its newfound desire to engage:

> We have set ourselves up to be completely open and transparent to local people. We want local people to come and visit us and discuss how the project can integrate fully into the lives of the community. We think Londoners as a whole will welcome this mosque—that's our aim. We want to ensure local people will benefit as well and we need your active participation to help. (Shahid 2008)

On the surface, TJ leaders had made the clearest indication of its significant change in the way it was to operate. For those who have been studying TJ in London, this shift in the methods of the movement came as a surprise. Movement leaders in London even claimed that "the Abbey Mills Mosque will be a symbol of unity and shared belief and a place for everyone to enjoy" (Shahid 2008). This was revelatory in light of the situation surrounding TJ's European headquarters in Dewsbury.

Based on his experiences of trying to access TJ's West Ham mosque in 2005, John Dunne (2006), a reporter for *The London Paper*, expressed a sense of surprise at TJ's change in strategy:

> Having been sent packing twice at the security barrier of Tablighi Jamaat's temporary mosque, I jumped at an invitation to Friday Prayers from a worshipper. Mujahid told me that he was a regular and that Islam was a religion that welcomed everyone. He was amazed that I had been turned away, saying that Islam was peaceful and inclusive. 'You can definitely get in with me, no problem at all', he said. However, after we took off our shoes, an official started frantically quizzing me about why I was there. Mujahid said I was with him. After a heated exchange, Mujahid came back and told me that journalists were under no circumstances permitted. He apologized and disappeared inside while I was ordered to leave the premises.

Dunne was expelled from the mosque a number of times between 2005 and 2006. This was during the period before TJ leaders in London had turned to "embracing" the media and could be due to the context of unfavorable media and think-tank coverage of mosques and terrorism (Friedman 2005; Burton and Scott 2008; O'Neill 2009). Another explanation of this is that TJ was a closed movement at that point and genuinely did not want "outsiders" attending.

This provides a clear example of the extent to which TJ claims to have changed following the hiring of Indigo. It progressed from no contact with the media to inviting the media on to the site. It is because of such a shift in approach in a short space of time that there are allegations of it not being a meaningful adaptation, but rather a short-term strategic and cosmetic move. As the new strategy does not correlate with past actions, it will take time and continued efforts on the part of TJ leaders to maintain their new approach to eventually change opinions.

For Alan Craig and opponents of the project, the open day was nothing more than a stunt to gain favor of the media. Behind the scenes, TJ had not changed. Craig termed the day "the not so open day."[12] Twenty-four hours prior to the event, Craig knocked on doors in the immediate proximity of the mosque. He found that many households had not received the pamphlet or any information regarding the open day. Craig speculated that only a select audience was invited. Craig further highlighted that TJ had not changed their ways. On September 7, 2007, members of TJ failed to attend a public debate in Stratford where local people were to discuss issues surrounding the mosque and overall construction project. Craig commented, "Tablighi Jamaat themselves are refusing to come tonight officially, they're refusing to participate in this open and democratic debate which is what they do!"[13] That TJ representatives did not attend signals a lack of credibility to their new claims-making and helps explain why sustained opposition to the project remains robust.

Opposition to TJ

Many illiberal and theocratic movements deal with opposition. This is especially true when a movement is linked to a religious ideology perceived as threatening by the wider society (Barker 1989). Opposition often necessitates adaptation in movements, developing their strategies, or modifying objectives. Opposition to TJ's plans added pressure on TJ leaders and acted as a catalyst in their decision to adapt strategies. Despite London TJ leaders making an overt effort to reframe the movement by engaging with the media, local residents, and government, opposition did not recede. Opposition to TJ increased between 2006 and 2008, with allegations that the movement's efforts to reframe themselves were PR stunts, and once the development plan was approved, TJ leaders would return to old methods. This is a problem that not only TJ has fact but something most theocratic movements initiating change in methods have experienced (El-Ghobashy 2005; Ashour 2009).

One of the most significant setbacks to TJ's mosque proposals came in the form of a 2,500 signature petition against its plans from local Newham Muslims. It was one thing for Alan Craig and the predominantly Christian-influenced Newham Concern to oppose the mosque, but different when local Muslims aired concerns and were willing to publicly sign a petition. Justifying the petition, Haras Rafiq, co-founder of the Sufi Muslim Council, commented that "Muslims in the area are concerned their children will become involved in an extremist ideology" and that TJ as an organization "is dangerous" (Haras Rafiq in Dunne 2006). This alliance between Newham Muslims and Craig's Newham Concern was to increase the pressure on TJ to abandon their traditional stance of isolationism and to begin the process of engagement.

While many Newham Muslims did not sign the petition, it is this coming together of a significant proportion of local Muslims in alliance with others who opposed the mosque that gave an extra layer of legitimacy to Craig's concerns. The significance of this alliance of opposition to TJ's project was not lost on Craig. In November 2006 he issued a press release to that effect. Craig (2006) argued that local Muslims and Christians alike were of the same opinion, that TJ "is an intolerant separatist sect within Islam that is radicalizing their young men, sending them off to Pakistani madrassas and causing disharmony." Through not responding to such concerns, TJ leaders were allowing themselves to be defined by their opponents and made the proposed construction plans untenable.

The Sunni Friends of Newham were also outspoken with their opinions regarding the project. Asif Shakoor, the leader of the organization and an organizer of the local Muslim petition, commented that TJ discriminates against non-Tablighi Muslims, and that TJ "radicalizes the younger generation" and demanded Muslims take a stand against the project (Asif Shakoor in Al-Alawi and Schwartz 2007). What emerges from this episode is that British Muslim communities are rife with doctrinal and theological disputes pertaining to the practice of Islam as developed on the Indian subcontinent over 100 years ago. These disputes are intensified and politicized in the British context, with different Muslim groups opposing others and their projects on the basis of historic disputes. This is not to take away from the significance or scale of the Muslim petition, but it is well known that Barelwis (the primary petitioners) and some other Muslims often object to TJ and with good historical cause, and to any project they may be pursuing.

In a further blow to the project, Dr Ghayasuddin Siddiqui, a prominent Muslim figure in Britain and co-founder of the Muslim Parliament of Britain, commented in London's *Evening Standard*, "we have too many mosques. I think it should not be built. What we need first is more integration between the existing mosques and the wider community" (Barney 2008). Other Muslims and Muslim organizations in Britain echoed his sentiments. The Muslim Public Affairs committee (MPACUK), an antizionist organization seeking to develop British Muslims' political awareness and produce "active and engaged" citizens, stated that they were against the project. They argued that TJ was not representative of Islam and that it would cause Muslims in Britain more problems than what it was worth. The MPACUK raised some concerns. For example, "Is there a need for the mega mosque to be built? Will it allow women on its committee, will members of the committee be democratically elected by those who use the mosque?" (MPACUK 2008).

By July 2007 there was full public and media debate surrounding TJ's proposals. It climaxed with a posting of a 270,000 signature petition against the project on the Downing Street e-petitions web-site.[14] E-petitions were created as an easy way for citizens to influence government and Parliament in Britain. Any citizen has the power to create an e-petition, and if it gets at least 100,000 signatures, it will be considered for debate in the House of Commons. The petition was organized by Jill Barham who later emerged as having close links with the far right British Nationalist Party (BNP). Her petition stated:

> We the undersigned, petition the Prime Minister to Abolish plans to build a £100 million mega mosque. We, the Christian population of this great country England, would like the proposed plan to build a mega-mosque in east London scrapped. This will only cause terrible violence and suffering and more money should go into the NHS.[15]

Although it was shown that many of the petition's signatories were not members of the BNP, nor knew of the petition's links to the BNP, there was an undeniable fact that Barham was so closely linked to the organization that helped to mitigate the petition's impact (Pieri 2012: 59). Interestingly, Craig and many of the Newham Concern supporters did not sign the petition, disagreeing with its exclusivist language, instead opting to support a broader local coalition.[16] The damage, however, had been done, and due to a common misperception that the antimosque campaign was a united one, allegations were made of a link among Newham Concern, The Christian Peoples Alliance, and the BNP. Craig and his supporters refuted the allegation. The BNP's entry into the debate managed to turn some of the tide of opinion in favor of TJ.[17]

The British-based *Guardian* newspaper reported on the size of the petition, but the main story was centered on the petition's links to the BNP (Bunglawala 2007). While the petition was damaging to TJ's ambitions, the discovered links to the BNP served to turn focus away from TJ. As such, it was not as disastrous as it could have been for them. In Inayat Bunglawala's opinion, the tone of Barham's petition was "embittered" and buying into existing anti-Muslim discourse (Bunglawala 2007). No matter how well a campaign is organized, unforeseen developments can serve to alter a context and thus provide opportunities that the "underdog" can exploit.

TJ leaders in London, now pursuing a strategy of engagement, were quick to seize the window of opportunity to mitigate some of the charges against the project. The BNP's involvement encouraged Muslims to stop and reflect on the situation. Pressure was put on the leader of the Muslim-organized petition, with TJ's website reporting that "the person who started this petition now supports the plan for the mosque."[18] TJ leaders in London were able to rely on the support of the then Mayor of London, Ken Livingstone, who entered the debate after it was suggested that public money would be used to pay for the mosque. Livingstone said allegations were "completely untrue" and reiterated that campaigns of "false information" "can damage good community relations."[19] This was a two-pronged attack. One on the Barham petition, which claimed that money could be better spent on the NHS insinuating that public money was to be spent on the mosque. The second was on the *Evening Standard*'s online poll. It asked whether Londoners wanted the mosque and anyone who wanted could vote and do so as many times as they wanted.[20]

The London TJ's website carried a headline article titled "False Mosque Claims," which reiterated what Lingstone said and expressed concerns about a malicious campaign being waged to influence the *Evening Standard*'s online poll.[21] Iqbal Sacranie, former head of the Muslim Council of Britain, supported TJ and called on Muslims to sign counterpetitions to the ones that had been negative to the project and said TJ is a peaceful and apolitical group.[22] There was an attempt to place the debate back into perspective, but similar debates over mosques, the state of Islam in society, and the belief that multi-culturalism exceeded itself were raging across Europe (Huetlin 2006; Spiegel 2006; Reimann 2007).

ALLEGATIONS OF TERRORISM

TJ publicly stipulated it is a peaceful and apolitical movement and that violence is not part of its ideology (Mohammed 2011). Despite TJ's nonviolence assertions, fears surrounding the movement's proposed mosque have not abated. Concerns are its potential as a radical-ization point for young men and for the promotion of terrorism in the United Kingdom (Friedman 2005; Burton and Scott 2008; O'Neill 2009). Apprehensions emerged from prominent British Muslims such as Ifran al Alawi, Ed Hussain, and Taj Hargey, and from local people in the London borough of Newham where the mosque is to be situ-ated. They reinforced the image of the proposed mosque as a poten-tial problem. Even though concerns stemmed from the securitization of Islam, there were also high-profile terrorist plots involving indi-vidual Tablighi worshipers.

In an interview, one TJ member said:

> Just because a handful of people, who may have used our mosques at some time in the past and behaved in an awful way by attacking others in the name of Islam it does not mean Tablighi Jamaat is a terrorist organization. It would be like saying that just because some people who have gone to Oxford University committed financial fraud, that Oxford University should be labelled as a training facility for financial misdemeanours. There's just no logic to it.

Those members implicated in terrorist plots, argued TJ leaders, rep-resent a very small proportion of TJ adherents. For Hedges this may be true, "but when viewed as the percentage of terror plots involving people somehow connected to the Tablighi, the correlation is unmis-takable" (2008: 6).

Following the 9/11 terrorist attacks on the United States, a num-ber of Western intelligence services reported TJ as having links to ter-rorism. In 2003, an article in *The New York Times* claimed that since 9/11, TJ "has increasingly attracted the interest of federal investiga-tors, cropping up on the margins of at least four high-profile terror-ism cases" (Sachs 2003). The article argued:

> Law enforcement officials say the group has been caught up in such cases because of its global reach and reputation for rejecting such

worldly activities as politics, precisely the qualities that are exploited by terror groups like Al Qaeda. "We have a significant presence of Tablighi Jamaat in the United States, and we have found that Al Qaeda used them for recruiting, now and in the past," said Michael J. Heimbach, the deputy chief of the F.B.I.'s international terrorism section. (Sachs 2003)

In 2003, in the context of the United Kingdom, this was not regarded as an issue of immediate concern. Not least because the July 7 attacks had not yet taken place, London had not yet won the bid to host the 2012 Olympic Games, and TJ had not yet proposed construction of what would be the largest mosque in Britain. It was the context of the July 7 attacks and the continued concern over terrorism that brought TJ under closer scrutiny. Individuals using the movement's facilities have been linked to instances of terrorism in Britain and abroad.

Specific allegations of acts of terrorism involving those who attended Tablighi mosques include Richard Reid the shoe bomber, a number of the July 2005 bombers, the August 2006 plot to bomb airlines going from London to the United States, and the attempted bombings in London and Glasgow in July 2007 (Friedman 2005; Doward 2006c; Burton and Scott 2008; O'Neill 2009). Reid is of British and Jamaican decent and currently serves a life sentence in the United States for terrorism crimes. He pled guilty in 2002 to his attempt to blow up a commercial airliner with explosives hidden in his shoes. Although he was a member of Al-Qaeda and not of TJ, he did attend TJ mosques (Briggs and Birdwell 2009: 17). Two of the July 7 attacks on London were carried out by regular TJ mosque attendees. Shehzad Tanweer and Muhammad Sidique Khan both attended TJ's Dewsbury seminary and were said to have had contact with a Jamaican convert there, Abullah el-Faisal. He radicalized them and was later deported for soliciting murder (Pieri 2012: 62). In 2006, a plot to blow up an airplane from London to the United States became headline news. Two of the plotters, Assad Sarwar and Waheed Zaman (arrested but not convicted), had attended TJ mosques. In July 2007, Kafeel Ahmed was one of the two protagonists who carried out an attack on Glasgow International Airport by ramming his jeep with full of gas canisters into the airport terminal. Ahmed is an Indian-born Muslim who was studying for a PhD in engineering at Anglia Ruskin University in Cambridge. As an adherent of TJ, "he was said by friends and neighbors of the Ahmed family in Bangalore to have changed dramatically three years before the attack, after joining the group" (Pieri 2012: 62).

Documents published by WikiLeaks suggest that people have been using TJ as a cover for Al-Qaeda operations. This is something TJ leaders say they have no knowledge of, and since missionary tours are open to all Muslims they have no way of knowing the exact background of each participant (Pubby 2011). Further to this, a report carried out by the Change Institute for the European Union Commission highlighted further problematic links between TJ and radicalization:

> Security experts assess them as potentially dangerous because of the training they organise in Pakistan. This training can be for some Muslims the start of an Islamist or even terrorist career. This assessment is also shared by the interviewed former Tablighi Jamaat member, who argues that the organisation can serve a catalyst function for radicalisation. Others argue that although the Tablighi Jamaat does not formally propagate violence they sometimes articulate some understanding or acceptance of violence that occurs, which might have a catalytic influence on some individuals. (Ahmad et al. 2008)

Such allegations and images of individuals linked to TJ appearing in British and international courts have been painful for TJ leaders and are still a sensitive issue.

Hedges argues that what is of even greater importance to Al-Qaeda is TJ's "ability to frame the world in a dialectic; Islamic and un-Islamic; good and bad; us and them; worldview as an unfettered, legitimate and protected part of Western civil society" (Hedges 2008: 11). Reference is made to Khaled Abou El Fadl, a professor of Islamic law at the University of California–Los Angeles. He warns that with TJ "you teach people to exclude themselves, that they don't fit in, that the modern world is an aberration, an offense, some form of blasphemy" and "by preparing people in this fashion, you are preparing them to be in a state of warfare against this world" (El Fadl in Conway 2009: 15). For Hedges, not all Tablighi members gravitate toward terrorism and violence, "but this foundation ensures its members will represent a pool of recruits far more susceptible to radicalisation than their cohorts" (2008: 11).

In an unprecedented move, Yusuf Suleri, a senior Tablighi at the movement's international world center in Nizamuddin, sought to put the record straight:

> I should make it very clear to you, the media and everybody who is interested in knowing our stand on the issue of Al Qaeda. We neither

indulge nor support any kind of violence on the name of Islam. In fact we condemn their doings on the name of Islam. violence which is done by people is unIslamic and the Jamaat condemns it in strongest terms. (Yusuf Suleri in Ali 2011)

Suleri continued to argue that any one who thinks TJ condones violence is misguided and defined the purpose of the organization as one that promotes "practice purifying and reforming people of worldly influence. We engage in perfecting *Namaz*, strengthening *Iman*, remembering Allah, treating everybody with compassion and brotherhood and helping people and preparing for the hereafter" (Yusuf Suleri in Ali 2011).

TJ leaders in Britain did not want to comment any further than what had been posted on the movement's London website in 2007: "We do not teach an extremist line, but we clearly can't speak for every single one of those who have ever attended our mosques. There are several thousand people at our weekly gatherings…We utterly refute any links to terrorism or terrorists."[23]

The Official Perspective: Newham Council and the London Thames Gateway Development Corporation

Amid the allegations of terrorism, radicalization, and media hype about TJ's proposed new mosque, its leaders worked hard to convince local planners that their project should be allowed to progress. The PR campaign to prove a commitment to engagement over the planning process did not always translate to actions expected of TJ leaders at the official level. This is ultimately why Newham Council decided to take enforcement action against the movement's temporary West Ham mosque.

Sunil Sahadevan, senior planning officer of London Borough of Newham (LBN) and chief case officer on the Abbey Mills project, has one of the most informed perspectives on the way TJ interacted with the Council since acquiring the site in 1996. Sahadevan suggested that from the Council's perspective, TJ in 1996 was an organization that managed to acquire the site by following the due legal process. Its leaders at the time were able to demonstrate that TJ was a responsible organization willing to engage with the Council to redevelop the site. What perplexed Sahadevan is why TJ did not follow that same due legal process, illegally erected temporary structures on their site, and contravened health and safety regulations: "I can't believe they don't have professionals in their congregation. Surely them acquiring the site in the first place took due legal process. Why does it come to an end as soon as they've acquired it? Why aren't the other requirements followed through?"

The discussion with Sahadevan continued to examine the way TJ leaders operated since 1996, and whether the apparent change in strategy since 2007 was reflected in interactions with the Council. Sahadevan commented:

> It's been since 2007 that they first got a PR firm on board, it was Indigo. Prior to that, there didn't seem to be that kind of angle at all. In terms of engaging with us and engaging with the community, when they first moved in, the local residents and businesses around there knew that they didn't have consent, and they were having large festivals which were causing noise and congestion. This was causing complaints so they probably didn't do themselves a lot of favours. They then started building structures on site. They were made aware that the council wasn't happy, and they then did retrospective applications for those structures. But when our members were undertaking site visits prior to those proposals being considered they saw other structures being built so there was a recklessness at that stage. Its not just the local authority they are on the wrong side of, but you have to give consideration to the local community who live at your doorstep and are aware that you are doing things without consent. That obviously causes friction.

Prior to 2007, TJ was not following due legal methods in the planning process. Information from the movement itself paints a picture of a group stifled by a long and laborious planning process, with younger TJ members taking law into their own hands and building temporary structures. There is indication that initial failures of TJ to comply with planning regulations were due to inexperience with the planning process. Sahadevan noted that since TJ leaders hired Indigo there had been a greater effort to communicate with the Council and hence to achieve a level of goodwill. This indicates that since TJ started receiving professional advice they have been learning to adapt to and negotiate the complex systems of the planning process.

The other planning body taking an active part in decision making over the proposed construction was the London Thames Gateway Development Corporation (LTGDC). Peter Minoletti, a senior planning officer there, explained that the LTGDC was set up in 2004 with a lifespan of ten years. It was charged to deal with strategic planning applications within Newham, Tower Hamlets, and other areas of East London. Minoletti was an employee of the planning department at Newham Council in 1996 when TJ acquired the site and, as such, is one of the few planners involved with the project since 1996.

Minoletti confirmed that since 2007 London TJ leaders were making an effort to engage with the media and the local Newham public. But he was less sure as to the actual long-term intentions of the movement. Minoletti said he welcomed TJ's newly found desire to develop a site in accordance with Newham Council's mixed development requirements, but questioned the extent to which the Council's definition of mixed development tallied with the TJ's. His comments capture the crux of the debate over TJ's adaptation:

> No matter how mixed [TJ's development] actually is, if you were not a member of their mosque or related mosque, how open would that facility be? For argument's sake, what sort of books will be in the library? If it's purely Islamic reserved books or all related to the Qur'an, who else might go there? What's on offer in the cafeteria? Also the school is an obvious one where you're unlikely to board there unless you're related to the mosque. If residential accommodation is provided on the site who's going to control who lives there?

Minoletti's point was that it is not enough to say the proposed facilities will be open to all. Those facilities must genuinely reflect the dynamics and diversity of the local community. In response to a question over whether TJ's PR strategy was a public face or whether TJ leaders had adapted and were behaving as expected under the planning rules, Minoletti argued that:

> You get the impression that the members of TJ that attend the official meetings are the ones who could understand a bit more about the arguments coming forward and would say, "oh yes we'll look at that or we want to do this"; "yes we want to have a library, we want to have a cafeteria." But once you prodded them or pushed them a bit about how inclusive will this facility be if I just walked off the street, how welcoming would I find it? Would there be material there that would be of a wider interest? They found it difficult to respond.

These are legitimate concerns, but the fact is that controlling these factors will for the most part be out of the hands of TJ leaders. It is the case that some Muslims will want to live next to, or nearby, the mosque more so than others. This will be the case if there is an increase in Muslim-friendly services. This relates to the role of the mosque as more than just a place of worship but rather the nexus of Muslim community events, and as such it is likely to draw in Muslims who want to live near these facilities. As documented by Kepel, Tablighi mosques can alter the demographics of an area. This can be observed in Dewsbury and in the vicinity of the TJ's main Paris mosque, "since the inauguration of the Omar mosque, indigenous French shopkeepers whose shops are situated on the path of the faithful have been continuously approached to give up their leases. Although some have resisted, the Islamization of the shops has progressed impressively" (Kepel 2000: 192).

Despite efforts of London TJ leaders to convince planners that they changed in modes of operation, an example of TJ's failure to properly understand the way in which the process works in Britain is through a comment made by a senior Tablighi in London to a planning officer. TJ own an island as part of the site which is one of the most polluted sites in the whole of Europe. The officer said. "the horror a few years ago when they [TJ trustees] said, it's alright the women and children can go on that site. I thought wow!"

Despite having hired some of the best consultants in London, it seems that the actual journey of engagement and adaptation for TJ in London has yet to reach its full conclusion. Of course, this is not a process that can be achieved overnight. It may indeed take a generation or two, and such comments coming from TJ leaders could hamper reframing the movement.

One of the most interesting discussions with Minoletti centered on whether he had noticed a change in TJ's engagement with or interaction with planning officials since 2007. Minoletti's response was telling of the situation. It was not simple but based on a number of factors. The way TJ's leaders were behaving had changed, but at the same time, part of the reason for change was not just out of a desire to change but due to opposition the movement was receiving. A reason for TJ upping it then was because there was a very active local councillor, Alan Craig. One of the interesting things in planning in recent years is the ability of the Internet to generate petitions for or against.

If TJ in London changed their stance due to opposition, it goes some way in showing that they have been adept at realizing that past strategies had not been successful and that responding to issues levelled against them is important. As already stated, it is difficult for theocratic movements to change without it looking as though the change has been due to opportunism, verses a genuine and rational desire to change.

What has come as most surprising for many TJ observers is the way London TJ leaders made a dramatic change in their strategy and discourse in 2007. Having gone from a movement that was closed and nonengaging—in short a retiring theocratic movement—to one that was attempting a mass PR campaign is intriguing. It is as though TJ leaders came to the realization that winning the battle over approval for construction was a matter of ticking the right boxes as well as saying what needed to be said. That is exactly what the London TJ did through Indigo, with public claims that the movement wanted the mosque to be a mixed-use site with a school, a library, a cafeteria, and a place for everyone. This marks an important watershed in the movement. By making these claims, TJ should be held to account. By the beginning of 2009, however, this strategy of overt engagement was being toned down. The PR campaign was not the success TJ leaders wanted, and a rethinking of strategy was needed.

CHAPTER 7

Tablighi Jamaat and the Politics
of Adaptation

INTRODUCTION

In 2011, Tablighi Jamaat (TJ) leaders and their hired team of professionals went to court to convince a planning inspector as to why they should not be evicted from the West Ham mosque and to defend the movement as one that is open, tolerant, and inclusive. TJ and its opponents attempted to draw on the wider history and international activities of the movement to make their cases. This chapter seeks to demonstrate that through starting a process of sociopolitical engagement, TJ leaders in London were learning what was expected of them. They were also gaining the ability to frame their activities within the broader concept of the community cohesion agenda, whether they believed in it or not. Initially this process of adaptation ignited discussions over the extent to which TJ had made a *genuine* change in its modes of operation. This was due to lack of (perceived) congruency between what TJ said and the way it acted. In short, TJ was caught in a juxtaposition between adapting to rules of a liberal state and the belief that the only way to achieve one's goals is through living a theologically authentic way of life.

This chapter uses the two Public Inquiries over TJ's West Ham site as a means to analyze the extent to which TJ in London managed to convince decision makers that it has made a long-lasting change in the way it operates. The chapter also examines TJ's submitted planning application for the proposed mosque and the ensuing public demonstrations for and against the project. The question of TJ's proposed London mosque has escalated to an issue of national importance. TJ, Newham Council, the supporters, and those in opposition of the proposed mosque have made their views clear. On the basis of evidence given to the second Public Inquiry, a planning inspector will make recommendations for or against the construction of TJ's new mosque. The ultimate decision, however, is in the hands of the Secretary of State for Communities and Local Government.

BACKGROUND TO THE FIRST INQUIRY

On Tuesday, February 8, 2011, the Public Inquiry into the appeal over enforcement action of TJ's site opened at Newham's Town Hall in East Ham. Planning inspector Graham Dudley delivered his verdict on May 23, 2011. The outcome of this inquiry did not determine whether or not the proposed mosque could be built, but whether TJ would remain on its current site for an extended period of 2 years. In this time a masterplan for the redevelopment and regeneration of the site would have to be submitted. Even though this inquiry was to determine whether the use of TJ's current facility should be extended for a further period of 2 years, TJ, Newham Council, and Newham Concern (NC) proceeded to act as though the final outcome of the project was to be determined. Issues surrounding the global nature of TJ and matters relating to community cohesion at times overshadowed the discussions over practicalities such as traffic and noise concerns.

Newham Council issued the Notice of Enforcement on TJ's site on January 21, 2010 on the grounds that TJ had consistently breached planning regulations on the site (LBN 2010: 1). TJ's use of buildings on the site was illegal since the authorization of temporary structures ceased in 2006. Ultimately, Newham Council did not believe that TJ made enough of a transition to make it an effective partner in the regeneration of the site, nor was TJ likely to do so in the near future. TJ was instructed to "cease the use of land and all buildings as a place of worship" (LBN 2010: 3), effectively meaning the closure of the current temporary mosque on the site. The Notice was to take effect starting March 4, 2010 "unless an appeal is made against it beforehand" (LBN 2010: 4). An appeal was made with the eventual result being the commencement of a Public Inquiry.

THE COUNCIL'S CASE: ENFORCEMENT ACTION

Talking from the perspective of planning officials involved with TJ's site, this section focuses on allegations that TJ in London consistently breached planning regulations, failed to engage with the Council's planning processes, and has been a significant factor in delaying the regeneration of the local area. The importance of these assertions is that they reveal TJ as having failed to fully adapt in London and lacking the ability to function within the parameters of the state. These claims are significant because London TJ leaders framed themselves as having done everything within their power to abide by regulations and blamed the local authority for hampering their plans for regenerating the site. This returns to the dispute over whether TJ has been able to present itself as a movement committed to sociopolitical engagement and community partnership and, more importantly, to also act in this way.

In its *Statement of Case*, Newham Council outlined case studies highlighting TJ's noncompliance with planning regulations as well as opposition to the cohesion of the local community. Newham Council further raised the issue that TJ's site is "heavily contaminated" and that questions regarding the "health and safety implications for occupiers and other users" remain (Waterman-Environmental 2007; Environment Agency 2010; Hegarty and Sahadevan 2010: 35; Crowcroft 2011: 11). Although TJ leaders had known at the time of acquisition of the site that it is one of the most contaminated lands in the whole of London, they had not taken adequate health and safety precautions. Indeed, when one senior planning officer raised the issue of the "highly contaminated Channelsea Island" with a TJ trustee, the response was that it should be adequate for women worshipers.

Comments such as the above provided ammunition to those who characterize TJ as a backward group and counter to the standards of equality in British society. Further to this, Newham Council explained:

> Adequate time has been given to the Trust to achieve acceptable redevelopment of the property or an alternative site for worship. The Council has warned the Trust on multiple occasions that the current development is unacceptable and that more appropriate redevelopment of the property was necessary. (Hegarty and Sahadevan 2010: 41)

Sahadevan stated that during his time as a planning officer for Newham Council, he had "never seen a masterplan" for the redevelopment of the site.[1] This raised questions over the extent to which TJ leaders seem to have changed. This accusation is one that TJ leaders in London worked hard to combat.

At some level, the inquiry came down to the question of whether TJ is a suitable group to construct Britain's largest mosque. From a planning perspective, this did not specifically raise questions over the religious affiliation of TJ, but rather the same core competencies required of any other group in the same position. That is the ability to properly function and provide the correct responses within the planning system—whether that system is alien to them or not. Initially, TJ leaders in London found this challenging as they had no previous experience with the planning processes. This difficulty in functioning within the system was highlighted by Sahadevan, who noted that throughout the 14-year period TJ owned the site, and despite repeated promises for submission of a masterplan, only one was submitted in 2003. That plan did not meet the requirements stipulated by Newham Council (Sahadevan 2011a: 13). There were allegations that TJ had not paid its hired professionals and that the eventual submission was deemed invalid (Sahadevan 2011a: 13). Indeed, the problem with the application had been the desire to develop "a homogenous religious use of the site, which TJ knew would be unacceptable to the Council" (Sahadevan 2011a: 13).

A homogenous religious use of the site was contrary to the *Memorandum of Agreement* that TJ leaders signed with Newham Council in 2001 (LBN 2001). TJ leaders wanted to develop the site in accordance with their own specifications (not wanting mixed use) and for building a large mosque and an Islamic boarding school. Sahadevan noted that until 2005, rather than hiring professional advisers to help them manoeuvre through the application process, TJ's consultants were members of the "trust's own congregation, and they did not have any previous significant master planning experience" (Sahadevan 2011a: 17). In many cases, groups with no previous planning experience may be naive as to the way the system works and go without realizing that the process of engagement provides a platform for such movements, socializing them into what is expected of them and giving them opportunities to operate and modify behavior.

By 2009, TJ's trustees in London attended a meeting with Council officials and were advised that "unless meaningful progress was made on the masterplan by the end of the year, the Council would be forced to pursue enforcement action" (Sahadevan 2011a: 19). Sahadevan reiterated that Newham Council "wanted to be reasonable and cooperate with the trust" and that the trust had been given numerous warnings regarding their "illegal use of the site."[2] According to him, despite these warnings the trustees did not approach the Council for any further meetings or consultations. They also made no contact with any of the Council's statutory partners.

By the end of 2010, Karen Jones, TJ's chief consultant at the time, contacted Newham Council requesting a meeting to "try and convince the Council why a single religious use of the site would be acceptable to the Council" (Sahadevan 2011a: 21). This was the last attempt by TJ leaders to develop the site in accordance with the movement's guidelines, although this changed to an acceptance of a mixed-use development at the inquiry. Sahadevan questioned the robustness of TJ's acceptance to a mixed-use development. He also raised doubts based on TJ's history of interactions with the Council and whether TJ leaders would be able to deliver on this promise.[3] For TJ leaders in London, however, the shift in their position marked an attempt to show that they understood what was expected of them and signaled readiness to comply. A failure to comply would risk the collapse of the proposed project, something that TJ leaders at the time were desperate to avoid.

For Newham Council, TJ did not adequately engage with the planning process, and where TJ had engaged, there was no adaptive effect. According to the Council, despite numerous meetings with TJ, its leaders still wanted a masterplan with a homogenously religious use of the site. It was not until the Public Inquiry that TJ leaders decided to pursue a practical agenda and came to understand the reality that the site could not be developed solely for religious purposes. There was a breakdown in trust between TJ and Newham Council, and the Council suspected that TJ had a double agenda. Based on its history of interactions with the movement, the Council feared redevelopment of the site would never come to fruition.

TJ RESPONDS

Solad Sakandar Mohammed, a senior member of London TJ, represented Tablighi leaders at the inquiry. He became a TJ member since he was a teenager in the 1970s and has been closely involved with the "management of the Riverine Centre since its acquisition."[4] In the words of Mohammed, TJ's objective is to:

> welcome people into our community so they can learn more about our faith, prayers, fellowship, sincerity in our deeds and betterment of character. It is our belief that a good Muslim is one with whom the person next to you feels safe. This is the ethos that drives our relationship with our neighbors and the wider community. (2011: 4)

That Mohammed chose to stress TJ's role as a good neighbor shows that TJ leaders viewed cohesion as a key consideration. Through referring to TJ's faith element and linking this with cohesion, TJ leaders have thought to frame the movement as having a balance between religion and politics and as abiding by the norms of the society. The goal was to portray that TJ leaders knew what was expected of them and were committed to it, and that TJ leaders have the ability to identify critical themes and deploy these in a way resonating with the inquiry, irrespective of their own views on the matter. It is at such instances that TJ leaders demonstrated they understand the planning system and have the sophistication to interact with it.

Rather than directly engaging with the planning issues at hand, Mohammed decided to turn to the proposed construction of the new mosque, arguing that the current site was not adequate for the purpose. A typical attendance on a Thursday evening (the mosque's busiest period) is "between 1,500–1,900 people," and with the numbers growing, the need for a larger and purpose-built place of worship arose (Mohammed 2011: 8).[5] Mohammed stated that the success of London TJ has been in its "apolitical message of peace...the success of the Center is testimony to the power of this message" (2011: 8). This exemplifies the sort of claim that TJ leaders made in public to reframe TJ as a movement with which business can be done. It is generally true that London TJ's success has been its framing of itself as an apolitical and peaceful movement, but more importantly because it managed to stay faithful to its principles and provided a familiar space for its members to operate in.

In a continuation of the cohesion theme, Mohammed asserted his belief that TJ's London site is a central aspect of the local community and that enforcement action would have a negative impact. In addition to the mosque's role as a place of worship, it also serves as a place of "faith studies, practical studies (application of holy teachings to modern life skills), occasional weddings, counselling services and eating facilities" (Mohammed 2011: 11). Having ensured that the Inspector and others at the inquiry knew that the mosque is more than just a place of worship, Mohammed continued to outline the implications of enforcement action. If the appeal was unsuccessful and the center was "forced to cease use, the impact on the participants will be long-lasting, dramatic and distressing" (Mohammed 2011: 13).

A point was made that between 50 and 60 percent of all regular participants in the mosque's activities are from the local area. The facility is being used by people from "42 different nationalities, all of whom trust the Center to be there for them" and that "no other Center has the strength of diversity that the Centre offers" (Mohammed 2011: 14). This countered the framing of TJ as a homogenous and closed group, rather presenting it as diverse, open, and multicultural, and actively engaged with many different sectors of the (Muslim) community. The argument resonated with the policies of community cohesion, reinforcing that the facility is not just for the few but open to vast segments of the local population. TJ leaders in London managed to gather and use facts to present themselves as being well-informed and able to engage to the level expected in a Public Inquiry. This exemplifies that the process of engagement had an effect on the way the movement operates irrespective of whether the new strategy is genuine or not. TJ was able to put personal convictions to one side, highlight information relevant to the planning process, and show an understanding of wider contextual factors as a means of advancing its objectives. In a sense, this signifies strategy above ideology in how TJ sometimes functions.

TJ leaders claimed that they were doing everything within their power to cooperate and engage with the local authority and to demonstrate how important the current use of the site is to the continued existence of the community. The rationale for them was that TJ is just as much a part of the community as is any other group and, as such, should have the right to continue practicing their faith in the local area, albeit recognizing that a more sincere approach to engagement is necessary. Russell Harris QC, speaking on behalf of TJ, suggested that the threat to TJ's existence has forced TJ to reassess its position (Pieri 2012: 69). The fear of the appeal failing "has concentrated their minds."[6] This comes as a guarded admission that TJ had short fallings in the past but had come to understand that there is a process to follow and that it should commit itself to that.

This is a theme that Karen Jones also noted. She said, "the threat of losing this [appeal] is enormous and they [TJ] will do everything to work with the Council to get a facility that is best for both parties." [7] Fear is the factor that played when Mohammed argued that if the mosque was "forced to close, it would be very difficult to restart it again" and that the success of TJ is "largely this notion of single geographical Centers; a single Center helps the community channel all its energy, spirit and resources into one place" (2011: 14–15).

This fear of the community disbanding if the mosque closed shows that TJ leaders were eager to convince the Inspector. Should this happen, a vital element of a diverse community could be lost. Expanding upon this, and again focusing on the theme of community, TJ leaders emphasized that their message is of benefit to everyone—a message that "encourages people to take responsibility of their own lives" and when combined with faith "unites people" (Mohammed 2011: 16).

Mohammed explicitly stated that TJ trustees took a firm resolution that any new development would be mixed-use and shall incorporate a school, community facilities, and retail units.[8] There has been further effort on the part of TJ to work against a drug culture in the wider community. Mohammed noted that TJ is "regularly in touch with parents who ask us to help their children and save them from falling into problems with crime, drugs or being manipulated by others and straying from the right path" (2011: 16). He outlined that this active community role was recognized by the Ministry of Justice—to use the mosque as a place where people can do community service. A letter from the London Probation Trust commented that the Abbey Mills site has been used as a place of community service since August 2010 and that the use of the facility was of benefit to those serving out their sentence (Goud 2010). If the site was to be closed, according to TJ leaders, "there is a significant risk that these younger members of the community would be lost and would revert to antisocial behavior" (Mohammed 2011: 16). There could be no stronger signal of TJ's active engagement with the wider community.

Despite the focus on cohesion and the consequences of the closure of the mosque, TJ leaders also had to focus on the actual planning issues the inspector was to adjudicate. One of the most significant claims made by Newham Council was that TJ consistently failed to submit a masterplan for the redevelopment of the site, stalling the regeneration of the area as a consequence. Karen Jones gave three key reasons why TJ in London failed to submit a masterplan (2011: 21):

1. Development plans outside TJ's control "safeguarded" the site for a canal and road. As such TJ was not clear about what part of their site could be developed.
2. An Olympics Compulsory Purchase Order (CPO) in 2006 proposed a proportion of the site would be acquired to build a walkway from West Ham to the Greenway.
3. The "financial crisis" between 2008 and 2010 impacted available funding for the redevelopment of the site.

None of these reasons suggests that TJ is a closed or fundamentalist group that failed to distinguish between faith matters and operate within the framework of the modern state. Of the three reasons given, the most important was the 2005 CPO on the site. Jones commented that once London had won the bid to host the Games, the Trust received advice from the London Thames Gateway Development Corporation (LTGD) "not to progress the Site's masterplan until they received further advice. The site may be needed for part of the Olympics" (2011: 24).

The CPO on a small area of the site was issued in 2005 and confirmed in 2006. This meant that the Trust had to reconsider the way the site was to be redeveloped. To complicate matters, there was a delay in the actual purchasing of the area, adding further uncertainty about what was going on, and it was not until 2009 that the ODA advised the Trust that in actuality the CPO would not take effect.

Douglas Edwards QC, representing Newham Council, argued that the Council never received any communication that TJ was having problems in submitting a masterplan due to the CPO. If the CPO was a real issue at the time, why did TJ leaders not relate this to the Council or LTGDC?[9] Further to this, Sahadevan challenged the assertion that TJ was told by the LTGDC not to progress with their plans. Only a small proportion of the site ever came under threat by the CPO and, as such, a comprehensive masterplan could and should have been developed, especially given TJ's claims of having an experienced team in place and promising a masterplan by December 2008 (Sahadevan 2011b: 6).

Karen Jones was adamant that the masterplan would emerge the next year. A failure to do so would be disastrous for TJ, effectively losing any goodwill left in the Council as well as being evicted from the site.[10] The new architect, Nicholas Champkins of Allies and Morrison, stated that new designs were being worked on and that the mosque would "include a maximum of two minarets" (Champkins 2011: 6).[11]

In a further bid to demonstrate need for extension of current use on the site to include a large mosque and to highlight TJ's proactiveness in assessing these needs, TJ leaders presented evidence to the inquiry of a report by ECORYS UK. The report stated that there are currently 31 mosques in Newham, with a combined capacity for approximately 16,000 worshipers. The largest is TJ's temporary mosque, the Masjid Ilays. If enforcement was taken, the combined capacity of worship spaces would drop by 3,000. This would be "a reduction in capacity of almost one fifth" (ECORYS 2010: 7). Through this, TJ leaders demonstrated that the current site performs an important role in the makeup of faith provision for local Muslims and offered a strong bid as to why the redevelopment of the site with a large mosque is a necessity.

Building upon this argument, interviews with the largest Deobandi mosques in Newham, as well as visits to these mosques during prayer time on Fridays "have provided clear evidence of the current capacity issues facing mosques in Newham" (ECORYS 2010: 8). This meant that if current use of the existing facilities on TJ's site were to cease, then the pressures on capacity in the other mosques in Newham would rise. The report stated that "there was universal agreement amongst these [local Deobandi mosque] representatives that the Riverine Center helps serve increasing local demand and mitigates the increasing demand pressures on their already stretched facilities" (ECORYS 2010: 22).

The survey, however, has come under much criticism, with Newham Council describing it as crude. Only 426 users of the site were interviewed, as well as the managers of the four largest Deobandi mosques in the area, who are naturally sympathetic toward TJ. Karen Jones, however, argued that the Muslim population in Newham increased by around 17 percent since the 2001 Census. The current mosque provision in the borough was inadequate for the current population. Closure of a TJ's center would make matters worse:

> There is enough evidence to support the fact that the Centre is so unique and established as part of the network of community services provided in Newham, that its loss would be hugely harmful and would be contrary to the planning processes. Furthermore, the idea that it could be located to another site runs contrary to the resistance of the Council to lose existing facilities which it must acknowledge have become well-established and at the heart of how a community functions, particularly that of an ethnic minority. (Jones 2011: 64)

Planning inspector Graham Dudley noted in his opinion that "the aspirations of the trustees have not changed" with regard to the desire to develop the site in a homogenously religious way. This is the trustees' ideal outcome; it was such in 1996 when they purchased the site and remains so today. What has changed according to Dudley's opinion is that TJ leaders have become pragmatic: "pragmatism dictates that it has to be mixed-use."[12] This is an important statement as it suggests that TJ leaders have in effect been able to put their ideal outcome as dictated by religious convictions to one side and reach a compromise for a mixed-use development.

The Role of NC

The third party to formally take part in the Public Inquiry was local interest group NC. It claimed to represent the views of local residents, including local Muslims, with support from a wider audience at the national level. NC states that its aim is to promote "our capital to be a model of social harmony between our many communities" (Craig

2011b). Its leader, Alan Craig, is one of the most prolific campaigners against the construction of the proposed mosque. His genius was to frame the issue as the "Mega Mosque," an epithet that soon became a synonym of large mosques being constructed around the world. For Craig, the issue has been about ensuring the cohesion of the local community:

> I am not against mosques, nor am I against mosque building. The UK is an open and tolerant society and I respect people's right to worship whatever their faith. What I do oppose however, is this specific mosque and the people behind this mosque. TJ are a closed and secretive sect, they discriminate against women, and if you look at their current headquarters in Dewsbury, you will see that it has become a parallel society. This is something that I don't want for London.[13]

NC's team argued that if TJ gained permission to construct its "Mega Mosque," the cohesion of the local area would face dire consequences. NC called on Muslim scholars and activists to testify that "TJ promotes hard-line separatism and intolerance, including of other Muslim denominations" and that it is misogynistic in "its refusal to open their current facilities to women." They further claimed that TJ "teachings run counter to the planning policy principles of social cohesion and integration which seek to underpin regeneration initiatives in East London's multi-cultural society" (Pugh-Smith and Deakin 2011: 2). NC centered its debate around cohesion, framing TJ's practices as contrary to planning policies.

NC had two witnesses, Imam Dr Taj Hargey of the Muslim Educational Centre in Oxford and Tehmina Kazi, Director of British Muslims for Secular Democracy. NC challenged TJ and called into question their record on cohesion. The aim of Hargey and Kazi was to demonstrate that even if TJ leaders embarked on a process of engagement, this would have no transformative effect on the movement and that new strategy is empty rhetoric. Contrary to Mohammed's assertion that the core ideology of TJ is peace, Hargey noted that "there is little doubt that most embrace religious interpretations that are largely indistinct from the fundamentalist Wahhabi-Salafi ideology that is the mainstay of Muslim militants" (2011: 5).

Hargey reframed TJ in a more sinister light, questioning whether an organization with links to militant activity should be in a position to build one of Europe's largest mosques. Taking this argument further, Hargey asserted that even though TJ adherents may not actively be involved in *jihad*, the fact that TJ leaders do not actively oppose it in their current teachings "is indirectly lending it sustenance and succour" (2011: 6). These comments are problematic for they do not distinguish between different forms of *jihad*, nor do they take account of TJ leaders' condemnation of terrorism. Going further, Hargey made reference to Marc Gborieau's belief that TJ's final goal is nothing short of "planned conquest of the world in the spirit of proselytizing jihad" (Hargey 2011: 10; see also Gaborieau 1999: 21).

Hargey proceeded to interact with policies on cohesion and argued that TJ is constrained by its ideology in how sincere its interactions with Newham Council and all non-Muslims can be:

> Since the TJ is at heart a fundamentalist movement, it embraces a conservative and undemocratic ideology. Aside from instructing its members to avoid entanglement in local politics, promoting the face-masking of women, opposing co-educational schools and banning social contact with non-Muslims, TJ encourages Muslims already disenchanted with life in the west (who are searching for their identity) to disassociate from the world by pursuing a transnational, self-imagined construct that can be exploited by extremists. (2011: 14)

For Hargey, TJ did not adapt to the British context in which they find themselves. Even though its professional team may be saying all the right things, the reality is that TJ operates at a different level to that of Newham Council (Pieri 2012: 41).

To promote this image of TJ as out of tune with the government's aspirations for cohesive communities based on equal opportunities, Hargey stressed that TJ is "scornful of secular democracy and Western values" and sees "voluntary apartheid as not merely beneficial, but crucial" (2011: 15). Hargey referred to the case of Zubair Dudha, the Dewsbury mufti who "tells parents that permitting their offspring to mix with non-Muslims is an evil that is bringing ruin to the holy moral fabric of Muslim society" (2011: 15). He regards this as evidence of cultural isolationism and as the polar opposite of integration. Should the eventual construction of the mosque be allowed, Hargey feared it would serve to "condition UK Muslims to divorce themselves from the mainstream to remain on the embittered edge of British society" and create a "distinctive separate enclave, a practical apartheid-like ghetto and a parallel society" (2011: 16–17). These are severe words and left the inquiry in no doubt as to some of the possible consequences if the mosque was allowed to be constructed. The inspector, however, was not adjudicating on the proposed mosque plans but rather whether TJ should be allowed to continue using their site for an extended period of 2 years.

Tehmina Kazi explained that she had been called to "explain why TJ doesn't promote social integration" with specific regard to women.[14] For Kazi, TJ is not conducive to furthering cohesion because TJ women are expected to be covered completely when out of the house. They are not allowed to leave their house without being accompanied by a close male relative.[15] While this highlights TJ's ethos toward women, it did not directly resonate with what the inspector was looking for in regard to TJ remaining on their current site for a further 2 years. Quoting the government's Cohesion Delivery Framework (2010), Kazi noted that TJ is acting in a contrary fashion:

> TJ discourages this kind of integration into British society, especially of female members, since they essentially do not communicate with non-Muslims. Instead, female members are kept secluded, and the values surrounding this seclusion are transmitted to their children. Therefore, the female members of this movement—as well as future generations—do not integrate into mainstream British Society. (Kazi 2011: 7; Pieri 2012: 45)

This argument, again, had little to do with the planning details over the illegality of the current structures on the site, but it did raise concerns on the overall project and of TJ as a global movement. It is these arguments over cohesion, the place of women in the movement, and allegations of TJ's fundamentalist nature that were picked up by the press and made the greatest impression to the public gallery at the Inquiry. Such comments highlight TJ as duplicitous and as having failed to adapt to the British context. Alternatively, many within the planning process go through its motions as a means to achieve objectives irrespective of actual intentions and could signify that TJ leaders recognized this. As such, the short fallings may not be on TJ leaders, but rather on the planning system. NC's argument was given that TJ is evidently "reluctant to engage in dialogue with people who are different" and which under normal circumstances promotes "self-segregation"—the answer should be no to the extension, and certainly no to the construction of a large mosque on the site.[16]

From TJ's perspective, Tablighi women, despite their apparent exclusion from public life, are not completely secluded in the house. The movement provides opportunities for women to break with their daily lives and gives them roles not limited to bringing up children. Agnes de Feo spent time living with and researching Tablighi women. She notes that Tablighi women strongly participate in the work of propagation of Islam as taught by TJ (Metcalf 2000; De Feo 2009).

For de Feo (2009), unlike other Islamist movements, "TJ does not confine women to the domestic sphere. On the contrary, according to the wishes of Ilyas and the rules established by his son Mohammad Yusuf, women are encouraged to get involved in *dawah*."

Including women in the *dawah* process gives them a new role in society, an escape from daily routine and domestic labor. Women obtain responsibility for teaching, explaining, discussing, reading, and concentrating on intellectual and spiritual activities. They learn how to preach other women and to use gentle behavior to convince the sisters to strengthen their faith. They spend time in a more valued activity, preaching other women to follow the path of Allah (de Feo 2009).

Inquiry Outcome

The Public Inquiry was at the time the single most important event in the history of TJ in Britain. For the first time in history, TJ leaders in London had to engage in a public and official way to frame the movement as open, dynamic, and in tune with modern Britain. More importantly, it had to defend its right to remain on the current site. The fact that senior members of the movement attended the inquiry in person, took to the stand to give evidence, and hired one of the most able and expensive teams to assist them throughout the proceedings highlights the importance TJ ascribed to the Inquiry and public engagement.

On May 23, 2011, Dudley announced his decision, "I allow the appeal, and direct that the enforcement notice be quashed" (2011: 2). This translated into victory for TJ. Permission to build the proposed new mosque was not granted, but TJ was allowed to remain on the current site for 2 more years. In this time, they had to submit a masterplan for the redevelopment of the site. Dudley conceded that the setup of the temporary mosque was failing to meet full standards of inclusivity, especially concerning the representation of women. TJ indicated this would be corrected with any future construction. Noting the important role the current TJ mosque has to play in the area, Dudley said:

> [TJ] has purchased this land, set up the temporary mosque and there are very large numbers of users that come to the facility. I attach substantial weight to the benefits provided by the current use. Because it has become established in this area, the forced relocation of the mosque would inevitably hit the current usage and harm users. The

overall use may well recover in time, with a build up of users from the area, but there would inevitably be considerable disruption to use should it be forced to move. (2011: 15)

Dudley also commented that TJ is a movement that recognizes the importance of being practical and is willing to compromise on some original intentions. Despite TJ leaders claiming they were always in favor of a mixed-use development, the facts show that "in the past the appellant has consistently not accepted the need for a mixed-use at the site, but wants to redevelop the site with mainly faith-based uses" and "even this year the appellant in correspondence sent to the LTGDC indicated that it still wants to see the site used as a religious and community complex" (Dudley 2011: 17). Dudley further commented that a solely faith-based site "remains the aspiration of the appellant, but in the light of the weight of the policy documentation requiring a mixed use for the site, [TJ] has reluctantly accepted that single use sought would not be achievable" (2011: 17).

TJ's recognition that the Council would reject any single-use religious development meant that even though TJ disliked the idea of a mixed-use development, they agreed and realized this was the only way they could win the appeal. What the outcome of the Inquiry shows is that state institutions have the power to set parameters in which movements function. TJ leaders realized that if they failed to conform to the rules set out in the planning process, then their objective of constructing the new mosque would fail. It is only at the Inquiry that TJ leaders gave into the prospect that their site would have to be mixed use. This is not what TJ wanted and would later try and ignore.

From Public Inquiry to Public Protest

At the Public Inquiry, TJ leaders made assurances to redevelop their West Ham site for mixed-use development. On the basis of this, the planning inspector granted a temporary 2-year consent for continued use of the site. This expired on May 23, 2013. TJ submitted its application for the redevelopment of the site and this was validated in September 2012. TJ's designs featured a mosque-centric proposal. According to the proposals, the mosque's prayer hall would accommodate up to 7,440 men with a separate prayer facility on an upper level accommodating a further 1,872 women. The facility would have an overall capacity of 9,312 people and would include two minarets. The mosque would facilitate night prayers and for festivals that fall during the Islamic year. Importantly, the mosque would be used for TJ's Thursday evening gatherings and Friday prayers.

As well as the mosque structure itself, the proposed plans indicated a multiuse center, comprising of areas for contemplation, study, prayer, and socializing. The development also contains two parallel wings of accommodation. These house ancillary facilities to the mosque that rise to approximately 25 meters above ground level. The prayer hall and external courtyard (riverside terrace) sit between these two wings. The main areas within the development, aside from the mosque, are the library with a collection of Islamic manuscripts, a visitors' center where members of the public can learn about the mosque and Islam, residential accommodation, overnight accommodation, a family room, meeting rooms, a sports pavilion, and a car park.

A week before Newham Council was to discuss TJ's newly submitted plans, Sheikh Haitham al-Haddad, a controversial, UK-based Muslim cleric,[17] issued a call on behalf of TJ. The call was for 15,000 supporters to demonstrate outside Newham's Town Hall on December 5 (the date of the decision). Al-Haddad (2012) wanted councilors voting on the proposals to know there was mass public support for the new mosque and a genuine need in the community:

> It is obligatory upon each and every Muslim to aid and help the establishment of this aforementioned [mosque]. This obligation is ever the more binding when we bring to our minds the unprecedented challenges the Muslim community in Britain is currently facing. This should oblige Muslims to be united and vigilant of any harmful or hidden agenda. I warn Muslims who are working and striving against the establishment of this mosque that they may in effect be aligning themselves with those who are classified as hindering people from the path of Allah as mentioned in the Quran.

On the evening of December 5, around 3,000 people turned up. This included those who regularly attend and participate in TJ activities, TJ elders, non–Tablighi-affiliated Muslims, as well as non-Muslims who supported the venture. Dubair, a local community activist and regular attendee at TJ's West Ham mosque, was present. In an interview that evening, he said he was there to demonstrate his support for TJ's proposed redevelopment plans and to express his frustration that the situation between TJ and Newham Council had been an ongoing struggle for 16 years. Dubair said that his purpose for being at the protest was to

> send message to the council and all the people out there that they need to give them [TJ] this application. There is dire need for that

application to go through for the community. There are 90,000 Muslims here in Newham, and for one third of the population, this centre will fulfill their requirements. Its land that was contaminated, no one wanted to buy it. It was bought and its been used for the last 16 years as a benefit to the community. Reducing crime and promoting peace, tolerance and respect. So its really frustrating to know that the media and other elements from the council itself is not not taken this in to consideration.[18]

Fayzan, another regular at TJ's mosque and who attends every Thursday, was present at the protest. He defended the new plans. He said the proposed mosque is a place to facilitate individuals to become better citizens. He placed his argument within an Islamic framework, but also ensured his message resonated with a wider audience:

> As our beloved Prophet said, the best Muslim is he who has the best manners and character, so with this [the proposed mosque] it is for the Muslims to become better Muslims, for them to practice Islam in a good way and take off the youngsters that are on the street doing all these bad things and try to get them to come to practice the real purpose of life, to become good citizens and serve the community. To become good people. This is the main purpose of this organization. And for them [Newham Council] to take this away, is very bad.[19]

Fayzan was able to rearticulate what TJ leaders were saying at the Public Inquiry and voice it in a very public and peaceful protest. This was not a message coming from a few articulate and elite leaders of the movement, but rather from grassroots members. There was a very clear understanding that the movement was now working within a context where community cohesion and a stronger emphasis on citizenship was key. TJ learned that if it stood any chance of succeeding in its desires, then a stance of claiming to be apolitical was not viable. Demonstrating in a peaceful way and articulating a strong, unified, and culturally resonant message would be TJ's best chance. In a continuation of his narrative on the benefits of TJ to wider London communities, Fayzan honed in on the issue of crime and gang culture and how TJ is able to make a positive impact:

> So this is what this organization is doing, finding youngsters that are really messed up in the head, they've got lots of problems in their lives, and you already know the problem with the economy. Obviously they've got lots of problems on their hands. But when they're spiritually strong they're better able to tackle the world, to deal with problems, to go to work every day. And the things they're doing on the street, they

could use that same energy to do something productive. And once they do something productive, they'll get a job, they'll be able to serve the community. This is the purpose of this organization.[20]

Shahid, a spokesman and active TJ participant present at the demonstration, made it clear that there were still issues of contention between TJ and Newham Council. The main one is, "we don't want the masjid to be mixed use. That's the point that we are fighting." Another TJ leader pointed out that studies conducted by TJ demonstrate that Newham Council's expectations of a redevelopment plan that is mixed use is not feasible, "there are already a lot of shops around. They want affordable housing, they want shops and everything there. But we said its our land, it was bought for the purposes of Muslims and it should stay in the hands of Muslims and for Muslim use." This was a clear indication that behind the scenes, and now publicly, the desire was still for a single-use facility. Talk of working with Newham Council to produce a genuinely mixed-use plan seems to have been a tactic to buy time from the planning inspector.

On the evening of January 5, 2012, as supporters of the proposed mosque were rallying outside Newham's Town Hall, borough councilors were inside voting on the proposed plans. After a tense wait, it was announced that all voting councilors had decided to vote against TJ's proposed plans. Explaining the decision, Conor McAuley, Newham's executive member for regeneration and strategic planning, commented that the "scheme was too large, there was not sufficient parking, it would have an impact on historic buildings nearby, and it failed to serve the needs of the community" (Martin and Razaq 2012).

As the throngs outside the Town Hall dispersed, TJ was left feeling disappointed and introspective. Despite claiming that the proposed facilities would be of benefit to the entire community and that TJ was willing to work with Newham Council to achieve this, councilors were unconvinced. The plans still centered on a large mosque with facilities that were for the most part geared toward the needs of Tablighi Muslims and with few commercial opportunities. Those who supported TJ saw the decision as politically motivated and unfair. In a statement to London's *Evening Standard*, one Tablighi supporter said, "It's a decision taken by a council, not in a court by legal professionals who'd consider the details properly. We'll certainly be taking it to a judicial review" (Martin and Razaq 2012).

Following Newham Council's decision to reject TJ's proposed plans, the Council also issued an enforcement notice on July 16, 2013. This was for TJ to discontinue the use of its site and demolish existing buildings (Atwal 2013). This meant TJ would no longer be allowed to use the temporary mosque and associated facilities on its site. With the proposed building plans rejected, TJ would have to seek an alternative home. TJ leaders in London appealed, and another Public Inquiry was set for June 2014.

DECISION POINT

In June 2014 a second Public Inquiry was held in London over TJ's appeal against Newham Council's decision to reject plans for the proposed mosque and for wanting TJ to vacate the site. Newham Council and NC argued that TJ should remove the temporary structures and vacate the site. Whereas, several advocacy groups backing the mosque, including Newham People's Alliance (NPA), an advocacy group backing the mosque, argued TJ was unfairly treated and that the building of the mosque should be allowed. At the end of the Inquiry, the planning inspector made recommendations to the Secretary of State for Communities and Local Government, who will decide if TJ will be granted permission to build their mosque.

Newham Council stated that TJ continuously violated planning policies, failed to develop a policy-compliant proposal for the site, and "are not particularly exercised or motivated in trying to find long term planning compliant solution for their site" (Sahadevan 2014: 21). Further, TJ's proposed mosque was described as "monolithic, and that it will be 'overly dominant' causing visual harm to the character and appearance of the area." Sahadevan expressed the Council's frustrations with TJ and argued that their proposed mosque is not designed for use by the local community, but rather to advance the Tablighi brand of Islam on a national and international scale:

> The proposals are of a scale that goes beyond meeting a local need, but one that is catered toward meeting a regional/national need. Catering for circa 10,000 worshippers will dwarf the next largest Tablighi Jamaat mosque in Dewsbury, West Yorkshire, which has a current capacity of 4,500. This suggests that the proposals have a national and international significance for this branch of Islam. The proposed facility will be the largest of its kind in the UK let alone London. (2014: 105)

From TJ's perspective, there is an "over-riding need for a mosque of this size" and the proposed mosque will be "a landmark building in its own right which will act as a symbol of regenerative change." Learning from the previous Inquiry, TJ leaders also highlighted the need for a large new mosque that will provide prayer space for women. This is an aspect of the mosque design that TJ was keen to stress and to combat the image of the movement as discriminatory against women.[21]

A major success for TJ at the Inquiry was that Tehmina Kazi, a key witness for NC, withdrew from giving evidence. In the past, Kazi gave evidence against TJ on the basis that it is "misogynistic." Alan Craig, director of the MegaMosqueNoThanks campaign, commented that Kazi was "intimidated by misogynist mosque supporters." On his blog, Craig (2004) wrote:

> While Tehmina's withdrawal was a disappointment it was not a complete surprise. The previous Saturday afternoon she called me from her holiday abroad to tell me that Muddassar Ahmed was pressurizing her ("intimidating" was her exact word) to withdraw. She said that Muddassar claimed he had obtained reassurances from TJ that they would treat women better in future, and he promised Tehmina "they will continue to become more liberal under his influence."

The interesting point is that Muddassar Ahmed is the founding CEO of Unitas Communications, a firm dealing in specialist public relations and reputations management, and also a key leader of NPA. This is the group that made a formal submission to the inquiry in support of TJ and the advancement of the proposed mosque. Craig (2014) added that Kazi had sent him text messages saying "Muddassar is not someone that you want as an enemy" and that he is "too well connected in the community." In response, Kazi said, "withdrawing was a decision I did not undertake lightly. I did it after consultation with several trusted people and a number of assurances on women's increased participation and involvement in the new facility" (Gledhill 2014).

Ultimately, for Newham Council as for NC, the issue of contention is that TJ failed to live up to the promises they made. At the Public Inquiry in 2012, TJ committed to advancing a policy-compliant mixed-use site. This did not happen. Instead TJ reverted to pursuing a primarily faith-based use of the site with a proposed mosque that would stand out above all else. For Newham Council and NC, this was not regarded as a form of development that would benefit the diverse communities living in Newham. Indeed, Sahadevan commented that rather than promoting community cohesion, the mosque would serve to segregate communities and create an "Islamic quarter" in an area that is in much need of inclusive regeneration:

In terms of sheer bulk, scale and massing it [the mosque] will dwarf other buildings in the area. This domination, coupled with its appearance, as an unmistakable place of worship will generate a clear perception of the site and the area around West Ham as a "religious quarter," in this case dedicated to Islam. The proposals will change the local townscape radically. I have concerns that this scale of development both visually and in terms of the whole site dedicated to a single faith-based use will generate the undesirable impression that the area has become a "cultural and community" quarter. (2014: 76)

Arguments were made for and against the proposed mosque and for and against TJ. As the Inquiry came a close, the planning inspector retired to consider the arguments and to put recommendations together, which will be sent to Erick Pickles, the Secretary of State for Communities and Local Government. This directly places the government at the center of the dispute, something it has managed to avoid thus far. The decision will go beyond the specifics of the so-called Mega Mosque and is likely to draw on questions relating to citizenship, identity, and integration. For example, what sorts of groups should be allowed to build places of religious worship in Britain? Should those places of worship be solely for the use of a specific religious community, or should they be of benefit to the wider public? The decision will also highlight how a liberal democracy balances between the religious needs of a given community and concerns that that community is promoting an illiberal and segregationist ideology. With an election looming in Britain in 2015, and given the contentious nature of the project, the decision is likely to spark as much controversy as the mosque itself.

PART IV

The Worldly Unworldliness of Tablighi Jamaat

CHAPTER 8

Tablighi Jamaat From Within

INTRODUCTION

Each week Tablighi mosques across the world hold gatherings where local Muslims are encouraged to attend, pray, and listen to a Tablighi preacher speak on Ilyas' six points. The talks culminate with the preacher inviting those gathered to donate their time in the cause of the movement and go out with Tablighis to call other Muslims to a Tablighi understanding of Islam. Tablighis believe this understanding to be the most authentic form of Islam and the ultimate way to salvation.

This chapter delves into TJ's core ethos and philosophies from the perspective of those who participate in its activities. The chapter is based on extensive ethnographic fieldwork of TJ in London. It has two primary aims. The first is to present the internal dynamics of the movement in the words of its own participants and preachers. The second specifically focuses on TJ in London and looks at what was happening during TJ gatherings at the time TJ leaders were most actively engaging over issues relating to the proposed mosque. This highlights how TJ leaders in London framed claims around the construction of a new mosque and how TJ members reacted to this. The chapter argues that in spite of their apparent strategic adaptation and promises made at the two public inquires, TJ leaders have not altered the message preached to grassroots members. In short, TJ is a salvation-oriented movement; its members are taught to strive for the eternal, and all else is secondary.

The chapter demonstrates a distinction between elite instrumentally aware leaders and rank-and-file grassroots members of TJ. As with leaders in other organizations, TJ leaders have to consider the larger context in which their movement operates and to strategize accordingly. TJ leaders in London articulate the movement's message in different a different way to its enrolled members at TJ gatherings from the way that same message is presented in public. Grassroots members do not always concern themselves with wider strategies and instead focus on what they regard as authentic interpretations of a given movement's doctrine. This at times gives the impression that there is disconnect between what TJ leaders say in public and what adherents are instructed in private. This reflects the ability of leaders to adapt to contextual changes and ensure the success of the movement. TJ in London, as in all parts of the world, is a movement whose main concern is, and always has been, the eternal. This is working toward the reorientation of one's life to the exact imitation of Mohammad and the early generation of Muslims, or what Reetz terms "living like the pious ancestors," as a means of salvation (Reetz 2003; Gugler 2007).

TJ leaders teach their adherents to abstain from worldliness, to focus on piety, self-reformation, and invitation of others to Islam—ultimately the salvation of the soul. This is best expressed in a popular Tablighi saying, "Concern yourselves only with the heavens above and the grave below, and never about the world in between."[1] In the context of modern liberal democracies, with concerns over Islamic terrorism and the pressures surrounding proposals for mosque construction, TJ leaders have become attune to the "here." That is, for TJ to become involved in the processes of engaging with the liberal state, which until 2006 had largely been avoided. TJ leaders in London, as in other Western cities, are often caught between seeking the sacred and having to adapt to practicalities of new contexts in the here and now.

RESPONSE TO ENFORCEMENT ACTION

In January 2010, Newham Council decided to take enforcement and considered the compulsory purchase of TJ's site. The atmosphere at the first Thursday evening gathering following the Council's decision was tense. The speaker that evening spoke of Joseph and Pharaoh. Joseph, the speaker reminded, "was stuck in a well, taken into captivity, bottom of the pile, but because he was sincere and remembered Allah, was taken by Allah and put at the top of the system." The speaker continued that it was Allah who granted Joseph the powers and respect that he commanded, and that without Allah he would have been nothing. The speaker argued, "we cannot achieve glories without the will of Allah. It does not matter what politicians say, what the media says, it is only through working for and remembering of Allah that we can succeed."

Although no direct mention of the enforcement action was made during the talk, there was a sense that this was a strategic rallying call to remind adherents that, no matter what action Newham Council wanted to take, the matter was in the hands of Allah. Tablighis could make a difference through reorienting their lives toward strict adherence of Islam, as well as through helping others to do the same. This theme was to return again:

> Don't curse your rulers and the people who are governing you. It is not they who bring bad decisions for you. Our own actions are the cause of the problems that are befalling us. We have to create such strength in our *iman* [faith], that following the commands of Allah become easy for us.

This is a classic Tablighi response. For TJ, problems that befall Muslims are ascribed to the lack of faith and failure to follow correct practise of Islam. The solution is to reorient one's life to becoming a better Muslim and inviting others to do the same. For TJ adherents in London, the ultimate success of the project does not rest in the powers of this world, but rather on the will of Allah and upon the amount of effort placed in promoting a "correct" version of Islam. This is the message expressed at Tablighi gatherings and is the view among the majority of dedicated grassroots adherents. TJ leadership, however, also realizes that to succeed with mosque construction in Britain, disengaging and leaving matters to the will of Allah is not an appropriate response (from the perspective of secular authorities). At least some attempt at public relations and civic engagement is necessary.

Grassroots Tablighis in London may have been advised to pursue traditional Tablighi solutions, but the leadership pursued a different strategy. Inspiring members to place an increased effort into the work of the movement, the leadership recognized that in order to achieve actual success in local politics, there were a number of rules to follow. Far from disengaging and turning inward to a traditional and unbending vision of Islam, London TJ leaders chose to pursue a policy of hiring professional consultants to present their case to the Council and to develop a media strategy to improve the image of the movement. This strategy was controversial—one that is in apparent contradiction to the ethos of the movement.

That TJ leaders in London were not totally in unison over this strategy is reflected in the start/stop relationships with their professional consultants. No member of the movement was willing to comment on the reasons for changing partnerships with media consultants, and the suggestion that the international leadership of the movement was opposed to such a large-scale development shows heated discussions within the movement (Taylor 2009). TJ leaders in London were split between seeking outside help and relying on Allah to provide for them. This by February 2011 was mainly resolved. A TJ spokesman said that the leadership realized that they have to be practical and, as such, decided to "hire the best team that money can buy."[2] It was not the government's policy of social cohesion, or of wanting to work in a multicultural way, that led TJ leaders in London to change their strategies. Rather, there was an understanding that being practical and abiding by the rules is the only way to convince the planning inspector of their suitability to redevelop their site.

Even though "innovative" methods such as media engagement and use of modern technologies may be needed to advance the project, the purpose of the construction will be to act as a beacon of correct Islamic practice in the area. The new mosque is to act as a base from which to coordinate and promote the sacred through the efforts of *dawah* and also represents the here and the profane. The accomplishment of the project will be a result of successful negotiation of issues arising from a modern, secular, and deeply political arena. Tablighi leaders were forced to adapt their methods and to engage. This is the means through which the project will succeed.

The initial inspiration for a departure from traditional TJ policy is found in the words of TJ's second international leader, Yusuf Kandhalawi:

> It is made clear in Q. 60:7–9 that this prohibition of a "moral alliance" with non-Muslims does not constitute an injunction against normal friendly relations with such of them that are not hostile to Muslims and their faith. By "those who are not of your kind," are meant only people whose enmity to Islam and its followers has become apparent through their behaviour and their utterances. (Maulana Yusuf in No'mani 2001: 132–133)

TJ is not barred from entering into alliance with non-Muslim consultants, nor is it forbidden from building partnerships with those in wider communities. The catch is that alliances may only be formed with those who facilitate the propagation of Islam and have not expressed enmity toward Islam.

One of the most popular parodies for the world frequently used in Tablighi circles, and which helps explain the way TJ leaders interact, is that of a toilet:

> This world is like a toilet. If a man needs to go but holds it in, people tell him to go or otherwise something bad will happen. So he goes

and soon he finishes and returns. But does anyone want to spend more time in the toilet than they have to? If they spend a lot of time there, people will worry and say why are they taking so long? Are they OK?

Going to the toilet is a necessity, but not a purpose. Just as with living in this world, Tablighis must not spend too much time in worldliness, but rather focus on the purpose, which is the propagation of Islam. Such popular sayings influence the way TJ leaders interact in public. The process of engaging over the construction of the proposed mosque has been treated in the same way as going to the toilet. One can spend some time and funds on furthering this ambition, but should be cautious not to fall into the trap of treating the process as ends rather than as means. This means that for TJ the process of engagement is not a worthy act in and of itself, but a steppingstone to goal attainment.

For TJ adherents, interaction with the profane should be limited to necessary tasks such as propagating Islam or working to support one's family. Tablighis are masters in using modern cultural references to argue against cultural trends viewed as un-Islamic and as a corrupting influence on society. In this sense, there is something to be said about the "worldly unworldliness" of TJ—a movement that preaches through culture against culture. A movement that so loves the world that they tirelessly work to convey what they see as the redeeming message of Islam and, at the same time, fundamentally believe that a failure to abide by that message is a ticket to deserved damnation.

DRESSING, EATING, AND SLEEPING: LIVING LIKE THE PIOUS ANCESTORS

TJ leaders in London in a sense adopted a dual strategy to the process of gaining permission to construct their mosque. The majority of this book focuses on the temporal approach of TJ leaders and their attempts at engagement. The other strategy was to renew traditional TJ messages to the grassroots, of turning away from secular society and pursuing a life on the path of Tablighi Islam. TJ as a movement does not view the modern world, the here and now, as a place where meaningful interaction other than for the propagation of Islam should take place, unless it is a necessity. For TJ adherents the world as it is now is in a state of *jahiliyyah*, or of darkness, ignorance, and abandonment of God. As Metcalf puts it, for Tablighis as for other Islamic revivalists, the belief is that "this is again a time of *jahiliyyah*, a time of ignorance classically understood as the pre-Mohammadan age in Arabia" (2009: 242).[3] From this perspective, the world has abandoned its dependence on Allah and drifted into a state of sin and frivolous immorality. This has happened because Muslims as the vice regents of Allah have become lazy and abandoned religious duties (Ali 2006: 182). Tablighis' lives are governed by strict imitation of the way Mohammad and the early generations of Muslims lived their lives. Any deviation from this path in the Muslim community contributes to the degeneration and decay of the *ummah*. Mohammad Ilyas recognized this state of the world at TJ's inception. The purpose of TJ is to counter this:

> In the beginning of Islam when *din* [religion] was weak and *dunya* [worldliness] was strong, the Holy Prophet went from house to house to meet the people empty of the want of *din*. The same weakness is present today. Therefore, we should visit in person the groups of impious and those who feel no interest in religion, who are empty of the want of *din*, and exalt the word of Allah among them. (Ilyas in, No'mani 2001: 67)

Other than for the purpose of propagating Islam as a means of countering the state of ignorance prevalent in all societies across the world, Ilyas saw little reason for engagement or involvement in the structures of those societies. Being an involved citizen was anathema to Ilyas. He believed there was little point in engaging in the systems of a corrupt society when what was important was to focus on the individual as the agent of change. What was essential was to overcome the state of ignorance prevalent in society. An antidote to this is following the correct proscription of rules of conduct in society as outlined by TJ. This involves rules around how members of the movement are to reorient their lives including ways of dressing, eating, and sleeping.[4] The severity of following these rules is highlighted consistently at TJ gatherings. Adherents are informed that "in our society, Muslims have become degenerate to the point where someone cannot tell if a Muslim is actually a Muslim." The speaker demonstrated the point as follows:

> There was once a man and he was involved in an accident and died. Some of the brothers did not know if he was a Muslim. He did not have a beard or wear Islamic dress. The only way to tell was to unzip him and see if he was circumcised.[5] This is what it has come to!

The point of this story is that it emphasizes that external markers of identity reinforced by Deobandis and Tablighis in the early twentieth century remain key to this day. The story further resonates with Tablighis who believe that many Muslims in Britain have integrated so well into British society that it is now difficult to distinguish Muslims from non-Muslims. The story buttresses the importance of Muslims maintaining marked characteristics of the faith and purity and segregation from what is going on in the wider world. This detachment allows one to focus on forming a bond with the creator. Clothing becomes an external indicator of an individual's religious zeal. It also acts as armor to protect that individual, serve as a reminder that they are Muslims, and that they should behave as Muslims at all times. For TJ, Muslims have to make an effort to be outwardly Muslim "because that reflects on the inwardness of the Muslim. To dress and act in the way of the Prophet and his companions is to be in the right direction of fulfilling Islam."

Through acting "in the way of the Prophet," the belief is that one's life should be completely oriented on the very same model of Mohammad. The rationale is as one adherent has put it, "if it was good enough for the Prophet, and he was the best of mankind, then who are we not to follow that?" Even so, it was perplexing to hear such an importance being placed on "outwardly" appearance, and that this would symbolize the inward reality of the individual. Indeed, by most standards of modern society, we are taught that it is what is on the inside that counts and not the exterior. One interviewee explained:

> Even though we may not be perfect Muslims if we start to dress like a Muslim we will start to act like a Muslim. If we are dressed like a Muslim it is like wearing your identity and you will start to be more regular in being a Muslim.

The participant commented that while he understood that some media commentators "made a big thing about Islamic dress," the reality is that if one is to base existence on imitation of the Prophet for correct living and sound structuring of society, then dress is an important aspect. Islamic dress, then, is one way in which Tablighis believe they can help counter the state of degeneracy around them. It is one way of maintaining the given order and rules as interpreted by TJ. The theme was again discussed where a different speaker admonished those gathered:

> Muslims now do not follow Islam properly and this is the cause of our troubles. Nine to five they go to work; they don't say their prayers; don't wear *salwaar kameez*; don't grow their beard; don't eat *halal* meat. As soon as they go home they become "Muslim" again. This is

not the true mark of a Muslim who should strive everyday to be fully Muslim.

One cannot understand TJ without realizing the extreme importance the movement places on correct Islamic practice in every single aspect of a Muslim's life. Being a Tablighi is not just about following a certain strand of Islam, it entails a complete way of life with rules governing every single action, as well as a belief that a failure to adhere to these rules is at the core of the *ummah's* decay. Indeed, one chapter of the *Fazail-E-Amal* details ways Muslims are to conduct themselves. Here are some examples (Elahi 2007):

- Do not eat from the center of the utensil, for the blessing of Allah descends at that point.
- Lick your fingers before washing your hands; it is mentioned in a *hadith*, "one does not know in which particle of the food the blessing is found in."
- Take you meal with three fingers and of the right hand.
- Clean the bed thrice before going to sleep.
- Lie on the bed on your right side, place your right hand under your cheek, and say "O Allah, in your name do I die and live."

The above actions were observable during time spent with many Tablighis. One Tablighi explained that while eating together he liked to finish his whole plate and lick his fingers clean because this would earn him ten blessings: "Allah is so good because not only does he provide food for us, but rewards us for being respectful and finishing what is on the plate." Many Tablighis assured me that following the proscribed rules for each action ensured the correct way of life as dictated by the *Shari'a*, and that if every Muslim did the same, then the state of the *Ummah* would be in a much better situation. As well as this, following the rules also helps to advance salvation of the individual. This way of living provides a firm structure on which adherents must base their lives. In an ever-changing and fast-paced society, many in TJ see this as providing stability, reassurance, and a purpose to their existence. It also leaves little room for engaging or interacting with wider non-Tablighi society.

Salvation and the Hereafter

For TJ there is more to life than life. Death and the hereafter is where they will spend eternity. One cannot underestimate TJ adherents' powerful belief in the Day of Judgment—in the yearning for salvation and an eternity in paradise far from the scorching fires of hell. For TJ adherents, life in this world is limited and one should constantly strive for the hereafter. This is a theme that TJ preachers consistently refer to—from gatherings in London to international congregational meetings in Bangladesh and Pakistan. One TJ speaker preaching in London said, "If we die with the kingdom of this world in our hearts," meaning with importance and riches "and not with the guidance of Allah, then we have failed." This clearly inverts the current meaning of success. The speaker clarified that we may think "someone who is poor and in rags has failed, but if they have the guidance of Allah, then they are much better than us. For those who fail there is eternal doom, woes and misery."

Congregations are reminded that a temporary taste of what is seen as success in this life (at the expense of obeying the commands of Allah) can result in an eternity of misery. At a different gathering, after the official proceedings had come to an end, a senior Tablighi made an impromptu speech. He delivered it to adherents in the English-speaking section of the mosque and spoke in an impassioned way:

> Before the Muslim could commit to living a genuine life here, he first had to commit to dying for the sake of Allah, for only once we have committed to dying—that is to accept that we will die, that we must die—will be able to live as true Muslims. Only then will we know when to laugh, when to cry and when to eat.

In a similar fashion, a different speaker commented:

> Just as Ibrahim [the prophet Abraham] was told to sacrifice his son, we must also sacrifice ourselves and go out in the path of Allah. [We must] make battle with ourselves, our inner desires, and battle with that, sacrifice that. This will give a person a high place in paradise. He will achieve the pleasure of Allah![6]

It is difficult to commit to living one's life as though nothing exists other than Allah. Only when a Muslim has come to terms with the principle that his life is not his own, but Allah's, will he be able to live in an appropriate way in this world. More than this, TJ view this as a matter of *jihad*—an internal struggle for the purification of mind, body, and soul. Although this is similar to the philosophy that Christian esthetics and monks subscribe to, this way of living is not one that is much recognized in the West. Archimandrite Vaselios of the Eastern Orthodox Church wrote that one of the most important lessons for a monk is, "He who loses his life in this world, will save it" (1984: 118). As with Tablighis, this should not be misconstrued to mean carrying out suicide attacks, but rather the realization that one has to completely detach themselves from the systems of this world and place complete and utter trust in the systems of God. The difference is that monastics know that it is difficult to do this and still claim to function as engaged members of a society in the ordinary sense. Instead, they reside in monastic communities dedicating their lives to prayer and supplications for the salvation of the world.

For Tablighis, this world is but a mere illusion, a testing ground, a place where one must pass through to reach the place where one's soul will reside forever:

> The real life is the life hereafter. The time in this world is like a needle dipped into the sea; just a small drop on the tip of the needle. The whole ocean is like the life hereafter. Very temporary is this life. Allah wants to bestow on us the success and favour of never ending life after death.

For Tablighis, the life hereafter is a real and looming factor. One never knows the time of death and as such has to be prepared at all times. As one interviewee put it, "Allah is just, he will judge according to our *iman* [faith] and *amal* [works] and if we have not followed his path then there is eternity in the fires of *jahanam* [hell]." The same interviewee presented me with a recording of a Tablighi sermon given by a Tablighi elder who traveled to Chicago. A main theme was the hereafter—a life of salvation or the threat of eternal damnation in the unbearable pits of hell. Listening to this talk, it is not difficult to see why Tablighis want to ensure they follow the movement's directives:

> Either a person will go into paradise or into the fire of hell *jahanam*. If a person is entered into paradise he will have luxuries and comfort forever, and if entered into the fire of hell, he'll suffer forever. The suffering will never end. For example, a person will feel thirsty for 1000s of years. For his thirst, he will not even get a sip of water. For trillions of years this person will continuously face hardships. For not even a fraction of a minute will there be any comfort or any ease. This person will be put into the fire of *jahanam*, he will see the end of *jahanam* like a person who is travelling in the sea and when he sees the shore, he will want to go to the shore. This person will want to go to the edge of the fire of *jahanam*. And he will request of Allah, "Grant me permission so that I can go to the edge of the fire of *jahanam*." And this person will go to the edge of the fire and to the border where

there'll be snakes. The snakes will be so huge, like a palm tree. There'll be scorpions the size of a mule. Other huge insects will get on this person and start biting him and this person will out of suffering say, "Oh Allah I cannot take this I do not want to stay at the border, I would rather go back to the centre of the fire." The fire of *jahanam* is so massive it has space for all the human beings.

For Tablighis, this is not a medieval description of what hell might be, it is the professed belief of the movement. These images of hell have such a deep impact on the psyche of TJ members and so strong is the belief that this could actually happen, it is no wonder members strive for salvation. This is a key motivating factor in the construction of the proposed mosque and for following innovative methods to achieve it. The mosque (for TJ) will act as a beacon of correct Islamic practice, to call individuals to Islam, and save them from the fires of hell. The proposed mosque is seen as an instrument of salvation, with innovative methods justifying the ends. In contrast to hell, the joys and eternal bliss of paradise are presented as follows:

Allah has made *jannat*—paradise. It is such a place that a person can fulfill all his desires in the highest standard that a person can think. If a person wants to eat food, the highest quality of food will be provided. If someone wants something to drink, the highest standard will be provided. If a person wants to listen to sweet and melodious voices, the highest quality of sound and voices will be provided. Everything will be top quality. Rasoolallah in his beautiful and sweet voice will recite the Holy Qur'an and because of that all the people of *jannat* will listen. Once a week Allah will invite the people of *jannat* in his court and hold a feast for them. Allah himself will recite the Qur'an, and when they listen they will get such enjoyment that they will enjoy it even more than the food. And with every word Allah reads, clouds of *noor* [light] will be made and it will shine on the people of *jannat*. because of that it will increase their beauty.

Tablighi speakers are apt at reminding followers that ultimate success does not reside in this life but in the life to follow. Ingrained into this worldview is the absolute fear of the power and ability of worldliness to corrupt and destroy the soul of a person, thus barring them eternal paradise. This was aptly put by one Tablighi interviewee who said, "all the things we have here, our businesses, our cars, our houses, our money—what good is this to us? When we die, can we take any of this with us? No! But just a little effort in the path of Allah will count in the hereafter." A different Tablighi told me that "we have to be sober in this life because we have been forbidden many things. The temptations are there, if you are patient you will be rewarded when the time is over." It is precisely this reward that motivates the actions of TJ members and a factor that should be recognized at the heart of the movement in London and the world over.

DAWAH

Equally as important as salvation, and something that should be seen as an instrument of salvation, is *dawah*. *Dawah* is the calling of people to Islam. *Dawah* is so important to TJ that it cannot be separated from any other goal or aspect of ideology. *Dawah* and the goal to construct the proposed mosque go hand-in-hand. The proposed new mosque will be a center from which to organize the missionary spread of Tablighi Islam. *Dawah* is so important that TJ's founder referred to it as "the backbone of the entire body of Islam" and as the "foundation, strength and success of Islam" (Ilyas in No'mani 2001: 240). At a gathering at TJ's West Ham mosque, one of the speakers informed that the purpose of life is to bring as many people as possible to Islam:

> It is not enough to give those in need food or clothes. If a man is starving and you give him food he will be hungry again. If you give him clothes then he will have them until they wear out. But true mercy is to inform them of Allah. True mercy is to teach them *salat* [prayer], because *salat* will last for life! We must not be content; we must not rest until every one around us learns *salat* and until everyone we know starts to come to the *masjid*.

While ambitious, the goal of spreading the Tablighi version of Islam as a means to benefit the whole community is a real and necessary goal for TJ. For TJ adherents, the goal is a matter of life and death. The person who accepts Islam is saved from damnation and will be able to taste the glories of paradise—a "gift" that TJ adherents want for all. It is here that the image arises of a movement that so loves the world that they desire for everyone to adopt the Tablighi form of Islam and be guaranteed the delights of paradise. At the same time, they insist that a failure to do so results in eternal and deserved damnation. The speaker continued, "our main goal in life is to think about how many people I have told about Islam this week, and how I can improve this. *Dawah* is to be the purpose of life." The speaker justified why *dawah* has to be the purpose of life. It is because:

Islam as a system is superior to every other form or system in life. It is above any other way of life. *Dawah* is the one thing that Muslims do that instills fears in the hearts of nonbelievers and this is because they know that Islam—through *dawah*—can overpower and overcome anything else.

Such sentiments express the climax of a rhetorical style that is aimed at mobilizing adherents into action. They are central to the rhetoric of the movement and something TJ adherents feel comfortable with. Though not controversial to Tablighis, these sentiments are problematic in the wider context of the community cohesion agenda. This is something the speaker recognizes but continued to rouse the congregation and informed them that "effort in the path of Allah is never wasted", even the "smallest of efforts can bring big changes." It is here that TJ recognizes its potential as a transformative movement, that individuals acting through the movement that it can change the nature of society. It is "through these efforts" the speaker argues that "there will come a time when we Muslims are in the majority." This again is a form of motivational claims-making aimed to give a purpose and meaning to the energy and efforts of adherents in pursuit of the movement's goals.

The *Fazail-E-Amal* goes further in reminding its readers that "Allah has also given assurances that true believers will always dominate over non-believers and that non-believers will be left without friend or ally" (Kandhlawi 2007a: 7). The speaker at one gathering argued that this is an important message to act upon, as it was a message of the Prophet Mohammad and a final revelation applicable for the rest of time. For Ilyas, if the "*ummah* neglects this duty, it will not fulfill the function for which it was raised" and "loose good grace from Allah" (Ilyas in No'mani 2001: 217). *Dawah* is the key to TJ's success—both in terms of new adherents as well as in the belief that through *dawah* Allah will bestow blessings on the movement and allow them to achieve other goals such as the construction of the proposed mosque. Even more than this, as a means of mobilizing the adherents to the work of *dawah*, TJ leaders have been adept at informing their congregations that they are the community of believers of which the *Qur'an* speaks. That is a chosen group that has "been made responsible for the reformation and well being of the entire *ummah*, rather all mankind to what is good" (Ilyas in No'mani 2001: 218).

Keen to see how Tablighis interpreted the talk, I interviewed Ali, an adherent who I spoke with regularly. Ali agreed with the speaker, commenting that "now I am thinking about how to intro-duce the topic of Islam to my boss tomorrow." Ali stated, just as the speaker said, "we have to engage all our neighbors; *dawah* is the purpose of our life." As well as this, Ali could sense that there was some unease surrounding the comments of the supremacy of Islam and noted that "we also have to be good Muslims and then people will see that they have nothing to fear." The important thing to note is that it is not false when TJ leaders comment in public that TJ is an open movement, one that is working for the cohesion of the local community. Indeed, TJ leaders view cohesion as stemming from the establishment of Islam, as the governing norm in society. In TJ's perspective, far from being oppressive, Islam is a system of liberation. Muslims, as one other interviewee put it, "have a heavy responsibility. Every single person that does not have *din* is our responsibility."

During Ramadan, the call for *dawah* as the solution to the ills of the world was intensified at TJ gatherings. Adherents were told that pursuing activities such as education, business, or family without time for going out in the work of Allah was a major error. For the speaker this was a reason for Allah not bestowing his full blessings on Muslims. He gave the following example:

> When I want to study, I go to school for 20 years. What I am learning there? Electron and bacteria. Study Allah, the ulama say, for 40 days and four months. But people say "no I don't need that." Where is our *yakim* [trust]? Our *yakim* is in bacteria and the devil's document, the certificate. If I get the certificate I will have a good job, and I will have a good house, but if I study Allah I won't have anything. To Allah belong the skies and earth. Allah says I own the world and the hereafter. But this certificate, it cannot feed you, cannot sustain you. They get this certificate for 20 years of study, but they still have plenty of problems. How many [people] take [exams for a] certificate but die when they get the certificate? And he pass away and without good deeds.

This serves to capture the "worldly unworldliness" of TJ, as well as highlighting the effectiveness of such strategy. An extraordinary amount of those gathered volunteered to take part in *dawah* mis-sions following this talk. During an interview the following week in London, a Tablighi university student, Jamal, noted that "going out in the path of Allah is the most important thing we can do, its only this that will bring benefit to our lives and to the lives of those around us." Jamal informed me that he had already been on a 40-day missionary tour, as well as shorter 3-day tours. For Jamal, the then current issues around the mosque were clearly linked to making efforts in the path of Allah. "Its only once we demonstrate that we can handle the responsibility through our proven efforts that Allah will be pleased and *inshallah* grant us the bigger responsibility of the new mosque." In this sense, the goal of *dawah* is very clearly tied to both salvation and success in the world.

Despite many Tablighis feeling that this is the only way to bring success, Birt and Lewis highlight instances where this ideology alienates Tablighis from the wider community. They underline views expressed by Mahmood Chandia, an academic at the University of Central Lancashire:

> Many students do not complete their examinations in science, medicine, law or journalism and use the excuse that we must give priority instead to revivalist tours of forty days, four months, or one year's duration—a central component of the activities of the Tablighi Jamaat. (Birt and Lewis 2010: 108)

In this sense, while the *dawah* work of TJ promotes success in the hereafter, it can also serve to contribute to stopping young people from achieving their potential in the here and now.

In a further bid to stress the primary importance of *dawah* as the essential and legitimate goal of the movement, one of the speakers utilized and played upon the language of human rights that have become so important in liberal democracies. TJ elevates *dawah* to the level of a human right. One speaker stated that "people have a right to hear about Islam" and that "your mission should be to ensure everyone the right to know about Islam, especially other Muslims, and to increase their knowledge and how those with no Islam can have Islam." These are in essence the goals of the movement, and the construction of the new mosque is seen as the means through which these goals will be achieved. The knowledge of possessing the truth and of propagating this through *dawah* acts to empower Tablighis. They see themselves as agents of human rights bringing the knowledge and right of salvation to others. As one senior member has put it:

> Tablighi Jamaat gives people a goal in life. TJ do not talk about politics, but actually go out and do. They help to reinvigorate the spirit of Islam in individuals. What better sense of mission could there be than going out in groups and aiming to bring back Muslims to Islam? You can see the rewards very quickly.

Dunya (Worldliness)

TJ as a movement wants to see a change in the way society is organized. The method of doing this is through reformation of the individual, and therefore a long-term objective. The individual is the agent of change through following the correct mode of living as proscribed by the *Shari'a* and as interpreted by TJ. Any indulgence in worldliness, or what TJ terms as *dunya*, results in intoxication. For TJ adherents, *dunya* is conceptualized as all those things that can be consumed, both physical and otherwise, the material and the worldly—the here. Good Muslims should move away from *dunya* and instead turn to the Tablighi way of life, seeking to improve and reorient their life to the attainment of salvation. So bad has the situation in our current societies become and so much has the love of *dunya* increased that, according to one TJ speaker, "this world is not even equal to one wing of a mosquito. This world is an example of something that is foul smelling, a very poor smell." For rank-and-file members of TJ, this perception of society's worth leaves little desire for engagement.

Modern conveniences are seen as having the ability to hold people back, to attach them to the profane, and to cause eschewing of responsibilities to Allah. For the most part, Thursday evening talks conveyed consumerism as the epitome of *dunya* and as something every Tablighi is to resist. It is TJ's belief that it is necessary to take consumerism and what they call "creation" out of our heart. "Creation stops us from reaching our potential. We are stunned by the way of the world and our heart deviates from the word of Allah." This signifies that material things have the power to take a person away from the path of Allah. Indeed this was the key point made at one gathering. "This world is too consumer oriented...too much faith is put in technology, in science and in non-religious education and too much effort in keeping up with the Jones."

The speaker argued that to make a success of life and of society as a whole, disengagement from all these frivolous activities and to take "time to focus on the unseen, on Allah and his angels" was necessary. These words had a deep impact on those gathered. Many present that evening sought spiritual dimension in their lives. The suggestion of unplugging from a fast-paced society with a heavy dependence on media and technology might be a good idea. Even though this is the message preached to the grassroots members at official Tablighi meetings, it is not the approach followed by TJ leaders in London with regard to the mosque project. It is this "worldly unworldliness" of

TJ—its ability to preach against culture through culture—that allows it to resonate with the everyday lives of its followers. One regular activist, Hamid, was aware of this fact when he said, "TJ lifts peoples' eyes to heaven and it allows them to fulfil a spiritual dimension that is seriously lacking in consumerist western societies and other movements that focus on politics and worldly issues."

TJ recognizes that there is a deep spiritual yearning among many Muslims (not to mention the wider population) and a belief that for all the conveniences of modern technology it has not done anything to improve the moral character of individuals. Participants reported that they see a rise in crime, drugs, and alcohol abuse in society, and on TV shows that profit from the exploitation of peoples' personal misfortune. TJ's message of abandoning worldly attachments and turning inwards to reexamine one's own life and to strive for salvation has been resonant with members.

There is no better example of TJ's "worldly unworldliness"—of its ability to highlight modern cultural practices to preach against those very same practices—than the following:

> Material wealth, play stations, cars and modern conveniences do not give you happiness. They do not give you the final status. What does matter is working in the path of Allah, because only Allah can give you what you want. Materialism breeds materialism and this is the cause of feeling depressed, of feeling anguished. Pills cannot cure this, medicines cannot cure this, and only Allah can cure this.

French academic Gilles Kepel noted similar sentiments at TJ gatherings in France and attributed this as part and parcel of TJ's ethos as a whole:

> Now there are people who go to the moon! And after that? There are more suicides in America than anywhere in the whole world. Every year more than 80,000 persons commit suicide there! That is the country that you find great and want to imitate! Why are there more than 80,000 people who hang themselves? This is because they have not found comfort in this world. Because they are farther from God. That is why they commit suicide. (Kepel 2000: 195–196)

In these instances, the speakers attempt to invert values that are important to liberal democracies—to show that modernity is not the antidote to the problems of the world, but rather part of the problem. At the same time, it is apparent that TJ is caught in this juxtaposition between the worldly and the unworldly. It recognizes that as the most important of Allah's creation, the world has been made for mankind, but at the same time, mankind belongs to Allah and, therefore, to the sacred. This was well put by one of the speakers: "This world is made for you, but you have been made for Allah." It is the same juxtaposition that TJ leaders have been caught in when discussing their approach to engaging with British institutions as a means to further the construction of their proposed mosque.

For the majority of the population, material wealth, physical possessions, and modern conveniences denote success in this life; for TJ, these signal a trap. Each resembles an attachment to the profane and a hindrance in being able to meaningfully engage with the spiritual. For TJ members, the way to achieve success in this world is through abandoning attempts at pursuing the material, instead focusing that energy on bringing others toward the Tablighi version of Islam. For TJ the current system we live in is a perversion of the true order of society. As one TJ speaker told me, "everything which we are told is good for us is actually not. Working for success, for power, for money, for position is nothing. Only Allah can grant those things."

TJ members are told time and again that:

> Riches are not success, armies are not success, and palaces are not success. All these have to be left behind. The Prophets did not come to make riches, or to promote people in their businesses, but to ask people to turn away from these and reconnect with Allah.

These attitudes are further reflected in TJ tracts. Ilyas warned his early followers that consumerism is the major disease of this age—that real disease is "concentration and absorption in worldly engagements—the things which have not left even a single moment spare in their lives for getting *din*" (Ilays in No'mani 2001: 255). Ilyas would go on to warn that these engagements and attachments are the "lords besides Allah" and "new idols of this age" (Ilays in No'mani 2001: 255). However, as part of their desire to construct the proposed mosque in London, TJ leaders were increasingly reliant on investing their time, effort, and funds in professionally hired teams and media consultants. Although the movement's messages may seem rigid, leaders have room to manoeuvre and to reinterpret traditions, especially if doing so will promote the expansion of the movement or allow it to succeed in its objectives.

The ideal for TJ adherents may be to disengage from the wider society and for all of one's energy to be focused on reorienting toward "Allah and his angels," but the leadership in London recognize the need to follow a practical agenda. In order for any major construction project to advance, one has to play by the rules of the existing system and that may mean temporarily following a strategy considered as a necessary evil. This is an important observation. It signals that, contrary to the cannon of Tablighi beliefs, movement leaders are more flexible and adaptable than they may first seem. TJ leaders in London reinterpreted their current situation as being similar to that of the Meccan period of Mohammad's life. This is the period when the Muslim community was still small and vulnerable and as a consequence had to establish good relationships with their neighbors in an atmosphere of coexistence (Peters 1991: 296). There was flexibility in the way Muslims conducted themselves with the wider non-Muslim society. TJ leaders in London view a similar level of flexibility as necessary today. This partly explains how the process of adaptation is negotiated within the movement. This flexibility with the political is further seen as a "necessary step in the path of ultimately establishing an Islamic state in the distant future" (Sikand 2007: 146).

Negotiating the Here and Now

For those who become increasingly committed to the work of TJ, the image of non-Tablighi society is one of *jahiliyya*. It becomes harder to fully partake in the activities of the wider community, because those activities are seen as sinful and as counter to the commandments of Allah. For Tablighi adherents, the ability to recognize this is a form of empowerment as it allows them to guard themselves against similar errors. In one of the movement's key texts, Maulana Zakariyya warns his readers that just because people in the West may engage in sinful activities and still remain successful in their economic dealings, it does not mean that they will have success in the hereafter. Zakariyya writes that:

> So much have some ignorant Muslims been troubled and perplexed that they even went to the extent to rejecting the tenants of the Shari'a. They went so far as to look at the nonbelievers and decided that those evils which are present in the nonbelievers were the very causes of their success. (Kandhlawi 2001: 94)

For Tablighi adherents a disengagement from what are perceived to be the sinful activities of the wider society—drinking alcohol, smoking, listening to popular rhythmic music, and intermingling of the sexes—is a way of bettering their chances of salvation. For those who engage in such activities—activities that are seen as a normal part of life in liberal democracies, the Tablighi's stance seems isolationist and disengaging. The emphasis for Tablighis is on the immaterial. Tablighis realize that material wealth is of no use once an individual dies. Whereas, following an Islamic way of life as interpreted by TJ may guarantee them eternity in paradise. There is often disconnect between such beliefs (which are also held by many religious people of different faiths) and the increasingly materialist views of many in liberal Western societies. This can label those who do not pursue a consumerist lifestyle as an "other."

Tablighi leaders recognize that the teachings of the TJ go against the grain of popular practices in Western societies. They bemoan the fact that society has lost its direction, that the balance of the universe has been disrupted, and that in actuality we have inverted good and evil, becoming blind to the realities laid down by Allah. One Tablighi preacher bemoaned, "Today the majority of people place value in mobile telephones, in houses, cars, money; these are the things that appeal to us." Another speaker announced that the majority of people have become slaves to desire, forgetting or even rejecting Allah: "No one is a slave of Allah. We are the slave of the environment that is governing our condition."[7] This resonates with Tablighi members who see consumerist practices on a daily basis among their neighbors or extended families and are agitated into participating in TJ efforts to counter such practises.

Tariq Jameel, an internationally renowned and popular TJ speaker, has said of the state of society:

> I bear Allah as my witness that even an animal as dirty as the pig feels embarrassed at the state of our society today. The world's most shameless animal today is embarrassed to see society like this. People have gone beyond the borderline of abomination. The veil covering people's dignity has been lifted by them.

It is this desire in the material, according to TJ leaders and adherents, that is the cause of society having lost its direction. The things that are of real importance are "*dawah, zakat,* justice, helping the poor and seeking knowledge of *din*." These are what TJ strives toward and which it wants others in the community to realize. "When we are able to see properly," the speaker said, "we will see that virtues are more valuable than material possessions." Aside from the Islamic element of TJ, such views of charity, justice, and neighborliness are in fact at the heart of discussions in liberal democracies as to how best to develop harmonious and cohesive communities. The issue for TJ is that there cannot be a separation of Islam from any of their actions and as such their message often fails to resonate with the broader society.

In a conversation with a senior member of the London movement, a modern example was used to highlight the juxtaposition between the worldly and unworldly, engagement and nonengagement of society, and the complex position of TJ regarding these matters. TJ has firm rules as to what is and is not acceptable in society. These values are being brought into question by a society that does not have any concept of the importance of an Islamic vision of morality. Focusing on the movement's proposed construction of the new mosque, the interviewee was particularly concerned about the way in which London's successful bid for the 2012 Olympic Games had changed the context of how Islamic movements are viewed—in particular, TJ's proposed new mosque near the Olympics Stadium. The interviewee stated that TJ, as part of an effort to show its commitment to values of openness, tolerance, and community spiritedness, was expected to actively show support for the Games:

> At best, TJ have become neutral to the Olympic Games, and this is a major step! How can the TJ or any other serious Islamic movement actively condone the Olympic Games? Scantily clad women running around and in full view of the mixing of sexes—this is very un-Islamic! The bursting open of champagne bottles for those who win on the podium; this is un-Islamic! Why should the TJ be expected to support or condone this?

The point is that as part of the effort to construct the new mosque, TJ is expected to show commitment to and support of what the movement may have traditionally considered sinful. TJ in London originally wanted the new mosque constructed in time for the Games. The mosque would act as a "Muslim quarter," "a hub for Islamic competitors and spectators" (Johnston 2006). For TJ in London, the role of providing a morally pure atmosphere for Muslim competitors and a chance to inform them of the Tablighi version of Islam would have mitigated some of their concerns surrounding such events. Once made public, the response to this suggestion from those outside of the TJ was negative. Most commentators noted that the Olympics are meant to bring people together, not keep them apart (Johnston 2006; Al-Alawi and Schwartz 2007). The situation became even more tense in the context of July 7 bombings. At the time, there was little room for goodwill or a deeper understanding of TJ's motivations and calls that it confirms to the same standards of society as prescribed by the government.

A different example, and one particularly susceptible to the adverse affects of Western society according to TJ, is the case of the youth who are easily led astray by the devil—*shaytan*. TJ aims to create a safe social environment, almost an alternative social order where its adherents have the best possible chance of working toward salvation. In some cases, and where possible, this extends to the education of children. Muslim children should not be subjected to a Western education. In one book on sale at TJ's West Ham mosque bookshop, the advice is:

> You should be convinced as to how disastrous it is to send young children to these non-Muslim institutions and how harmful it is to their *din* and character. Our children tend to become isolated from *din*, emblazoned by the emblem of disbelievers and become flagrant violators with regard to beliefs, actions and characters. (Al-Mashaat 1993: 9)

The warning here is that a Western secular education is not beneficial to Muslim children due to the secular curriculum of Western schools. The book on education promoted by TJ espouses a negative view of society and education in the West. It warns parents that they have a responsibility to protect their children from the traps laid out in Western schools that draw children away from Islam. It even argues that forming friendships with non-Muslims is enough to entrap one in the fires of hell for eternity (Al-Mashaat 1993: 11). This is problematic on a number of levels, and not least due to inconsistencies with messaging propagated by TJ leaders in public, that the movement is open and inclusive and that all will be welcome to the new mosque.

For TJ, disengagement from society and focusing on the work of Allah does not necessarily denote a detachment from society. Devoting one's life to going out on *jamaat* transforms the lives of those who take part and makes them better citizens. Interviewees spoke of men who had gone on *jamaat* and returned changed men—"more caring husbands, loving fathers, better Muslims." The boldest statement was that TJ has a better vision for society, a vision that would enhance communities. The claim was that many people who go out on *jamaat* were in to "drinking, drugs, women, and sex outside of marriage. But with the grace of Allah, and through the effort of Tabligh, they left their gangs, gave up alcohol and drugs. Now they are hard working pious people."

Should TJ's scheme be implemented, it could transform communities. This signals a positive ideal of wanting to help the community, but it also entails that the community as a whole convert to Islam and reorient their lives and efforts toward TJ. This is not something that is realistically achievable in secular liberal democracies. More recently, TJ leaders claim that they aim to imbue self-respect and self-control in its members, as well as the ability to abstain from the wrongs of society and not to be drawn into the subcultures of their local areas. Just as in London, TJ in Australia, according to Jan Ali, follows the same method:

> In Australia I have seen, for example, a lot of drug addicts and gangsters becoming involved in the religion because of the Tablighi Jamaat. They left the bad things and they don't do bad things…they pray. The Tablighi Jamaat has provided the environment for the people to have more self-respect, something that's not found in wider Australia. There are a lot of misbehaving teenagers and dysfunctional and dismantled families…Tablighi Jamaat has a lot of good affect on them. (TJ adherent in Ali 2006: 208)

TJ members are attune to the problems of the world and are not as disengaged as they may first appear. The issue is that Britain, as with the majority of states in the West, is far from having Islamic contexts, and TJ's message has little resonance with the wider society.

CHAPTER 9

Conclusions

In 2015, a final decision will be made as to whether Tablighi Jamaat (TJ) could build its proposed mosque and, if so, what shape and size this should take. The Secretary of State for Communities and Local Government will make the decision. For the first time, this places the British government at the center of the dispute. The decision will go beyond the specifics of the so-called Mega Mosque and will draw on questions relating to citizenship, identity, and integration in modern Britain. For example, what sorts of groups should be allowed to build places of religious worship in Britain? Should those places of worship be solely for the use of a specific religious community, or should they be of benefit to the wider public? The decision will also highlight how a liberal democracy balances between the religious needs of a given community and concerns over the illiberal nature of that community. With an election looming in Britain in 2015, and given the contentious nature of the project, the decision is likely to spark as much controversy as the mosque itself.

The controversy over the construction of TJ's mosque brings to the forefront a wider debate over the role of religion, and specifically Islam, in Western liberal democracies. At the same time, the place of religion in liberal democracies generates profound questions over the moral basis and legitimacy of liberalism. As Raymond Plant argues, this is because the "legal and regulatory requirements of a liberal political order in many respects challenge religious practices and the ways which religious beliefs are manifested" (2013: 9). Examples of this have been the banning of the veil in France, the banning of minarets in Switzerland, and an increased number of court cases over the role of religion and religious symbols in public across Europe.

The reemergence of religion as a force in society (and in this case specifically Islam) not only challenges the basis of the authority of the liberal state but also "challenges religion within it and in particular whether a religion seeking a role in a liberal society can do so only if it is a liberalized form of that religion" (Plant 2013: 9). In short, this has been the crux of the dilemma for TJ. In order for TJ's mosque to succeed, TJ leaders have to demonstrate that their version of Islam fits within the boundaries of religion acceptable to the liberal state in Britain. That is a form of religion that is open, inclusive, and tolerant—a liberalized Islam. Again, as Plant argues, the effects of this are immense. This is because for such religious groups, being part of a liberal political order will have "radical effects on the integrity of the beliefs held by those who espouse them by requiring that such beliefs should be held in a liberal way as a precondition of playing a part in the liberal order" (Plant 2013: 9).

Central to the book are attempts to explain why TJ leaders in London undertook a process of sociopolitical engagement. This episode has been unique to TJ in London and somewhat puzzling in the context of how TJ as a movement operates. TJ has traditionally preached a detachment from society and takes considerable efforts to avoid controversy or publicity. As an organization, TJ does not maintain a website, does not have official publications, and claims not to keep any records of members. Since 2007, TJ in London adopted new methods that veered from traditional practices. These included the use of social media such as YouTube and the establishment of a website and better relationships with journalists and members of the public. TJ leaders both in Britain and abroad made strong statements against acts of terrorism and were at pains to distance TJ from any form of violent action. In essence, TJ leaders wanted to present TJ as a movement that was part of the fabric of a liberal democracy and a movement with which business could be done.

It is clear that through wanting to construct a large and iconic mosque in London, TJ leaders for the first time had to think about the movement's place in British society and politics. By the end of 2011, TJ leaders had done much to demonstrate that TJ, at least in London, was a changed movement. Promises were made that TJ would develop mixed-use plans for their site and in a way that would benefit the wider community. The recognition was that TJ may have faulted in the past, but moving forward TJ leaders would be committed to working in partnership with Newham Council to develop a sustainable and community-oriented site. Why is it that TJ leaders in London veered so far from traditional Tablighi practices? What does this tell us about how illiberal and theocratic groups operate and their abilities to adapt in liberal democracies such as the United Kingdom?

TJ leaders in London sought to strategically reframe the image of the movement as a means of gaining permission to construct the proposed mosque. It is as simple as that. The context in London following the terrorist attacks of July 7, 2005, ushered in a period where Islam was securitized and one that demanded TJ leaders to demonstrate in a public way that TJ was becoming attune to the British context. In essence, this meant TJ leaders had to present TJ as open, tolerant, and willing to engage with government and wider communities to develop a mosque site that would not only benefit them but also the wider community. Failure to do so would result in the collapse of the project.

Where pressure was not placed on TJ, for example in Dewsbury where the movement's British and European headquarters are based, there was no attempt by TJ there to reframe their activities. Outside of London, no branches of TJ in Britain made attempts to engage with the state or with wider communities. This is important for it shows that illiberal and theocratic movements are not homogenous but have the ability to function in different ways according to the demands of the local context and depending on the gaols of the movement in a given location. It is further significant because the case shows that where contextual pressures are sustained and implemented from the top down, groups may have but little choice to reframe their activities.

The hypothesis was that illiberal or (retiring) theocratic movements that begin a process of sustained engagement (whether strategic or otherwise) would undergo transformative change. Engagement is seen as a powerful tool having the ability to transform those who participate or at least engender an adaptive course. This has not yet happened with TJ or at least with not enough members for it to affect change in the movement as a whole. It is clear that a small group of TJ leaders in London pursued engagement and believed that the process would be beneficial to the movement. For those TJ leaders, engaging with political elites and institutions was seen as the fastest way to gain permission to construct their mosque. They acknowledged that without the correct paperwork, without public relations, without the goodwill and partnership of the local authority and community, their application is unlikely to succeed. It is necessary to play by the rules that have been established.

The process of sociopolitical engagement, however, did not go according to plan. TJ leaders in London were not united over the process, with some fearing that too much trust had been placed in people from outside of the movement and in innovative and secular methods.

TJ's traditional recourse is to renew efforts in bringing Muslims back to a correct understanding of Islam as perceived by the movement and, through doing so, gaining Allah's pleasure. TJ believes that it is Allah who will make the ultimate decision over whether the mosque will be built or not. Further, there was opposition to the new tactics from other branches of TJ in Britain that argued that the controversy was bringing too much focus on the movement as a whole in the United Kingdom. Furthermore, at TJ international headquarters in Nizamuddin, there were questions over the size of the proposed mosque by TJ elders, who felt the project was too ambitious and was bringing the movement into an unwanted limelight. At the same time, engagement did not yield the results that TJ leaders were looking for. Instead the movement became embroiled in controversy after controversy that resulted in sustained media attention.

Ultimately, TJ leaders veered too far from traditional Tablighi beliefs, creating disconnect between what they taught their members and what they were saying to the media and government officials. By the time of the second Public Inquiry into TJ's redevelopment plans in 2014, TJ leaders toned down their discourse, and plans for the redevelopment of the site indicated the prominence of a TJ mosque. In a sense this signaled that engagement had not worked, although TJ leaders still tried to emphasize some of the nonreligious aspects of the proposal. The demands being made by Newham Council and the community cohesion framework were too much for TJ. Rather than continue to invest in a strategy that had not yielded results, TJ leaders decided to propose what they really wanted—that is, a mosque-centric site. A number of Tablighi interviewees commented that if the proposed mosque is not granted, TJ will reconsider its options. It may be that instead of having one big mosque, three or four smaller ones could be built in different locations in London, and London divided into a series of zones for missionary activities.

As contentious episodes over the nature of religion in liberal democracies are only likely to increase in the near future, further study is needed on how religious groups negotiate and adapt to liberal contexts. What factors precipitate adaptation and what measures could be introduced to ease the process? Governments in liberal democracies will have to better articulate and explain the ways in which they deal with religion, as well as justify why the liberal approach is the best one. An interesting line of further study would be to compare the ways in which other retiring illiberal movements have attempted to engage in liberal societies and what impact this has on those movements. It would further be insightful to identify cases in which engagement has been prolonged and whether this has engendered a process of adaptation or accommodation of the movement in question.

What remains in this study is that TJ is no ordinary Muslim group and its proposed mosque is no ordinary mosque. The project has raised significant questions about mosque construction in Britain, who should be allowed to build mosques, as well as what size such structures should be. TJ leaders argued that the purpose of their proposed new mosque is to serve local Muslims. Yet, the size of the proposed mosque signals that it will be something much more than this. It is to be a new Tablighi world center that will provide not only space for prayer and congregational gatherings but also act as a coordination and dispatch center for missionary activities throughout the world. TJ is a movement with 80 million adherents worldwide and dedicates its time to reorienting Muslims to what TJ regard as a purer understanding of Islam. It is traditionally disengaged from Western liberal societies in which it finds itself, viewing them as corrupt and immoral. Instead, TJ leaders preach a message of turning inward to a life dedicated to shunning worldliness and materialism and moving in the path of missionary endeavors. The Secretary of State for Communities and Local Government will have to decide whether there is room in Britain for such a mosque, and if not in Britain, then where?

NOTES

I INTRODUCTION

1. This process is also described by Eva Hoffman in her book *Lost in Translation* (1998).
2. All interviews with TJ members were carried out between October 2009 and December 2013. The interviews took place at a number of locations, including coffee shops, local restaurants, and homes, but the majority were at TJ's West Ham mosque—the Markaz Ilyas. Interviews with planning officials and those opposing TJ's mosque proposals took place over the same time period and at a number of different locations in East London.

3 CONCEIVING TABLIGHI JAMAAT

1. For a more in-depth analysis of Waliullah, see Rizvi (1980) and Baljon (1986).
2. According to Haq, there was a personal link between Shah Waliullah and Ilyas. Muzaffar Husayn, the maternal grandfather of Ilyas, was a pupil of Shah Muhammad Ishaq who was himself a distinguished student and grandson of Shah Abdul-Aziz, the son of Shah Waliullah. Shah Muhammad Ishaq was chosen as the successor of Shah Abdul-Aziz since the latter had no sons.
3. This school would go on to be associated with its own strand of Islam—the Deobandi—and it was from this that TJ would later emerge.
4. The heightened religious tensions centered on the battle for the souls of neo-Muslims or those belonging to late-converted groups who had retained non-Islamic customs in their social etiquette.
5. Society of Nobles, a Hindu nationalist movement, founded in 1875.
6. A Hindu "Purification" movement.
7. Conversion and reconversion are traditionally alien concepts to Hinduism.
8. For further analysis on Hindu nationalist movements and competition over conversions with Muslims, see Mayaram (1997), and for a general introduction to relations between Hinduism and Muslims in India, see Char (1997).
9. These Muslim organizations and movements included the Barelwi *Anjumam Ridai Mustafa* (1923), the *Tablighi-i-Islami* in Ambala,

the *All India Anjuman Tablighi Islam, Tanzim* in Amristar, *Markazi Jamiat Tabligh Islam* in Poona, and the *Tablighi Mission* (Masud 2000b: lii).

10. This has been a practice, as will emerge later, of the TJ in Britain, and some commentators claim it is a bar to effective community engagement.

11. Such divine inspiration for the movement is a common feature of many revitalization movements, with Wallace identifying this as a key factor in all the revitalization movements he had examined (Wallace 1956).

12. In reality, as Mewat was such a "backward" area, the majority of children were still needed to contribute to family stability through work in the fields, even if education was available.

13. One *Chillah* lasts for 40 days.

14. In the beginning the demand was only for one *chillah*. It is not clear whether this service for a period of 4 months was expected once in a lifetime or once a year. Recent thought is that it is a one-off event. Indeed, while at the *Masjid Ilyas* in London, as part of my field work, I was informed by a Tablighi that the 40-day endeavor was expected from each Tablighi man once in their lifetime and preferably toward the start of his commitment. He went further to say that one should think of the 40-day endeavor like the "old rechargeable batteries" whereby the first time they are charged they need a long period of time, followed by shorter bursts (author interview, Thursday, October 22, 2009, Masjid Ilyas, West Ham, London).

15. While the *Qur'an* does not explicitly use the word *tabligh*, words from the *b-l-gh* root are rather frequent (5:67, 33:39, 7:62, 68, 79, 93). All are associated with communication or the revelation of a message. The Qur'anic usage, according to Masud, signifies that "communication of the message alone is the objective—conversion is not the duty or the mission of a prophet or a preacher; this is left to the free choice of the addressees" (2000b: xx).

16. The main anthology of texts used by the TJ, translated as "The Virtues of Good Deeds."

17. TJ is so focused on this text as the guide to their everyday actions, that its critics have accused the movement of raising it above the *Qur'an*. TJ's critics also accused the *Fazail-E-Amal* as containing mainly weak or fabricated *Hadith* that serve to further the purposes of the movement as opposed to the strict message of Islam. In refutation of this, a senior scholar at Deoband stated: "It is a total misconception that *Fazail-E-Amal* is the guidebook of TJ. This book only consists of the virtues of good deeds. The concept of TJ was not derived from this book, nor is the Jamaat dependent on this book to do the work of *tabligh*. They thought it necessary to stipulate such

NOTES ✦ 165

a book that would encourage people towards good deeds, and this book served the purpose; therefore, the people who join this work are advised to stipulate a specific time for the reading of this book. However, it is not compulsory upon each an every person who joins this effort to read this book." http://www.sunniforum.com/forum/showthread.php?29176-Objections-on-Fazail-e-Aamal-Answered-by-Darul-uloom-Deoband (accessed January 15, 2012).

18. Conversation over dinner with two committed Tablighi members, November 22, 2009, London.

4   TABLIGHI JAMAAT: ORGANIZATION, STRUCTURE, AND METHODS

1. These were Hafiz Muqbal Hasan, Qari Daud, Mawlawi Ihtisham ul-Hasan Kandhalawi, Mohammad Yusuf Kandhalawi, Mohammad Inamul Hasan Kandhalwai, and Sayid Rada Hasan Bhopali.

2. The three senior colleagues were Maulana Zakariya, Maulana Abdul Qadir Raipuri, and Maulana Zafar Ahmad. This process of appointing the *amir* was supposed to reflect the process used for the appointment of the successor of the second Caliph of Islam Omar bin al-Khattab. Omar, however, asked his six companions to choose from among themselves rather than from another group who had no say in the matter.

3. As Gaborieau notes, the movement is centered around an exceptionally tight endogamous patrilineage (2006: 57).

4. This notion, however, has been hotly contested by other Islamic scholars who claim that there is no mention in either the *Quran* or the hadith relating to the Prophet sending out individual groups for 3 or 40 days to towns to proselytize others.

5. The movement is also increasingly organizing *jamaats* for women, in which they are led by a husband of a woman in the group, and their message is directly aimed at other Muslim women.

6. The author witnessed this on several occasions during fieldwork and was invited to join an evening meal in the mosque.

7. Of the several hundred people at the first TJ meeting, only a small number of people (possibly 10 to 15) volunteered to go on Tablighi tour.

8. This is based on my observation research at the Markaz. It should be noted that due to Markaz Ilyas being one of the main TJ centers in the United Kingdom, it is likely to have a much higher level of volunteers than "ordinary" TJ mosques, as people from all over the United Kingdom come here to listen to talks.

9. Another justification for the 3-day option is that Prophet Jonah "stayed in the belly of a whale for three days and three nights" and completely focused on praying to God (Elias 2004: 16).

5 TABLIGHIS IN BRITAIN: ADAPTING TO SHIFTING CONTEXTS

1. Information taken from statements made by the trustees of the Tablighi Jamaat at a Public Inquiry in London, June 3 to June 20, 2014.

6 TABLIGHI JAMAAT IN TRANSITION: 2005–2010

1. The same pattern can be found in other European countries too; for example, in Germany in the 1990s there were approximately 2,400 improvised and largely invisible Muslim places of prayer found in cellars, shops, and factories. See Jonker and Kapphan (1998).
2. http://www.myaa-arq.com/ (accessed May 2, 2011).
3. Ibid.
4. Several Tablighis repeated this to me during the course of fieldwork.
5. www.abbeymillsmosque.com.
6. www.megamosquenothanks.com.
7. www.abbeymillsmosque.com/AMILLS/page.php?PBN=TablighiJamaatHome (accessed October 27, 2007).
8. www.abbeymillsmosque.com/AMILLS/page.php?PID=48 (accessed October 27, 2007).
9. Ibid.
10. http://www.youtube.com/user/AbbeymillsMosque#p/u/4/z01c7ICaUn4 (accessed April 27, 2009)
11. www.abbeymillsmosque.com/AMILLS/page.php?PID=58 (accessed October 27, 2007).
12. Interview with Alan Craig, Thursday, February 12, 2009.
13. Alan Craig, Public Debate over Abbey Mills Mosque plans, September 7, 2007, Ithaca House, Stratford, London.
14. www.petitions.number10.gov.uk/ (accessed March 28, 2010). This at the time was the largest petition to have been posted on the Downing Street e-petitions website.
15. http://petitions.number10.gov.uk/ScrapMegaMosque/ (accessed May 24, 2011).
16. Interview with Alan Craig, Thursday, February 12, 2009.
17. *The Evening Standard* reported that the paper "has learned that the antimosque campaign has been infiltrated by the British National Party, which has told its members to sign the Downing Street petition. The petition was originally posted on the No 10 site by a Right-wing extremist called Jill Barham" (Anon. 2007).
18. www.abbeymillsmosque.com/AMILLS/page.php?PID=48 (accessed October 27, 2007).
19. www.abbeymillsmosque.com/AMILLS/cache_PID_59.html (accessed October 27, 2007).

20. Craig also commented on the unfairness of the poll noting that allegations had been made that Muslims in the United Kingdom had contacted Muslims in India asking them to vote on the poll.
21. www.abbeymillsmosque.com/AMILLS/page.php?PID=52 (accessed October 27, 2007). The *Evening Standard* poll, which is referred to here, is the decision by the *Evening Standard* to ask their readers to vote online whether in their opinion the construction of the "mega mosque" should go ahead. The poll was marred due to a malicious email campaign trying to influence peoples' votes through arguing that the mosque would be bigger than St. Paul's Cathedral, and that public money could be better spent on hospitals—even though no public money had been pledged for the project.
22. http://www.islamonline.net/servlet/Satellite?c=Article_C&cid=1 164545880054&pagename=Zone-English-News%2FNWELayout (accessed March 27, 2008).
23. www.abbeymillsmosque.com/AMILLS/page.php?PID=48 (accessed October 27, 2007).

7 TABLIGHI JAMAAT AND THE POLITICS OF ADAPTATION

1. Examination of Mr Sunil Sahadevan (Planning Officer LBN) by Douglas Edwards QC, Public Inquiry into the Enforcement Action at the site of the Abbey Mills Centre, East Ham Town Hall, London Borough of Newham, February 18, 2011, morning session.
2. Cross-examination of Mr Sunil Sahadevan (Planning Officer LBN) by Russell Harris QC, Public Inquiry into the Enforcement Action at the site of the Abbey Mills Centre, East Ham Town Hall, London Borough of Newham, February 18, 2011, morning session.
3. Ibid.
4. Examination of Mr Solad Mohammed (trustee of the Anjuman-E-Islahul-Muslimeen of London) by Russell Harris QC, Public Inquiry into the Enforcement Action at the site of the Abbey Mills Centre, East Ham Town Hall, London Borough of Newham, February 15, 2011, morning session.
5. From my own observations, I would place the average Thursday evening attendance figures at over 2,000 worshipers.
6. Mr Russell Harris QC, Public Inquiry into the Enforcement Action at the site of the Abbey Mills Centre, East Ham Town Hall, London Borough of Newham, February 18, 2011, morning session.
7. Examination of Ms Karen Jones (Consultant, Cushman and Wakefield) by Russell Harris QC, Public Inquiry into the Enforcement Action at the site of the Abbey Mills Centre, East Ham Town Hall, London Borough of Newham, February 15, 2011, afternoon session.

8. Cross-examination of Mr Solad Mohammed by Douglas Edwards QC, Public Inquiry into the Enforcement Action at the site of the Abbey Mills Centre, East Ham Town Hall, London Borough of Newham, February 15, 2011, morning session.

9. Douglas Edwards QC, Public Inquiry into the Enforcement Action at the site of the Abbey Mills Centre, East Ham Town Hall, London Borough of Newham, February 16, 2011, morning session.

10. Proposals for the redevelopment of the site emerged in February 2012, with an open exhibition of the plans being held at Markaz Ilyas.

11. In February 2012, London TJ held an exhibition of their new plans at Markaz Ilyas. The plans propose a 9,500 capacity mosque with two large minarets. The plans also included a library, nature trail, visitor center, housing, and retail units (Jacobs 2012).

12. Mr Graham Dudley (planning inspector), Public Inquiry into the Enforcement Action at the site of the Abbey Mills Centre, East Ham Town Hall, London Borough of Newham, February 16, 2011, morning session.

13. Interview with Alan Craig, Thursday, June 10, 2010, London Newham.

14. Examination of Ms Tehmina Kazi by Mr John Pugh-Smith, Public Inquiry into the Enforcement Action at the site of the Abbey Mills Centre, East Ham Town Hall, London Borough of Newham, February 17, 2010, afternoon session.

15. Ibid.

16. Ibid.

17. He is alleged to have made anti-Semitic and homophobic comments; see Schipper (2012).

18. Interview conducted on Message TV, "Stratford Demonstration for Riverine Centre West Ham Markaz," aired December 6, 2012.

19. Ibid.

20. Ibid.

21. TJ leaders and their hired team made this clear during the Public Inquiry, June 3, 2014.

8 TABLIGHI JAMAAT FROM WITHIN

1. This is a common mantra that TJ interviewees repeated on a number of occasions.

2. Conversation with Mr Solad Mohammed (trustee of the Anjuman-E-Islahul-Muslimeen of London), February 9, 2011.

3. This is a concept that Islamists such as Qutb and Maududi also developed (Qutb 2006).

4. This sort of totality in religious rules governing one's life is a common feature of theocratic groups—for further discussion, see Swaine (2006).

5. This is particularly relevant to the context of the United Kingdom where most men are not circumcized.
6. Gathering and talk at Markaz Ilyas, Thursday, June 24, 2010, West Ham, London.
7. Ibid.

GLOSSARY

Alim	expert trained in the Islamic sciences
Amal	action or effort
Amir	leader
Bayan	Islamic sermon
Chillah	period of 40 days, of particular significance in Sufism
Dawah	invitation, spreading of the faith
Din	religion, Islam
Dunya	this world, worldliness
Eid	festival
Fatiha	first chapter of the Qur'an
Fatwa	legal opinion
Fazail-E-Amal	"Virtues of Good Deeds," collation of readings used by the TJ
Hadith	sayings or acts ascribed to Prophet Mohammad
Hajj	pilgrimage to Mecca
Halal	allowed/permitted
Haq	truth
Harram	forbidden
Hijra	migration, usually referring to that of Mohammad from Mecca to Medina
Ijtima	congregational gathering, rally
Iman	faith
Inshallah	God willing
Jannat	heaven/paradise
Jahanam	hell
Jahiliyyah	a state of extreme ignorance and disbelief in God
Jamaat	group, community
Jihad	struggle
Kalima	Islamic creed of confession
Madrassa	Muslim school or center of education, seminary
Markaz	center, large mosque
Masjid	a building designated for prayer, mosque
Miswak	tooth-stick, generally procured from trees

Namaz	prayer
Niqab	a cloth that covers the face except the eyes
Pir	"old person," guide, teacher, Sufi master
Purdah	veil, literally "curtain"
Sahaba	companions of Prophet Mohammad
Salaf	predecessors, first three generations of Muslims—the "pious ancestors"
Salat	prayer
Shalwar Kaemeez	baggy trousers and shirt
Shari'a	Islamic law
Shaykh	Sufi spiritual preceptor
Shaytan	devil
Shirk	associationism, polytheism
Shuddhi	literally "purification"; Hindu missionary movement
Shura	consultative committee
Tabligh	literally "to communicate"; Islamic missionary work
Tayyibah	purity
Ulama	plural of alim
Ummah	the entirety of community of Muslim believers
Yakhim	trust
Zakat	the poor-due, obligatory on all Muslims who can afford it

Bibliography

Abbas, T. ed. 2005. *Muslim Britain: Communities Under Pressure*. London and New York: Zed Books.

Abdul, T. 2006. "Veil teacher was obeying a fatwa," *The Sunday Times*, 29 October.

Adler, R. P., and Goggin, J. 2005. "What do we mean by 'Civic Engagement?'," *Journal of Transformative Education*, 3 (3): 236–253.

Ahmad, A., Aydin, H., Barou, J., Kakpo, N., Rizvi, S., and Birt, Y. 2008. *Studies into Violent Radicalization; Lot 2 The Beliefs, Ideologies and Narratives*. London: Change Institute.

Ahmed, M. 1991. "Islamic fundamentalism in South Asia; The Jamaat-i-Islami and the Tablighi Jamaat of South Asia." In *Fundamentalism Observed*, ed. M. Marty and R. S. Appleby. Chicago and London: University of Chicago Press.

Al-Alawi, I., and Schwartz, S. 2007. "Ken's Mega-Mosque will encourage extremism," *The Spectator*, January.

Alexiev, A. 2005. "Tablighi Jamaat: Jihad's stealthy legions," *The Middle East Quarterly*, 12 (1): 3–11.

Al-Ghazali, M. 2004. *The Socio-Political Thought of Shah Wali Allah*. New Delhi: Adams Publisher and Distributors.

Al-Haddad, H. 2012. "Urgent message from Sheikh Haithum al-Haddad about Mega Mosque in London," *YouTube*, November 27. Available from https://www.youtube.com/watch?v=37aOxsJoI0w

Al-Mashaat, H. 1993. *Muslim Youth and Western Educational Systems*. Azaadville: Madrsah Arabia Islamia.

Ali, J. 2006. *Islamic Revivalism: A Study of the Tablighi Jamaat in Sydney*. Sydney: University of New South Wales.

———. 2012. *Islamic Revivalism Encounters the Modern World: A Study of the Tablighi Jama'at*. New Delhi: Sterling Publishers

Ali, M. D. 2012. "No shelter for terrorists: Tablighi Jamaat hits back at WikiLeaks," TwoCircles.Net, 2011. Available from http://twocircles.net/2011may11/no_shelter_terrorists_tablighi_jamaat_hits_back_wikileaks.html

Allievi, S. 2010. "Mosques in Europe: Real problems and false solutions." In *Mosques in Europe: Why a Solution Has Become a Problem*, ed. S. Allievi. London: Alliance Publishing Trust.

Anon. 2007. "BNP is linked to petition against new 'megamosque'," *London Evening Standard*, July 20.

Ansari, H. 2009. *The Infidel Within: Muslims in Britain Since 1800*. London: Hurst & Company.

Arshad, S. 2007. "Tabligh, or the enigma of revival," *The Times of India*.

Ashour, O. 2009. *The De-Radicalization of Jihadists: Transforming Armed Islamist movements*. London and New York: Routledge.

Asim, M. 2014. "Demise of Tablighi Jamaat Ameer spread sadness among Muslims," Two Circles Net, March 21. Available from http://twocircles.net/2014mar21/demise_tablighi_jamaat_ameer_spread_sadness_among_muslims.html#.U53Df9y4llJ

Bagguley, P., and Hussain, Y. 2005. "Flying the flag for England? Citizenship, religion and identity among British Pakistani Muslims." In *Muslim Britain: Communities Under Pressure*, ed. T. Abbas. London and New York: Zed Books.

Baldwin, T., and Rozenberg, G. 2004. "Britain 'must scrap multiculturalism' race chief calls for change after 40 years," *The Times*, April 3.

Baljon, J. 1986. *Religion and Thought of Shah Wali Allah Dihlawi 1730 – 1762*. Leiden: Brill

Barger, W., and Ernesto, R. 1994. *The Farm Labor Movement in the Midwest: Social Change and Adaptation Among Migrant Farmworkers*. Austin: University of Texas Press.

Bari, M. 2005. *Race, Religion & Muslim Identity in Britain*. Swansea: Renaissance Press.

Barker, E. 1989. *New Religious Movements: A Practical Introduction*. London: HMSO.

Belien, P. 2005. "Jihad against Danish newspaper," *The Brussels Journal*.

Benford, R., and Snow, D. 2000. "Framing processes and social movements: An overview and assessment," *Annual Review of Sociology*, 26: 611–639.

Birt, J., and Lewis, P. 2010. "The pattern of Islamic reform in Britain: The Deobandis between intra-Muslim sectarianism and engagement with wider society." In *Producing Islamic Knowledge: Transmission and Dissemination in Western Europe*, ed. M. Van Bruinessen and S. Allievi. London: Routledge.

Boyer, M. C. 2001. *The City of Collective Memory: Its Historical Imagery and Architectural Entertainments*. 5th ed. Cambridge and London: The MIT Press.

Brady, H. 1999. "Political participation." In *Measures of Political Attitudes*, eds. J. Robinson, P. Shaver, and L. Wrightsman. San Diego: Academic Press.

Briggs, R., and Jonathan, B. 2009. *MICROCON Policy Working Paper 7: Radicalization Among Muslims in the UK*. Brighton: MICROCON.

Bunglawala, I. 2007. "A maliscious campaign," *The Guardian*, July 18.

Burgess, R. 1984. *In the Filed: An Introduction to Field Research*. London: Allen and Unwin.

Burnett, J. 2004. "Community, cohesion and the state," *Race and Class*, 45 (3): 1–18.

Burnham, P. 2004. *Research Methods in Politics*. Basingstoke: Palgrave Macmillan.

Burr, V. 1995. *An Introduction to Social Constructionism.* London and New York: Routledge.

Burstein, P. 1999. "Social movements and public policy." In *How Social Movements Matter,* eds. M. Giugni, D. McAdam, and C. Tilly. Minneapolis and London: University of Minnesota Press.

Burton, F., and Scott, S. 2008. *Tablighi Jamaat: An Indirect Line to Terrorism.* Austin: Stratford Global Intelligence.

Cameron, D. 2011. "PM's speech at Munich Security Conference," Munich, February 5. Available from https://www.gov.uk/government/speeches/pms-speech-at-munich-security-conference

———. 2014. "British values aren't optional, they're vital. That's why I will promote then in every school," *Daily Mail,* June 14. Available from http://www.dailymail.co.uk/debate/article-2658171/DAVID-CAMERON-British-values-arent-optional-theyre-vital-Thats-I-promote-EVERY-school-As-row-rages-Trojan-Horse-takeover-classrooms-Prime-Minister-delivers-uncompromising-pledge.html

Cantle, T. 2001. *Community Cohesion: A Report of the Independent Review Team.* London: Home Office.

———. 2006. "Multiculturalism – A failed experiment?," *Index on Censorship,* 35 (2): 91–92.

Cesari, J. 2005. "Mosque conflicts in European cities: Introduction," *Journal of Ethnic and Migration Studies,* 31 (6): 1015–1024.

CSJ. 2013. *Qualitative Research Report: Savile Town Dewsbury.* Bristol: CSJ Planning.

Champkins, N. 2011. "Note of evidence: Nicholas Champkins of Allies and Morrison." In *APP/G5750/C/10/2125895.* London: Cushman and Wakefield.

ChangeInstitute. 2009a. *Summary Report: Understanding Muslim Ethnic Communities.* London: The Change Institute/Department for Communities and Local Government.

———. 2009b. *The Bangladeshi Muslim Community in England: Understanding Muslim Ethnic Communities.* London: The Change Institute/Department for Communities and Local Goverment

———. 2009c. *The Pakistani Muslim Community in England: Understanding Muslim Ethnic Communities.* London: Change Institute/Department for Communities and Local Government.

———. 2010. *Summary Report: Understanding Muslim Ethnic Communities.* London: The Change Institute.

Char, S. V. D. 1997. *Hinduism and Islam in India: Caste, Religion and Society From Antiquity to Early Modern Times.* Princeton: Markus Wiener Publishers.

Conway, D. 2009. *Disunited Kingdom.* London: Civitas

Craig, A. 2006. "Press Release: Muslims and non-Muslims unite in opposition to West Ham Olympics Mega-mosque." London: Christian Peoples Alliance.

———. 2011a. *Olympics Mega Mosque Threat Is First Test for Cameron's Speech Against Extremist Islam.* London: Christian Peoples Alliance

Craig, A. 2006. 2011b. *Welcome*. Newham Concern. Available from http://www.megamosquenothanks.com/
———. 2014. "Muddassar's dirty tricks at the Mega-Mosque Inquiry," *Alan's Angle*, June 28. Available from http://www.alansangle.com/?p=1485
Crooke, W. 1906. *The Castes and Tribes of the North-Western Provinces and Oduh*. Calcutta: Office of the Superintendent of Government Printing.
Crowcroft, P. 2011. "Proof of evidence of Philip Crowcroft on land contamination issues." In *APP/G5750/C/10/2125895*. London: London Borough of Newham.
Dalrymple, T. 2004. "Why Theo Van Gogh was murdered," *City Limits*, Novemeber 15. Available from http://www.city-journal.org/html/eon_11_15_04td.html
Dalrymple, W. 2008. *The Last Mughal*. London: Bloomsbury Publishing.
Davies, D. 2000. *The Mormon Culture of Salvation: Force, Grace and Glory*. Aldershot: Ashgate.
De Feo, A. 2012. "Behind the veil, in the ranks of the Tablighi Jamaat," *World Religion Watch 2009*. Available from http://www.world-religionwatch.org/index.php?option=com_content&view=article&id=284&Itemid=57
DeHanas, D, and Pieri, Z. 2011. "Olympic proportions: The expanding scalar politics of the London 'Olympics Mega-Mosque' controversy," *Sociology*, 45 (5): 798–814.
Dispatches. 2007. "Undercover Mosque," *Dispatches*. United Kingdom: Channel 4.
Doward, J. 2006a. "Battle to block massive mosque: Project for 40,000 worshippers has links with radical Islam," *The Guardian*, September 24.
———. 2006b. "Mega-mosque falls foul of planning laws," *The Observer on Sunday*, November 5.
———. 2006c. "The Karachi connection," *The Guardian*, August 13.
Dudley, G. 2011. *Appeal Decision*. Bristol: The Planning Inspectorate.
Dunne, J. 2006. "Mystery of the 'mega-msoque'," *thelondonpaper*, November 28.
Dwyer, C. 2000. "Contested spaces: Mosque building and the cultural politics of multiculturalism." In *Symposium on New Landscapes of Religion in the West*. Oxford: University of Oxford.
Eade, J. 1996. "Nationalism, community, and the Islamization of space in London." In *Making Muslim Space in North America and Europe*, ed. B. Metcalf. Berkeley and London: University of California Press.
ECORYS. 2010. *Riverine Centre Needs Assessment: Final Report*. London: ERCOYS UK.
Elahi, A. 1992. *Six Points of Tabligh*. Delhi: Rasheed Publications.
———. 2007. "Six fundamentals." In *Fazail-E-Amal*, ed. Z. Kandhlawi. New Delhi: Islamic Book Service.
Elias, A. H. 2004. *Tabligh Made Easy*. Karachi: Zam Zam Publishers.
El-Ghobashy, M. 2005. "The metamorphosis of the Egyptian Muslim Brothers," *International Journal of Middle East Studies*, 37 (3): 373–395.

Environment Agency. 2010. "Environment Agency Written Statement." In *APP/5750/C/10/2125895*. London: The Environment Agency.

Esposito, J. 2010. *The Future of Islam*. Oxford: Oxford University Press.

Faust, E. 2000. "Close ties and boundaries: Tablighi Jama'at in Britain and Germany." In *Travellers in Faith: Sudies of the Tablighi Jama'at as a Transnational Movement for Faith Renewal*, ed. M. Masud. Leiden, Boston, and Koln: Brill.

Fetzer, J., and Soper, C. 2005. *Muslims and the State in Britain, France and Germany*. Cambridge: Cambridge University Press.

Fitzgerald, M. 2014. "How the Mormons conquered America: The success of the Mormon religion is a study in social adaptation," *Nautilus*, June 12. Available from http://nautil.us/issue/14/mutation/how-the-mormons-conquered-america

Fourest, C. 2008. *Brother Tariq: The Doublespeak of Tariq Ramadan*. New York: Encounter Books.

Friedman, D. 2005. *Tablighi Jamaat Dossier*. Washington: Centre for Policing Terrorism.

Gaborieau, M. 1999. "Transnational Islamic Movements: Tablighi Jama'at in Politics?," *ISIM Newsletter* 3.

———. 2000. "The transformation of the Tablighi Jamaat into a transnational movement." In *Travellers in Faith: Studies of the Tablighi Jamaat as a Transnational Islamic Movement for Faith Renewal*, ed. M. K. Masud. Leiden: Brill.

———. 2006. "What is left of Sufism in Tablighi Jama'at?," *Archives de Sciences Sociales des Religions*, 135 (juillet-septembre): 53–72.

Gardner, K. 2002. *Age, Narrativ and Migration: The Life Course and Life Histories of Bengali Elders in London*. Oxford: Berg

Gest, J. 2010. *APART: Alienated and Engaged Muslims in the West*. London: Hurst & Company.

Ghosh, B., and Mich, D. 2010. "Islamophobia: Does America have a Muslim problem?," *Time*, August 19.

Gilliat-Ray, S. 2005. "Closed worlds: (not) accessing Deobandi dar ul-uloom in Britain," *Fieldwork in Religion*, 1 (1): 7–33.

———. 2010. *Muslims in Britain: An Introduction*. Cambridge: Cambridge University Press.

Gilliat-Ray, S., and Birt, J. 2010. "A mosque too far? Islam and the limits of British multiculturalism." In *Mosques in Europe: Why a Solution Has Become a Problem*, ed. S. Allievi. London: Alliance Publishing Trust.

Gilligan, A. 2014. "Islamist plot: six schools face Ofsted special measures," *The Telegraph*, April 19. Available from http://www.telegraph.co.uk/education/educationnews/10776607/Islamist-plot-six-schools-face-Ofsted-special-measures.html

Githens-Mazer, J. 2008. "Locating agency in collective political behaviour: Nationalism, social movements and individual mobilisation," *Politics*, 28 (1): 41–49.

Geldhill, R. 2014. "Intimidation controversy on day one of mega-mosque inquiry," *Lapido Media*, June 3. Available from http://www.lapidomedia. com/intimidation-controversy-day-one-mega-mosque-inquiry

Goud, J. 2010. "Letter from the London Probation Trust to the Planning Inspectorate," London, December 23, 2010.

Gugler, T. 2007. "Parrots of paradise – Symbols of the Super Muslim: Sunnah, Sunnaization, and self-fashioning in the Islamic missionary movements Tablighi Jama'at, Da'wat-e-Islam and Sunni Da'wat-e-Islami." In *Vortrag, gehalten auf der 20th ECMSAS, Panel 41: Pakistan in Transition, Session 3: The Politics of Difference*. University of Heidelberg.

Hailes, S. 2014. "Cameron's 'British values' are a 'tasteless soup' says academic," *Lapido Media*, July 2. Available from http://www.lapidomedia. com/camerons-british-values-are-tasteless-soup-says-academic

Haq, M. A. 1972. *The Faith Movement of Maulana Muhammad Ilyas*. London: George Allen and Unwin Ltd.

Hardy, P. 1972. *The Muslims of British India*. Cambridge: Cambridge University Press.

Hargey, T. 2011. "Taj Hargey: Proof of evidence." In *APP/5750/C/10/2125895*. London: Newham Concern.

Harper, C., and Bryan, L. B. 1993. "The social adaptation of marginal religious movements in America," *Sociology of Religion*, 54 (2): 171–192.

Hasan, M. 1997. *Legacy of a Divided Nation: India's Muslims From Independence to Ayodhya*. Boulder: Westview Press.

Hasani, M. 1982. *Sawanih Hazrat Maulana Muhammad Yusuf Kandhalawi*. Lucknow: Maktaba Darul-ulum Nadwatu'l-Ulama.

Hedges, J. 2008. *Tablighi Jamaat: The Premier Latent Network*. Washington: The Fund for Peace.

Hegarty, T., and Sahadevan, S. 2010. "Statement of case of the London borough of Newham." In *APP/5750/C/10/2125895*. London: London Borough of Newham.

Hellyer, H. 2007. "Ruminations and reflections on British Muslims and Islam Post 7-7." In *Islamic Political Radicalism: A European Perspective*, ed. T. Abbas. Edinburgh: Edinburgh University Press.

———. 2009. *Muslims of Europe: The 'Other' Europeans*. Edinburgh: Edinburgh University Press.

Hicks, T. 2009. "On assignment: While thousands gather," *The New York Times*.

Hobsbawm, E. 2003. *The Age of Empire, 1875–1914*. London: Abacus.

Hoffman, E. 1998. *Lost in Translation*. London: Vintage.

Home Office. 2005. "Improving opportunity, strengthening society: The government's strategy to increase race equality and community cohesion." London: HMS.

Horstmann, A. 2007. "The Tablighi Jama'at, transnational Islam and the transformation of the self between southern Thailand and South Asia," *Comparative Study of South Asia, Africa and the Middle East*, 27 (1): 26–40.

Huetlin, T. 2006. "Feeling foreign at home," *Spiegel Online*.

Huntington, S. 1997. "The erosion of American national interests," *Foreign Affairs*, 76 (5).

Hussain, A. 2006. "Focus: Undercover on planet Beeston," *The Times*, July 2.

Ilyas, M. 1967. *Six Points of Tabligh*. Karachi: Darul-Ishaat.

Imamuddin, A, Hassan, S., and Sakar, D. 1985. "Community mosque – A symbol of society." In *Regionalism in Architecture*, ed. R. Powell. Singapore: Concept Media.

Izzard, J. 2008. "Battle for Britain's largest mosque," *BBC News*, March 16. Available from http://news.bbc.co.uk/1/hi/england/london/7299037. stm

Jacobs, L. 2012. "New proposals for West Ham 'mega-mosque' unveiled," *London24*. Available from http://www.london24.com/news/ new_proposals_for_west_ham_mega_mosque_unveiled_1_1210084

Jacobson, D. 2013. *Of Virgins and Martyrs: Women and Sexulaity in Global Conflict*, Baltimore: The Johns Hopkins University Press.

Jenkins, P. 2011. "Securitizing Islam: An interview with Professor Stuart Croft." Available from http://www2.warwick.ac.uk/knowledge/themes/ terror/securitizingislam/

Johnston, P. 2006. "The shadow cast by a mega-mosque," *The Daily Telegraph*, September 25.

Johnston, P., and Foster, P. 2007. "The 'peaceful' group linked to radical Muslims," *The Daily Telegraph*, July 11.

Jones, K. 2011. "Proof of evidence and summary proof on planning issues on behalf of the trustees of Anjuman-E-Islahul-Muslimeen of (London) UK." In *APP/G5750/C/10/2125895*. London: Cushman and Wakefield.

Jones, K. 1981. "Religious identity and the Indian census." In *The Census of British India: New Perspectives*, ed. N. Barrier. Delhi: Manohar Publications.

———. 1989. *Socio-Religios Reform Movements in British India*, Vol. 3. Cambridge: Cambridge University Press.

Jonker, G., and Kapphan, A. 1998. *Moscheen und Islamisches Leben in Berlin (Mosques and Muslim Life in Berlin)*. Translated by P. Heinrich. Berlin: Die Auslanderbeauftragte.

Kalra, V., and Kapoor, N. 2008. *Interrogating Segregation, Integration and the Community Cohesion Agenda*. Manchester: Cathie Marsh Centre for Consensus and Survey Research.

Kandhlawi, Z. 1997a. "Stories of the Sahaaba." In *Fazail-E-Amaal*, ed. Z. Kandhlawi. New Delhi: Islamic Book Service.

———. 1997b. "Virtues of Tabligh." In *Fazail-E-Amal*, ed. Z. Kandhlawi. New Delhi: Islamic Book Service.

———. 2001. *Al-Eti'daal*. Translated by Anon. New Delhi: Islamic Book Service.

———. 2007. *Faza'il-E-A'maal*. 2nd ed., Vol. 1. New Delhi: Islamic Book Service.

Kandhlawi, I. H. 2007. "Muslim degeneration and its only remedy." In *Faza'il-E-Amal*, ed. Z. Kandhlawi. New Delhi: Islamic Book Service.

Kanmaz, M. 2002. "The recognition and institutionalization of Islam in Belgium." *Muslim World*, 92 (1–2): 99–114.

Kazi, T. 2011. "Proof of evidence: Tehmina Kazi." In *APP/5750/C/10/2125895*. London: Newham Concern.

Kepel, G. 2000. "Foi et Pratique: Tablighi Jama'at in France." In *Travellers in Faith: Studies of the Tablighi Jama'at as a Transnational Islamic Movement for Faith renewal*, ed. M. Masud. Leiden: Brill.

———. 2005. "Europe's answer to Londonistan," *Open Democracy*. Available from http://www.opendemocracy.net/conflict-terrorism/londonistan_2775.jsp

Khan, W. 1986. *The Tablighi Movement*. New Delhi: Islamic Centre.

Khattak, I. 2009. "Tableeghi Jamaat leaders denounce gunpoint Sharia," DAWN.COM. Available from http://www.dawn.com/wps/wcm/connect/dawn-content-library/dawn/news/pakistan/12-tableeghi-jamaat-leaders-denounce-gunpoint-sharia-bi-12

Klandermans, B. 1992. "The social construction of potest and multiorganizational fields." In *Frontiers in Social Movement Theory*, ed. A. Morris and C. Mueller. New Haven: Yale University Press.

Knofel, U. 2008. "Europe's mosques move from back alleys to boulevards," *Spiegel Online*.

Lambat, S. 1998. *Tablighi Jamaat in the Words of the Founder Maulana Muhammad Ilyas*. Leicester: Time Publication.

Lambert, R. 2010. *The London Partnerships: An Analysis of Legitimacy and Effectiveness*. Exeter: University of Exeter.

Langley, W. 2006. "Authorities probe little-known Islamic group's alleged ties to extremists," *The Sunday Telegraph*, August 21.

Langley, W., Nikkah, R., Orr, J., Bamber, D., and Ansari, M. 2006. "Army of darkness," *The Daily Telegraph*, August 21.

Lapido Media. 2010. "Exlusive: Unknown to Western media – but bigger than the Hajj," *Lapido Media*. Available from www.lapidomedia.com/unknown-to-western-media

———. 2011. "Salafi mosque gets go-ahead – led by team that looks after royal palaces." In *Ladipd Media: Religious Literacy in World Affairs*. London: Lapido Media.

LBN. 2001. "Memorandum of agreement between Anjuman-e-Islahul Muslimeen (London) of the UK Trust & The London Borough of Newham." London: London Borough of Newham.

———. 2010. "Enforcement notice – Material change of use and operational development." In *07/00186/UCU*. London: London Borough of Newham.

Lent, A. 2001. *British Social Movements Since 1945: Sex, Colur, Peace and Power*. Houndmills: Palgrave.

Lewis, P. 1994. *Islamic Britain: Religion, Politics and Identity Among British Muslims*. London and New York: I.B. Tauris.

———. 2007. *Young, British and Muslim*. London: Continuum International Publishing Group.

———. 2011. "Muslims and non-Muslim relations in Britain: Why relations are difficult and ways forward." In *University of Exeter Sociology Seminar Series*. University of Exeter.

Lynch, R. 2001. "Appendix C: An analysis of the concept of community cohesion." In *Community Cohesion: A Report of the Independent Review Team*, ed. T. Cantle. London: Home Office.

Mackie, P. 2014. "Islamic takeover plot in Birmingham schools investigated," *BBC News*, March 7. Available from http://www.bbc.com/news/uk-england-birmingham-26482599

Malik, K. 2001. "The real value of diversity." In *Connections*. London: Commission of Racial Equality. Available from http://www.kenanmalik.com/essays/diversity.html

Malik, M. 2005. "Muslims in the UK – Discrimination, equality and community cohesion." In *Muslims in the UK: Policies for Engaged Citizens*, ed. T. Choudhury. London: Open Society Institute.

Manco, U., and Kanmaz, M. 2005. "From conflict to co-operation between Muslims and local authorities in a Brussels Borough: Schaerbeek," *Journal of Ethnic and Migration Studies*, 31 (6): 1105–1123.

Martin, E., and Rashid, R. 2012. 'Muslims fight after Newham mega-mosque plan is rejected," *London Evening Standard*, December 6. Available from http://www.standard.co.uk/news/london/muslims-fight-after-newham-megamosque-plan-is-rejected-8388931.html

Masud, M. K. 2000a. "Growth and development of the Tablighi Jamaat in India." In *Travellers in Faith: Studies of the Tablighi Jamaat as a Transnational Islamic Movement for Faith Renewal*, ed. M. K. Masud. Leiden: Brill.

———. 2000b. "Introduction." In *Travellers in Faith: Studies of the Tablighi Jamaat as a Transnational Islamic Movement for Faith Renewal*, ed. M. K. Masud. Leiden: Brill.

———, ed. 2000c. *Travellers in Faith: Studies of the Tablighi Jamaat as a Transnational Islamic Movement for Faith Renewal*. Leiden: Brill.

Mayaram, S. 1997. *Resisting Regimes: Myth Memory and the Shaping of a Muslim Identity*. Oxford and New York: Oxford University Press.

MCB. 2003. *Muslim Statistics Archive*. The Muslim Council of Britain. Available from http://www.mcb.org.uk/library/statistics.php

McRoy, A. 2006. *From Rushdie to 7/7*. London: The Social Affairs Unit.

Meijer, R. 2009a. "Introduction." In *Global Salafism: Islam's New Religious Movement*, ed. R. Meijer. London: Hurst & Company.

———, ed. 2009b. *Global Salafism: Islam's New Religious Movements*. London: Hurst & Company.

Metcalf, B. 1982. *Islamic Revival in British India: Deoband, 1860–1900*. Princeton: Princeton University Press.

———. 2000. "Tablighi Jama'at and women." In *Travellers in Faith: Studies of the Tablighi Jama'at as a Transnational Islamic Movement for Faith Renewal*, ed. M. K. Masud. Leiden: Brill.

Metcalf, B. 1982. 2004. "Traditional Islamic activism: Deoband, Tablighis and Talibs." In *Islamic Contestations: Essays on Muslims in India and Pakistan*, ed. B. Metcalf. Oxford: Oxford University Press.

———. 2009. "Jihad in the way of God: A Tablighi Jama'at account of a mission in India." In *Islam in South Asia in Practice*, ed. B. Metcalf. Princeton and Oxford: Princeton University Press.

Miah, S. R. 2001. *A Guide Book of Tabligh*. 2nd ed. Dhaka: Tabligi Kutubkhana.

Modood, T. 2005. "Remaking multiculturalism after 7/7," *Open Democracy*, September. Available from https://www.opendemocracy.net/conflict-terrorism/multiculturalism_2879.jsp

———. 2007. *Multiculturalism: A Civic Idea*. Cambridge: Polity Press.

Modood, T., Berthoud, R., Lakey, J., Nazroo, J., Smith, P., Virdee, S., and Beishon, S. 1997. *Ethnic Minorities in Britain: Diversity and Disadvantage*. London: Policy Studies Institute.

Mohammad, O. 1996. *The Role of the Mosque*. London: The Islamic Book Company.

Mohammed, S. S. 2011. "Proof of evidence: Solad Sakandar Mohammed." In *APP/SSM/1*. London: The Planning Inspectorate.

Mortimer, E. 1988. *Faith and Power: The Politics of Islam*. New York Vintage Books.

MPACUK. 2008. *It's Blind Puppet Muslims Who Are Unislamic – Not MOACUK!* MPACKUK. Available from http://www.mpacuk.org/content/view/4644/

Nadwi, S. 2002. *Life and Mission of Mohammad Ilyas*. Translated by M. Kidwai. Lucknow: Academy of Islamic Research and Publications.

Naqshbandi, M. 2010. *Islam and Muslims in Britian*. London: City of London Police

Nawhami, A. 2013. *London – Muslim Population 2011*. Available from http://londonisoc.buzzislam.org/2013/01/02/london-muslim-population-2011/

Nielsen, J. 1987. "Muslims in Britain: Searching for an identity," *New Community*, 13 (3).

Nocera, K., and Goldsmith, S. 2010. "Imam building Islamic center near Ground Zero urges worshippers to fight against backlash with peace," *New York Daily News*.

No'mani, M. 1991. *Malfuzat Hazrat Maulana Muhammad Ilyas*. Translated by H. S. Muhammad. New Delhi: Idarah Isha' at Dinyyat.

———. 2001. *Words and Reflections of Hazrat Maulana Muhammad Ilyas (R.A.)*. Translated by S. Muhammad. Lahore: Iqra Books.

Noero, J. 2003. "Architecture and memory." In *Global Cities: Cinema, Architecture and Urbanism in a Digital Age*, ed. L Krause and P. Petro. New Brunswick and New Jersey: Rutgers University Press.

Norfolk, A. 2006. "How bomber's town is turning into an enclave for Muslims," *The Times*, October 21.

Oberoi, H. 1994. *The Construction of Religious Boundaries: Culture Identity and Diversity in the Sikh Tradition.* New Delhi: Oxford University Press.

OFSTED. 2011. *Institute of Islamic Education Independent School Standard Inspection Report.* Manchester: OFSTED.

Olick, J., and Robbins, J. 1998. "Social memory studies: From collective memory to the historical sociology of mnemonic practices," *Annual Review of Sociology,* 24 (1): 105–141.

O'Neill, S. 2009. "Airline terror plot – The three convicts were all Tablighi followers," *The Times,* September 16.

O'Neill, S., and Boyes, R. 2006. "Islamic missionary group links alleged plotters," *The Times,* August 17.

ONS. 2011. *Population Estimates by Ethnic Group 2002–2009.* London: Office for National Statistics.

———. 2012. *Religion in England and Wales 2011.* London: Office for National Statistics.

Panton, S. 2014. Appeal from the High Court of Justice Queen's Bench Division His Honour Judge Seymour QC, Case Number A2/2013/1548, April, London: Royal Courts of Justice.

Parekh, B. 1998. "Integrating minorities." In *Race Relations in Britain,* ed. B. Parekh and P. Saunders. London and New York: Routledge.

Peach, C. 2006. "Muslims in the 2001 Census of England and Wales: Gender and economic disadvantage." *Ethnic and Racial Studies* 29 (4): 629–655.

Pearson, H. 2008. *Islamic Revival and Reform in Nineteenth-century India.* New Delhi: Yoda Press.

Penderson, L. 1999. *Newer Islamic Movements in Western Europe.* Aldershot: Ashgate Publishing Ltd.

Perlez, J. 2007a. "A battle rages in London over a Mega-Mosque plan," *The New York Times.*

———. 2007b. "Pakistani group, suspected by West of Jihadist ties, holds conclave despite ban."Available from http://www.nytimes. com/2007/11/19/world/asia/19jamaat.html?_r=1

Peters, F. E. 1991. "The quest for the historical Muhammd," *International Journal of Middle East Studies,* 23 (3): 291–315.

Pieri, Z. 2012. *Tablighi Jamaat: Handy Books on Religion in World Affairs.* London: Lapido Media.

———. 2014. "Any one for Tabligh?" In *Critical Muslim: Sects,* eds. Z. Sardar and R. Yassin-Kassab. London: Hurst.

Pieri, Z., Mark, W., Mariani, Y., Ibrahim, H., and Inayah, R. 2013. "Commanding good and prohibiting evil in contemporary Islam: Cases from Britain, Nigeria and Southeast Asia," *Contemporary Islam,* 8 (1): 37–55.

Plant, R. 2013. "Religion in a liberal state." In *Religion in a Liberal State,* eds. G. D'Costa, M. Evans, T. Modood, and J. Rivers. Cambridge: Cambridge University Press.

Pubby, M. 2012. "Tablighi Jamaat Qaeda Delhi Cover 2011." Available from http://www.indianexpress.com/news/tablighi-jamaat-qaeda-delhi-cover/787813/

Pugh-Smith, J., and Deakin, A. 2011. "Opening statement on behalf of Newham Concern." In *APP/5750/C/10/2125895*. London: Newham Concern.

Rabinowitz, D. 2010. "Liberal piety and the memory of 9/11: The enlightened class can't understand why the public is uneasy about the Ground Zero Mosque," *The Wall Street Journal*, August 4.

Reimann, A. 2007. "Far-Right mobilizes against Cologne Mega-Mosque," *Spiegel Online*.

Reetz, D. 1999. "Mediating the external: The changing world and religious renewal in Indian Islam." In *Dissociation and Appropriation. Responses to Globalization on Asia and Africa*, eds. F.-S. Katja, P. Heidrich, and E. Schone. Berlin: Das Arabische Buch.

———. 2003. "Living like the pious ancestors: The social ideal of the missionary movement of the Tablighi Jama'at." In *Salafi Phenomenon Panel*. DAVO Conference, Hamburg.

———. 2004. "Keeping busy on the path of Allah: The self-organisation (Intizam) of the Tablighi Jamaat." In *Islam in Contemporary South Asia*, ed. D. Bredi. Rome: Oriente Moderno.

———. 2006. *Islam in the Public Sphere: Religious Groups in India 1900–1947*. Oxford and New Delhi: Oxford University Press.

———. 2008. *The Faith Bureaucracy of the Tablighi Jamaat: An Insight into their System of Self-organization (Intizam)*. Oxford and New York: Oxford University Press.

Reetz, D., and Gugler, T. 2009. *Strategies of Adaption and Dissociation: Islamic Missionary Groups from South Asia in the European Diaspora – The Tablighi Jama'at and the Da'wat-e-Islami*. Zentrum Moderner Orient 2009. Available from http://www.zmo.de/muslime_in_europa/teilprojekte/tp1_en.html

Rex, J. 1979. *Colonial Immigrants in a British City: A Class Analysis*. London: Routlege and Kegan Paul.

Richards, J. 1995. *The Mughal Empire (New Cambridge History of India)*. Cambridge: Cambridge University Press.

Richter, C. 2011. "The Egyptian Muslim brotherhood movement and its media strategies: The mobilising effect of religion in contentious politics." In *Religious Action in the Public Sphere: Means, Objectives and Effects*, eds. J. Haynes and A. Henning. London: Routledge.

Rizvi, S. 1980. *Shah Wali-Allah and His Times: A Study of Eighteenth Century Islam, Politics and Society in India*. Lahore: Suhail Academy.

———. 2012. "Supervison meeting," *Exeter*, December 1.

Robinson, D. 2005. "The search for community cohesion: Key themes and dominant concepts of the public policy agenda," *Urban Studies*, 42 (8): 1411–1427.

Robson, C. 2004. *Real World Research.* 2nd ed. Massachusetts: Blackwell.

Roy, O. 2002. *Globalised Islam: The Search for a New Ummah.* London: Hurst

Runneymede Trust. 1997. *Islamophobia – A Challenge for Us All.* London: The Runneymede Trust.

Sachs, S. 2003. "A Mulsim missionary group draws new scruitiny in U.S," *The New York Times,* July 14.

Saggar, S. 2010. *Pariah Politics: Understanding Western Radical Islamism and What Should be Done.* Oxford: Oxford University Press.

Sahadevan, S. 2011a. "Proof of evidence of the London borough of Newham." In *APP/G5750/C/10/212589.* London: London Borough of Newham.

———. 2011b. "Proof of evidence of the London borough of Newham: Rebuttal Proof." In *APP/G5750/C/10/2125895.* London: London Borough of Newham.

———. 2014. "Proof of evidence of the London Borough of Newham." In G5750/C/13/2203432. London: London Borough of Newham.

Sardar, Z. 2004. *Desperately Seeking Paradise: Journeys of a Sceptical Muslim.* London: Granta Books

———. 2006. "Watch this grass-roots group carefully," *New Statesman.* Available from http://www.newstatesman.com/200609040026

Sassen, S. 2003. "Reading the city in a global digital age: Between topographic representation and spatializsed power projects." In *Global Cities: Cinema, Architecture and Urbanism in a Digital Age,* eds. L. Krause and P. Petro. New Brunswick and New Jersey: Rutgers University Press.

Schimmel, A. 1991. "Sacred geography in Islam." In *Sacred Places and Profane Spaces: Essays in the Geographics of Judaism, Christianity and Islam,* eds. J. Scott and P. Simpson-Housley. New York: Greenwood Press.

Schindall, J. 2009. "Switzerland's non-EU immigrants: Their integration and Swiss attitudes," *Migration Policy Insitute,* June 9. Available from http://www.migrationpolicy.org/article/switzerlands-non-eu-immigrants-their-integration-and-swiss-attitudes

Schipper, J. 2012. "Radical cleric determined to debate in Amsterdam," *Radio Netherlands Worldwide,* February 16. Available from http://www.rnw.nl/english/article/radical-cleric-determined-debate-amsterdam

Schudson, M. 1998. *The Good Citizen: A History of American Civic Life.* Cambridge: Harvard University Press.

Schwartz, S. 2010. "A mosque grows near Brooklyn: The dubious financing of 'Cordoba House' deserves scrutiny," *The Weekly Standard,* July 17.

Shahid, A. 2008. *Abbey Mills Mosque Open Days.* London: Tablighi Jamaat.

Shams, S. 1983. *Meos of India, Their Customs and Laws.* Delhi: Deep and Deep.

Shipman, T. 2014. "Muslim teacher spoke of 'white prostitutes' to children in assembly," *The Sunday Times,* June 8. Available from http://www.thesundaytimes.co.uk/sto/news/uk_news/Education/article1420173.ece

Shryock, A. 2010. "Introduction: Islam as an object of fear and affection." In *Islamophobia/Islamophilia Beyond the Politics of Enemy and Friend*, ed. A. Shryock. Bloomington: Indiana University Press.

Shukra, K., Back, L., Keith, M., Khan, A., and Solomos, J. 2004. "Race, social cohesion and the changing politics of citizenship," *London Review of Education*, 2 (3): 187–195.

Siddiqui, A. 2001. "Issues in co-existence and dialogue: Muslims and Christians in Britain." In *Muslims Christian Perceptions of Dialogue Today*, ed. J. Waardenburg. Leuven: Peeters Publishers.

Sikand, Y. 2002. *The Origins and Development of the Tablighi Jamaat (1920–2000): A Comparative Study*. Hyderabad: Orient Longman.

———. 2006. "The Tablighi Jamaat and politics: A critical re-appraisal," *The Muslim World*, 96: 175–195.

———. 2007. "The reformist Sufism of the Tablighi Jama'at: The case of the Meos of Mewat, India." In *Sufism and the Modern in Islam*, eds. M. Van Bruinessen and J. Howell. London and New York: I.B. Tauris.

———. 2010a. "The Tablighi Jamaat in Mewat – Part 1." TwoCircles. net. Available from http://twocircles.net/2010apr13/tablighi_jamaat_mewat_part_1.html

———. 2010b. "The Tablighi Jamaat in Mewat – Part 2." TwoCircles. net. Available from http://twocircles.net/2010apr16/tablighi_jamaat_mewat_part_2.html

Singh, D. 2007. *Our Shared Future*. London: Commission on Integration and Cohesion.

Singh, K. S., ed. 2004. *People of India: An Anthropological Survey*. Delhi: Tarun Enterprises.

Snow, D. 1979. "A dramaturgical analysis of movement accommodation: Building idiosyncrasy credit as a movement mobilization strategy," *Symbolic Interaction*, 2: 23–44.

Spiegel. 2006. "Europeans have stopped defending their values: Interview with German Islam expert Bassam Tibi," *Spiegel Online*.

Steyn, M. 2005. "Wake up and listen to the Muezzin," *The Daily Telegraph*, November 29.

Swaine, L. 2006. *The Liberal Conscience: Politics and Principle in a World of Religious Pluralism*. New York: Columbia University Press.

Tarrow, S. 1996. "States and opportunities: The political structuring of social movements." In *Comparative Perspectives on Social Movements: Political Opportunities, Mobilizing Structures, and Cultural Framings*, eds. D. McAdam, J. McCarthy, and M. Zald. Cambridge and New York: Cambridge University Press.

Taylor, J. 2009a. "Megamosque sect split over plans," *Lapido Media*. Available from http://www.lapidomedia.com/megamosque-sect-split-over-plans

———. 2009b. "Taking tea with the Tablighi Jama'at," *Lapido Media*.

Tilly, C., and Tarrow, S. 2007. *Contentious Politics*. Boulder and London: Paradigm Publishers.

Torrekens, C. 2011. "Political opportunity and Muslim leadership in Brussels." In *Religious Actors in the Public Sphere: Means Objectives and Effects*, eds. J. Haynes and A. Henning. London and New York: Routledge.

Upadhyay, R. 2003. "Shah Wali Ullah's political thought – Still a major obstacle against modernisation of Indian Muslims." South Asian Analysis Group.

Vaselios, A. 1984. *Hymn of Entry: Liturgy and Life in the Orthodox Church*. New York: St. Vladimir's Seminary Press.

Vaughan, R. 2007. "Coup at mega-mosque as Allies and Morrison pushes Mangera Yvars aside," *The Architect's Journal*.

Venkatesh, S. 2008. *Gang Leader for a Day: A Rouge Sociologist Crosses the Line*. London and New York: Allen Lane.

Vetrovec, S. 2007. "Super-diversity and its implications," *Ethnic and Racial Studies*, 30 (6): 1024–1054.

Wainwright, M. 2006. "Dangerous attack or fair point? Straw veil row deepens," *The Guardian*, October 7.

Wallace, A. 1956. "Revitalization movements," *American Anthropologist, New Series*, 58 (2): 264–281.

Waterman Environmental. 2007. *Risk Management Strategy: The Riverine Centre, Abbey Mills*. London: Waterman Environmental.

Wax, R. 1983. "The ambiguities of fieldwork." In *Contemporary Field Research*, ed. R. Emerson. Boston and Toronto: Little Brown and Co.

Wedeen, L. 2008. *Peripheral Visions: Publics, Power and Performance in Yemen*. Chicago: University of Chicago Press.

Wehr, H. 1960. *A Dictionary of Modern Written Arabic*, ed. J. Cowan. Beirut and London: Librairie du Liban.

West, P. 2005. *The Poverty of Multiculturalism*. London: Civitas: Institute for the Study of Civil Society.

Wheatcroft, G. 2009. "Cartoon characters 2006." Available from http://www.slate.com/id/2135820/

Williams, R. 2014. "Rowan Williams: I didn't really want to be Archbishop: Interview with Cole Moreton," *Sunday Telegraph*, April 27. Available from http://www.telegraph.co.uk/news/religion/10789740/Rowan-Williams-I-didnt-really-want-to-be-Archbishop.html

Wogan, P. 2004. "Deep hanging out: Reflections on fieldwork and multisited Andean ethnography," *Identities: Global Studies in Culture and Power*, 11: 129–139.

INDEX

Public Inquiries, 9, 81, 110, 113,
115, 118, 122–3, 125, 127–8,
160, 166–8
public relations, 9, 27, 28, 53, 85,
90–3, 97, 103–5, 107
purity, 34, 60, 80, 139, 172

Qur'an, 124, 165

radicalization, 20, 97, 101–3
Raiwind, 56–7
Ramadan, 42, 82, 146
Reetz, Dietrich, 34, 36, 46, 52, 53,
56–8, 60, 61, 63, 134
riots
Danish cartoons, 19, 174
North of England, 18, 22
Notting Hill, 70

sahaba, 33, 43, 59, 172
Sahadevan, Sunil, 103–4, 111–13,
117, 127–8, 167
salaf. *See* pious ancestors
Salafism, 46–7
salat, 43, 144, 172
salvation, 10, 31, 37, 43, 55, 58–9,
63–4, 85, 133–4, 140–4,
147–8, 151, 154
Sarbuland, Sohail, 91
Saudi Arabia, 38, 51, 76, 92
Savile Town, 54, 67, 74, 76–8
Secretary for Communities and
Local Government, 19, 81,
110, 127, 129, 157, 161
secularism, 13, 21, 33, 39–40, 75,
78–80, 119–20, 135–7, 154–5,
159
segregation, 18, 24, 76, 121, 129
shari'a
law, 3, 5, 35, 40, 47, 60, 140, 172
marker of identity, 8, 34–5, 47,
140, 148, 151
zones, 20
shaytan. *See* devil
shura, 53–4, 172
Sikand, Yoginder, 75–6, 80

sin, 45, 138, 151
Six Points of Tabligh, 43–5, 55, 62,
63, 83, 133, 165
social cohesion, 10, 119, 136
Social Movement Theory, 8, 13–14,
27–8, 36–7, 49, 86, 96–7, 123, 159
society, 4, 5, 10, 15–17, 19, 23–8,
45, 67, 69, 70, 75, 80, 92, 111,
114, 119–22, 137–40, 146,
148, 152–5, 157, 158
Sociology of Religion, 26–7
students, 33, 44, 74, 78–80, 83,
146, 147, 163
Sufism, 38, 47, 62, 97, 171, 172,
177, 186
Sureli, Yusuf, 102–3
Swaine, Lucas, 3, 15–17, 168

Tablighi Jamaat
apolitical, 25, 47, 81, 85, 99, 100,
114, 125
elites, 49–52, 55, 102–3, 135–6,
145–6, 152–5
etymology, 41–2
grassroots, 5–6, 49–50, 57–9,
133–7, 148
ideology, 4, 42–7, 84, 88, 100,
115, 119–22, 129, 144–7
structure, 49–50, 52–3, 55, 57
terrorism, 100–3, 120
women, 40, 57, 77, 98, 106, 111,
119–23, 128, 153, 165
Tablighi Jamaat in Australia, 4, 155
Tablighi Jamaat in London
membership, 5–6, 83–4, 118
Open Day, 94–6
opposition to, 35–6, 96–100,
106, 109, 111
public relations strategy, 27–8, 85,
91–3, 96, 104, 107, 135, 159
website, 85, 91–3, 99, 103
Taliban, 35
technology, 78, 94, 148–9
terrorism, 18, 86–7, 96, 100–3,
120, 134, 158–9
Thanwi, Ashraf Ali, 38

Lightning Source UK Ltd.
Milton Keynes UK
UKOW05n0020210415

249959UK00005B/114/P